Wrath

WRATH

America Enraged

PETER W. WOOD

BOOKS

NEW YORK · LONDON

First American edition published in 2021 by Encounter Books,
an activity of Encounter for Culture and Education, Inc.,
a nonprofit, tax-exempt corporation.
Encounter Books website address: www.encounterbooks.com

Manufactured in the United States and printed on acid-free paper.
The paper used in this publication meets the minimum requirements of
ANSI/NISO Z39.48-1992 (R 1997) (*Permanence of Paper*).

FRIST AMERICAN EDITION

LIBRARY OF CONGRESS CATALOGING-IN-PUBLICATION DATA

Names: Wood, Peter, 1953– author.
Title: Wrath: America Enraged / Peter W. Wood.
Description: First American edition. | New York: Encounter Books, 2021. |
Includes bibliographical references and index. |
Identifiers: LCCN 2021016450 (print) | LCCN 2021016451 (ebook) |
ISBN 9781641772198 (hardcover) | ISBN 9781641772204 (ebook)
Subjects: LCSH: United States—Social conditions—21st century. |
Anger—Social aspects—United States. | Popular culture—United States—
Psychological aspects. | Political culture—United States. |
National characteristics, American.
Classification: LCC HN59.2 W6833 2021 (print) | LCC HN59.2 (ebook) |
DDC 306.0973—dc23

LC record available at https://lccn.loc.gov/2021016450
LC ebook record available at https://lccn.loc.gov/2021016451

1 2 3 4 5 6 7 8 9 20 21

Contents

Preface

WHAT IS THE DIFFERENCE between wrath and anger? *How dare you ask* – that's anger. *I will destroy you!* – that's wrath. Wrath is more intense and usually more sustained than anger. *That's unacceptable*, says the angry diner to the rude waiter. *I will track down the names and locations of your family members and post them on the internet*, says the wrathful political partisan.

Some wrath, I believe, is justified. The popular will of Americans has been thwarted by a combination of careerist elites, progressive ideologues, an unprincipled press, and a business class more attuned to global opportunities than to domestic flourishing. Because traditional forms of political protest have been tourniqueted by mass arrests, censorship, and decisions by law enforcement and the courts to stand aside, many Americans see themselves as having been denied a legitimate voice in their own governance. They are right in that judgment, and it is the kind of judgment that turns anger into wrath.

That wrath is further prodded by a progressive elite that seems to take sadistic delight in devising new ways to torment ordinary Americans. "Antiracism" is a psyops campaign aimed at institutionalizing discrimination against Whites. The 1619 Project is an attempt to erase American history and put in its place an elaborately constructed lie in which slavery explains everything. "Critical race theory" (CRT) further amplifies the message that American success is built entirely of the bricks and mortar of White racial supremacy. The elite preaches and now practices the benefits of abolishing our national border and flooding the country with illegal immigrants, at the expense of working-class Americans. Apologists for rioters demand we "defund the police." Progressive climate alarmists pursue policies aimed at driving up the cost of energy, knowing full well that cheap energy makes American prosperity possible. Progressives up-arm government agencies while pressing for antigun laws aimed at disarming the American public. Progressives manipulated the Wuhan virus epidemic by turning a manageable health crisis into a major economic disaster, an excuse for stripping Americans of their civil liberties, and an incitement of mass hysteria. And progressives, claiming the need to protect "voter rights," seek to lock into place the subterfuges they used to steal the 2020 presidential election.

To mention any one of these things is generally enough to get an employee fired, a professor canceled, a social media acquaintance defriended, a book delisted from Amazon, or a blog suspended. For Hollywood actors, it could be career-ending. For public figures daring to dine out, it could come with a side of noisy harassment. Perhaps none of these things by itself would prompt wrath – but, poked and prodded by all of them, people begin to move beyond mild irritation.

What form will this populist wrath take? Will it really become a movement aimed at *destroying* its foes?

Let's distinguish between the intense feelings of people who feel betrayed and the actions they are likely to take. The wrath is real, but it is unlikely to manifest itself in armed rebellion – although that can't be ruled out. Americans – at least, conservative Americans – love law and order. But they abhor corrupt law and coerced order. When those are imposed on them, Americans choose the path of defiance. A great deal of defiance can be achieved short of violence. Rejection of illegitimate authority in the form of widespread civil disobedience is the better path for the wrath that many Americans now feel.

That wrath has targets besides the people occupying high

offices in Washington. It includes much of the mainstream press and the billionaire oligarchs that control our digital communications. An especially intense form of this wrath is directed toward establishment Republican politicians who did nothing to oppose the organized corruption of the 2020 election and then counseled the public to accept the results. Another category in the white-hot center of the wrath are the so-called Never-Trumpers: political pundits who spent the four years of the Trump administration chastising Americans for electing him and then working as hard as they could to unseat him.

These opening paragraphs may suggest that this is a book that will be spent disputing the results of the 2020 election and attacking the character of those who claimed victory. But no. This is not that book. Rather, this is a book about how emotions – especially anger – have entered into our politics. Rather than incite anger, I aim to describe and analyze it, and, by doing so, I hope to help those in the midst of angry rejection of our current regime figure out a way to direct their legitimate fury to a constructive end. We often think of anger as a great stimulant to action. It can be. Anger can make a man fight back against an attacker. But anger can also lead to a kind of paralysis, a feeling of being utterly overwhelmed and helpless. Or it can lead to foolish decisions. Anger can make one rush headlong into a fight with no sense of strategy.

I don't want to dampen anyone's anger. I just want to step back from the immediate sense of wrath to help us figure out where and how we can direct it. And if your anger is beginning to fade and you are concluding that we can wait this out, I want to remind you that your anger is worth sustaining. You will need it.

This book, thus, occupies a seemingly peculiar space. It offers an intellectual argument addressed to Americans who are often treated as incapable of making serious intellectual distinctions. The "educated" class of Americans tend to look down on the people to whom I address these pages and of whom I consider myself one. Condescension toward the "deplorables," clinging to their guns and Bibles and other insignia of their benighted lives, is well established among those who see themselves as upholding "progressive" ideals. The progressive class does not countenance the idea that deplorables write and read serious intellectual books of their own, and they tend to be irritated when they run into a book such as J. D. Vance's *Hillbilly Elegy* or Michael Anton's essay *The Flight 93 Election*.

In 2006, I published *A Bee in the Mouth: Anger in America Now*, a book in which I traced the rise of what I called "new anger." New anger differs from older styles of anger in America, mainly because it is unmoored from the traditional ethic of self-control. In this book, I keep that distinction, but I go several steps further by considering that intensified and sustained form of anger: wrath.

But that introduces a complication. Wrath isn't just "new anger" carried to an extreme. Anger in all its forms, old and new, always carries the potential to become wrath. What turns anger into wrath? Two things: first, a significant number of people who share the sentiment and who sense their common affront; second, their collective sense that they face an impossible situation. For anger to become wrath, it needs not only a group of people gripped by the same sense of grievance, but also a realization in that group it has encountered an obstacle that is unjust and insurmountable. Anger doesn't become wrath if we think the sheriff or the judge will prevail over the malignant forces that provoke us. Only anger inflated by the crowd and with nothing left to lose becomes wrath.

The wrath of the decade at hand has some roots in old anger – that is, anger that sought to contain itself but occasionally broke out. The American Revolution, the abolitionist movement, the Civil War, and the civil rights struggle stand out as examples of old anger that sometimes turned wrathful. We know when anger turned to wrath, because that's when the muskets were fired or the buildings burned.

The wrath right now, however, draws on the cultural dynamics of new anger. We can see the difference in several ways. This wrath is self-consciously and conspicuously theatrical. Pussy hats are new anger–style wrath. Cancel culture is too. And Black Lives Matter, a total inversion of the civil rights movement, is new anger writ large and in flames. It is wrath as a charter for living.

Before diving into these matters, however, I should say a little about the larger subject.

Anger is an old theme and one that never goes out of style. Quarreling is in our nature, and wars are never far removed from quarrels. Nor are humans the only entities to lose their temper from time to time. We might not know exactly how a dog or a cat experiences anger, but it is plain that any animal with a limbic system can feel rage. Even insects can "express anger, terror, jealousy and love," wrote Charles Darwin in 1872, and modern science has found supporting evidence among honeybees.[1]

The biological facts of anger, however, lie somewhere in the background of our stories of anger. Whether we start with the Sumerian epic of Gilgamesh from 4,000 years ago or the epic Hollywood franchise *John Wick* (2014, 2017, 2019), about a hitman seeking revenge for the killing of his pet dog, anger is the deep well for the motives that propel heroes into action. Achilles would still be sulking in his tent and the Trojan War still dragging on if he hadn't been roused to fury.

Fictional stories of anger tell us a great deal about the people for whom those stories were first told. The stories capture what sorts of insult, indignity, or aggression gave rise to anger and what sorts could be shrugged off. They also tell us what the angry man does with his anger – in contrast to what the angry woman does with hers. And the stories help us see that people in different times and places treat anger in surprisingly different ways.

I came to the subject of anger in the early 2000s, when I was working on a book about the rise of the *diversity* movement in the United States. I kept meeting people who insisted they were very angry over the injustices in their lives but whose actions and general demeanor didn't seem angry at all – except that, given the right occasion, they could put on a display of towering verbal anger. I began making notes on this "performative anger," as I called it. My observations became the basis for *A Bee in the Mouth*.

That title misled some readers. The book was not about *hymenoptera* – bees and wasps – though I played with the conceit throughout. Rather, it was about a shift in American culture, roughly over the period 1950–2005, in which an older ethic of emotional self-control was gradually replaced by a new ethic of vivid emotional expression. The emotion at the forefront of this cultural change is anger. Because I was focused on the cultural construction of this emotion and not on the universal biological phenomenon, I labeled it "new anger."

New anger and all the old forms of anger, of course, have plenty in common. What distinguishes new anger is its flamboyant self-regard. New anger is anger mixed with the pride of being angry and finding impressive ways to project it. New anger is not the anger of simmering resentment or the anger of sudden outburst from an otherwise calm person. It is rather the anger that commands: "Notice me! See how angry I am!" And it is as much or even more of a lifestyle than an episode brought on by some specific aggravation.

This style of ostentatious anger wasn't just invented one thunderous day in 1950, and it didn't become rampant in the course of one year or one decade. The patterns of emotional control that prevail in a society are determined by how children are taught to deal with their emotions. Generation by generation, the expectations placed on children can and do shift, but it is impossible to rewire a culture's emotional character all at once. Our national shift from a culture that aspired to overcoming the temptations of anger to a culture that celebrates effusive displays of anger involved many intermediate steps. *A Bee in the Mouth* attempted to retrace those steps.

The study of how emotional expression and the emotions themselves differ among cultures is a small branch of my academic discipline, anthropology. The cross-cultural study of emotions is not my academic specialty, but I've read widely in the field for twenty years. In this new book, however, references to other cultures and anthropological analyses are few and far between. I am writing for a broad American audience, not fellow anthropologists.

One anthropological idea, however, stands at the center of the whole book: the idea that emotions are socially patterned. This is hard for some people to swallow. We feel that our emotions are authentically our own – and, perhaps, our most authentic part, inseparable from our sense of self. To suggest that we feel what we feel because our "culture" shapes us to feel those feelings can come across as insulting or as an arrogant intrusion on our privacy. These defensive reactions are understandable but mistaken. We find our authentic selves (if that is what we are looking for) in the materials that a culture provides. No one becomes a Christian, a Buddhist, an existentialist, or an Antifa out of thin air. We learn these things from each other; and, just as we learn belief systems from others, we learn emotional control and emotional expression from others – from our experiences in our families, schools, and churches; on the playground, on the internet, and in the workplace; and in sports, romantic relationships, and feuds. We also learn emotional styles from movies, books, music (especially songs), the arts, and all forms of imaginative engagement.

Gustave Flaubert's novel *L'Éducation sentimentale* (1869) gives us a useful term: "sentimental education." Flaubert wasn't referring to education by means of Hallmark cards or tear-jerking stories; he was referring to men and women growing up and discovering *how* to feel. Each of us has his own sentimental education, as we find our capacities to love, hate, rejoice, envy, welcome, regret, fear, yearn, empathize, scorn, and express a thousand other shades of feeling. Our personalities are woven of these threads, some of them acquired young but many altered by experience. A sentimental education isn't always for the better. We can learn to be mean, boastful, unforgiving, and worse. The world of new anger doesn't bring out the best in us.

Instances of boastful anger, of course, can be found throughout history, but they stand out as instances, not as cultural norms. The Roman satirist Juvenal was, by all accounts, a very angry man who railed against the vices of his age. For his troubles, he was exiled, probably to Egypt. Not many Romans aspired to be like him. In the fifteenth century, the Dominican friar Girolamo Savonarola led a campaign to destroy secular art and culture in Florence after preaching against the moral depravities of Renaissance Europe. He gained influence and followers, but in 1498 he and his closest associates were publicly hanged and burnt. Savonarola's writings, like those of Juvenal, inspired other reformers, but his persona as a fiercely angry castigator didn't become something that other Florentines regarded as admirable. America has not lacked for prominent scolds of its own, among them John Brown, Carrie Nation, and Malcolm X.

Over-the-top anger could always get you noticed, but it was a tricky career path. And it is hard to find social worlds where volatile anger is regarded as a positive character trait. Accusing *other* cultures of excessive anger is another matter.

The ferocious political and ideological battles of 2020 and 2021, I argue, should be seen through the prism of what I call "new anger": that self-regarding, self-rewarding, flamboyantly expressive, and narcissistic form of performative rage. New anger often gets in the way of our better judgment, but that doesn't mean that the underlying anger is necessarily foolish. We may be angry for the right reason but angry in the wrong way.

A Bee in the Mouth warned against the consequences for our culture of indulging too freely in the celebration of anger. We've seen that warning about some hard-to-pin-down or imaginary catastrophe sometimes pays off handsomely. Al Gore managed it, and Greta Thunberg has had an auspicious start to marketing her inauspicious pronouncements. But other warnings often go unheeded. My 2006 warning about the coming swarm of anger hornets did attract a number of attentive readers, and I still get letters from people who have only lately come across the book.

What I hope for in this new book, however, is very different. I hope to inspire confidence in those who are determined to wrest their nation back from the elites who have taken it away.

Their efforts must overcome the silencing, censorship, criminalization of dissenting opinion, and other forms of persecution that are becoming the standard operating procedure of the illiberal regime now in power. To those who feel angry about this but who are ridden with doubts about how to contest this new order, this book offers the counsel that, in some circumstances, your wrath is your best defense. But wrath is a dangerous weapon, and you must use it wisely to avoid self-injury.

I am mindful of Aristotle's counsel in his *Ethics* that we should strive to be the person who "is angry at the right things and toward the right people, and also in the right way." The self-celebratory new anger seldom meets any of Aristotle's criteria, and it violates what he calls the virtue of "mildness." Aristotle does not regard it as virtuous, however, to remain indifferent or resigned when one has good cause to be angry. Can wrath sometimes be the right response to sustained injustice? Presumably over the right things, toward the right people, and in the right way. Let's take care that our wrath is planted in virtue, not folly.

In the years since I published *A Bee in the Mouth*, I became the president of the National Association of Scholars (NAS), leaving behind more than two decades as a professor and college administrator. NAS is a membership group made up mostly of academics but open to all. I thus sit on the borderlands of higher education as a watchdog, but a watchdog especially watchful for the bad ideas that originate in the academy and gradually spread their poison through the rest of society. Almost all the really terrible ideas that blight contemporary America started on campus, including the new rationalization for suppressing free speech, the eagerness to discard the Bill of Rights and "interpret" the Constitution into nothingness, the expansion of identity-group rights and privileges, and the corruption of everyday language to give words the opposite of their old meanings. These are all techniques aimed at manipulating the public and speeding the acquisition of still more power by the elite. My work is to teach Americans how to fight back against this perversion of our culture. *Wrath* is meant as a contribution to that effort. It offers a sentimental education of its own. It teaches, I hope, how to put some righteous anger to good use in the effort to save our country and our civilization from an approaching barbarism.

How to Read This Book

———————

W<small>RATH</small> <small>IS</small> <small>MORE</small> <small>OF</small> an exploration than an argument. As it explores contemporary anger, it invites disagreement. It is a conflicted book about emotional conflict. *My* conflict is whether to endorse the wrath that has been summoned by the vile behavior of our political, social, and economic elites or to caution Americans to hold that wrath in check in order to avoid still greater pain and destruction. Fight or flight? Take it to the punks, or stay committed to higher ideals?

I honestly don't know, but I am increasingly pushed in the direction of obstinate defiance of state edicts that have no real basis in law. The states that have found ways to countermand the extra-constitutional actions of the administration point to one good way to fight back. The rise of alternative digital media outside the vicious control of the media oligarchs point to another way our wrath can be channeled to good ends. But, plainly, these steps by themselves will not be enough to restore our liberty, our rights, and our elections.

My book reflects my uncertainty about what to do next, and I dedicate it to those who share my quandary. I have no answers, easy or otherwise, to those who seek counsel about how to recover our country from a profound betrayal by a self-serving class of powerful people. What I have is a reflection, twenty years in the making, on anger in America.

Chapters 1, 2, and 10 deal with the political anger of the 2020 presidential election. Chapter 3, "Bees," identifies the pervasive but barely noticeable smog of anger in contemporary life. Chapter

3 and the following five chapters build on ideas in *A Bee in the Mouth* and, in a few cases, borrow from that book. Chapter 4, "Pollyanna Meets Tar-Baby," deals with the *representation* of anger in American popular culture. It also introduces the idea that our sense of anger has changed dramatically over time: we have gone from a culture that prized self-control to a culture that prizes self-expression, which often means unleashed anger. Chapter 5, "Temper, Temper," focuses on how we *talk about* anger: whether we try to tame it or flame it, to leash it or license it. Chapters 3, 4, and 5 overlap, because all three deal with the materials of cultural expression. Chapters 6 and 7 deal with aspects of self-control. Chapter 6, "Self-government," deals with interplay between *pretending* to be angry and actually *being* angry. The boundary between the two is poorly marked, and that bears on contemporary politics. Chapter 7, "Taking Charge," examines figures in American history who exemplified self-control or who proudly renounced it. Chapter 8, "Yester-Anger," focuses on the 1994 midterm elections – the so-called Gingrich Revolution, the success of which was attributed by the left to the rise of "angry White males." This political era saw the emergence of the angry racial and sexual-identity politics that came front and center again in the 2016 presidential election. Chapter 9, "The Revolution in How We Feel," registers some of the changes in the ways Americans instructed themselves in how to experience injustice. Chapter 10 brings the story back to Trump and the aftermath of the 2020 election.

Wrath combines two topics: wrath and my analysis of how we got here. The how-we-got-here part covers a lot of ground. The wrath part expresses my search for the meaning of what the country has recently endured and, I expect, will continue to suffer. The wrath chapters can also be read by themselves, though plainly I hope the reader will see this as one book that puts the present together with a recent past and an older history. And I hope it will help some readers find a way out of the maze in which we seem to be trapped.

Chapter One

WRATH RIGHT NOW

WRATH. THE CRACK of the whip across the sneering face of your foe? A burning coal gripped tight in your hand? Wrath aims to punish the enemy but, notoriously, takes its toll on the punisher as well. Still, when wrath seizes us, we are elated at the prospect of triumph over the wretches who have provoked us. The cost to ourselves comes later. Not always a great deal later.

As I write this in February 2021, a news report (with video!) tells of a quarrel between a Pennsylvania couple, James and Lisa Goy, and a neighbor, over where to shovel snow from their parking spaces. Vulgar insults were traded back and forth until the neighbor, Jeffrey Allen Spaide, went into his house and returned with a gun. The insults flew again; Spaide displayed the gun, only to be mocked by Lisa. He then shot both the Goys to death, pumping extra bullets into Lisa as she lay on the ground. Having given wrath its due, Spaide returned to his house and shot himself to death.[1]

America right now has plenty of wrath. It is not limited to snow-shoveling madness. Nor is this the first time America as a whole, not just individual Americans, has descended into the warm embrace of righteous antipathies. We have a national song about it.

"He is trampling out the vintage/Where the grapes of wrath are stored," proclaimed Julia Ward Howe in "The Battle Hymn of the Republic." Her lyrics were a substitute for an anthem already pop-

1

ular with Union soldiers in the Civil War, the antislavery song "John Brown's Body."[2] Howe's version invokes the wrath of God against the defenders of slavery. Howe was drawing on a verse from the book of Revelation (14:19): "And the angel thrust in his sickle into the earth, and gathered the vine of the earth, and cast it into the great winepress of the wrath of God."

In her version of God's wrath, "He hath loosed the fateful lightning of his terrible swift sword," and

> *He has sounded forth the trumpet that shall never*
> *call retreat,*
> *He is sifting out the hearts of men before His judgment seat.*

But "The Battle Hymn of the Republic" stirred more than battle-hardened White Union soldiers. Black Union soldiers adapted it to express their own wrath. Their version begins:

> *Oh, we're the bully soldiers of the "First of Arkansas,"*
> *We are fighting for the Union, we are fighting for the law,*
> *We can hit a Rebel further than a white man ever saw,*
> *As we go marching on.*

> *Glory, glory hallelujah.*
> *Glory, glory hallelujah.*
> *Glory, glory hallelujah.*
> *As we go marching on.*

> *See, there above the center, where the flag is waving bright,*
> *We are going out of slavery; we're bound for freedom's light;*
> *We mean to show Jeff Davis how the Africans can fight,*
> *As we go marching on! (Chorus)*

> *We have done with hoeing cotton, we have done with*
> *hoeing corn,*

We are colored Yankee soldiers, now, as sure as you
*   are born;*
When the masters hear us yelling, they'll think it's
*   Gabriel's horn,*
As we go marching on. (Chorus)

They will have to pay us wages, the wages of their sin,
They will have to bow their foreheads to their colored
*   kith and kin,*
They will have to give us house-room, or the roof shall
*   tumble in!*
As we go marching on. (Chorus) [3]

As it happens, the song started out as a Southern camp-meeting spiritual with Black roots at "open-air services attended by blacks and whites, slaves and free individuals." The first known lyrics were published in 1807, "Say Brothers Will You Meet Us? On Canaan's happy shore."[4] So the soldiers of the "First of Arkansas" – that is, the First Arkansas Volunteer Infantry Regiment (African Descent)[5] – were re-appropriating a song that had already been twice appropriated, although every version looked beyond slavery to human brotherhood.

Julia Howe's version of "The Battle Hymn of the Republic" survived the Civil War to become a versatile expression of righteous indignation, adaptable to almost any cause. The song's historians, John Stauffer and Benjamin Soskis, noted that the University of Georgia made it its official anthem in the 1890s, on the grounds that the South had also "fought for God and freedom."[6] The hymn surged in popularity with the Spanish-American War of 1898, with the added lyric "Let us furl again Old Glory in the name of Liberty."[7] Teddy Roosevelt "treated it as his personal Anthem," as well as a Progressive Party fight song.[8] The U.S. entry into World War I brought the song back into popularity among soldiers with another added lyric, "We have heard the cry of anguish from the victims of the Hun." The radical labor union of the time, the International Workers of the World, rewrote it as "Solidarity Forever (The Union Makes Us Strong)."[9] The evangelist Billy Graham – a Southerner and grandson of Confederate soldiers – restored the hymn to its camp-meeting origins by making it part of his "crusades."[10] Martin Luther King, Jr., popularized it as a civil rights anthem and quoted from it in the powerful ending of his "Address at the Conclusion of the Selma to Montgomery March," March 25, 1965.[11] The song also reaches out in other contexts, such as the title of John Steinbeck's 1939 novel about Dust Bowl migrants, *The Grapes of Wrath.*

So Americans have sung about, preached about, talked about, and written about *wrath* for a long time. What's different today?

Carthage

The Wrath Right Now – WRN – comes from several compass points. It is partly the snow-shovel wrath of Jeffrey Allen Spaide and others who foolishly abandon themselves to bloodthirsty anger. But our wrath right now is a lot more than out-of-control personal grievances. It is the wrath of those who believe that "systemic racism" is behind the police killings of Black Americans. WRN is the equal and opposite wrath of people who believe that accusation to be false and bigoted. It is the wrath of Americans who believe that Donald Trump was a disgrace to the office of president and someone who empowered the forces of ignorance and intolerance in our society. But WRN is also the wrath of Americans who believe that Trump accomplished great good in office and that his reelection was stymied by voter fraud and other forms of electoral manipulation. It is the wrath of Americans who believe that our society is founded on lies and suppression of those who seek social justice. And WRN is the wrath of those who see efforts to impose "social justice" as intent on destroying our self-governing republic by imposing a dictatorial regime that would vacate our basic rights.

These forms of wrath have some commonalities, but they differ in crucial ways. One side – the self-named *progressive side* – dominates the elected and appointed offices in the federal government; maintains a near monopoly on the establishment press, both print and digital; finds its policy preferences fiercely advanced by social media; enjoys a large margin of popularity among the titans of medicine, investment, banking, industry, and commerce; has almost exclusive control over higher education and teaching in the K–12 realm; and enjoys lopsided support among Americans who have bachelors' or advanced degrees from colleges and universities.

The other side – often called "populists" – finds its support among blue-collar workers; small entrepreneurs and shopkeepers and other members of the traditional bourgeoisie; churchgoing members of traditionally minded Christian denominations; Jewish conservatives; Black, Hispanic, and Asian Americans who reject the identity politics of the "communities" that are organized by progressives around ethnic resentments; and a large but amorphous category of Americans who see themselves as upholders of our *national* identity as opposed to wearing some kind of global, post-national bracelet.

These distinctions make differences in not only what we get angry about, but also how we express and even how we inwardly experience that anger.

But both sides are engaged not just in ordinary anger – anger that gets over itself – but in *wrath*. And not just murderous snow-shoveling wrath, but a deep, collective, civil-war-ish mutual hatred. I'm setting apart that Wrath Right Now with the initials WRN to avoid conflating it with other moments of mutual antipathy that have gripped the nation from time to time. WRN has not, at the time I write, broken out in the form of widespread armed conflict, although many on both sides entertain that possi-

5

bility. The Biden administration has summoned the National Guard and surrounded the Capitol with barbed wire, in apparent expectation that the arrival of a latter-day Confederate Army is imminent. Citizen militias in the backwoods of Michigan and Washington practice guerilla-warfare tactics in apparent expectation that Ruby Ridge–style federal assault teams are waiting to arrive. Both, I believe, are mistaken, although the hugely excessive force used by the FBI to arrest alleged participants in the January 6, 2021, Capitol riot gives more weight to those who anticipate federal overreach.

But strife need not become a war fought with bullets to wreak destruction on the country or to render America ungovernable or so weakened as to be vulnerable to hostile foreign powers. These are matters to consider in due course.

The great difference between anger and wrath is that wrath aims at obliterating its foe. It does not rest until Carthage is destroyed. At the end of the Third Punic War, in 146 BC, the Roman general Scipio Aemilianus burned Carthage to the ground – as some say, "leaving not one stone on top of another." The rhetoric, if not always the reality, of wrath is war. Wrath demands the enemy be vanquished and humiliated. If it gains its way, it wants the survivors to feel their defeat utterly.

I should qualify this description by observing that the God of the Bible is frequently spoken of as having wrath toward transgressors of divine law. God's wrath often results in obliteration of the guilty (Exod. 22:24, "And my wrath shall wax hot, and I will kill you with the sword; and your wives shall be widows, and your children fatherless"), but God also, on occasion, draws back (Ps. 85:3, "Thou hast taken away all thy wrath: thou hast turned thyself from the fierceness of thine anger"). Citing Biblical injunctions may seem a fair distance from our national situation, but only if we allow our prevailing secularism to blind us to its cultural roots. The unleashed passions of our historical moment owe more than a little to an American past saturated with moral absolutes from the Biblical tradition and with the ever-twisting attempts to requisition those absolutes for the causes we favor. It is not for nothing that the "Battle Hymn of the Republic" reemerges during dark times. "His truth is marching on."

The wrath that is present among us now has, so far, broken out only in limited ways. For this we should be thankful, though it is clearly a cause of impatience among some who would prefer to say, "Bring it." Why should we restrain ourselves? A little counsel from our ancestors might be in order. The Babylonian Talmud cautions, "He who gives vent to his wrath destroys his house."[12] That's because wrath blinds us. A medieval Persian poet warned, "The fire of wrath falls first on the wrathful man."[13]

The desire to annihilate the enemy is not praiseworthy, but it almost always rises to the surface in war. Can the impulse be yanked back into recognition that civic amity is the higher good? The trouble is that even a truce requires a modicum of trust in the goodwill of the other side, and that trust is hard to summon after repeated betrayals. When both sides feel that they have been betrayed, finding a place to parley is very difficult.

To caution against wrath is not to deny the provocations that give rise to it or to ask those who feel those provocations to submit to injustice. Rather, it is to ask that we put our wrath under strict supervision. Let's master it, rather than let it master us.[14]

Was It Fraud?

This is a book written with keen sympathy for what I have called the populist side of our current discontent and with aversion to the progressive side. I doubt that I will sacrifice many readers by acknowledging this affinity at the outset. Some readers who regard themselves as progressive may venture into these pages in the hope of learning more about what their opponents think – and, if you are among those, you are welcome. I hope to gratify your curiosity. But first let me acknowledge that I am not an appointed spokesman for the populist view, nor do I wholly identify with it. I am an anthropologist – one who spent many years teaching that academic discipline – and a former college administrator. Neither of those biographical details are likely fits with American populism. Moreover, as I will explain later, I was highly skeptical of Trump when he emerged on the scene as a political figure, and I retain strong reservations about his character and some of his approaches to governance. To the extent that *Wrath* is a book that upholds the social and political movement that he ushered into contemporary American life, it is a book that treats that movement with *sympathy*, not with ardor. The populist movement, in my view, gets certain fundamental things right that the progressive movement gets profoundly wrong. The details of that judgment are embedded in the body of the book, and I'll refrain from saying more outside of the context of particular disputes.

I will add, however, that my own wrath was kindled by what I take to be the Democratic Party's significant electoral mischief in the 2020 presidential election. I'm fully aware of how contentious it now is to say the election was "stolen," though I believe it was. I also believe that anyone who has been willing to look squarely at the nature of voter registration, mail-in balloting, vote-counting procedures, monitoring of vote counts, judicial unwillingness to examine the substance of complaints, irregularities in the use of voting machines, interruptions and delays in vote counting, ploys to neutralize the legal authority of state legislatures to set election rules, "consent agreements" on balloting, and – above all – results that are statistically impossible or nonsensical cannot but conclude that the election was marred by electoral fraud.[15] Whether such fraud was decisive in the election of President Biden is technically an open question, but it is "open" only because the pertinent evidence has been either destroyed or ignored.

In February 2021, *Time* magazine published an extended

report, "The Secret History of the Shadow Campaign That Saved the 2020 Election," which, in considerable detail, documented many of the quasi-legal and extralegal tactics that the Democratic campaign employed to turn the election.[16] The article was written in the voice of approval: that these steps were warranted by the danger that Trump would win reelection. Now that the threat of Trump's victory was past, *Time* could acknowledge the "conspiracy" – its word for what transpired – with approbation.

We live with the results, which I believe are woeful for America. But I have little more to say on that topic in these pages, which deal instead with some of the emotional dynamics of America – how we got here and where we are likely to go. We are in the midst of wrath, perhaps even something we could call "The Wrath" – or *the fire*, as James Baldwin, quoting a Black spiritual that elaborates on God's promise never again to destroy the earth by flood – Genesis 9:11 – suggested when he titled one of his books *The Fire Next Time* (1963).

Minneapolis Burning

After the death of George Floyd in Minneapolis on May 25, 2020, following his arrest for passing counterfeit currency, race riots ensued in many American cities. The *New York Times* counted more than 2,000 cities and towns that saw post–George Floyd protests by June 13.[17] Many months later, the *Times* inexplicably reduced its count to "at least 140 cities," the lower number perhaps representing the protests that involved significant violence.[18] The word "protests" in the *Times'* accounts requires attention. Many of these events may have been peaceful, but some were full-scale riots. The rioters inflicted more than a billion dollars in property damage in the first ten days alone, and counting only insured property.[19] By the end of 2020, more than a dozen people had been killed in George Floyd–related violence.[20]

The ostensible cause of the mayhem was Floyd's supposed killing by police officer Derek Chauvin, who had restrained Floyd by kneeling on his neck. The official autopsy determined that Floyd was not injured by this restraint but died of other causes stemming from his heart disease and intoxication with various drugs, including fentanyl.[21] A subsequent examination commissioned by Floyd's family came to a contrary conclusion.[22] This is a matter for the courts to sort out, but the verdict in the street seemed immediate: Floyd, who was Black, had been killed by a White police officer as part of a long pattern of heedless disregard for the lives and safety of Black people.

The post–George Floyd riots were kindled anew in the following months wherever a Black suspect died in confrontation with police. Floyd's death was seized upon by the organization Black Lives Matter (BLM), the name of which became a slogan and a rallying cry well beyond the organization itself. Distinguishing the formal group from the broader movement and the sentiment it inspired is important but cannot be done with any precision. BLM, the organization, is an avowedly Marxist-Maoist group that originated (by its own account) "in 2013 in response to the acquittal of Trayvon Martin's murderer." The phrasing is tendentious in that George Zimmerman, who fatally shot Trayvon Martin in self-defense, is not a "murderer," but it is to be understood that BLM had, from the start, an agenda that aimed at challenging the legitimacy of American jurisprudence. The BLM organization, time and again, would attempt to reframe cases in which violent criminals died in the midst of brutal acts or while resisting lawful authority as instances of police misconduct or White oppression. BLM's stated purpose is "to eradicate white supremacy and build local power to intervene in violence inflicted on Black communities by the state and vigilantes."

BLM's website was scrubbed in 2020 to erase some of its other declarations of purpose, which included its opposition to the "Western-prescribed nuclear family structure." That opposition can be misunderstood out of context, so here is BLM's original statement:

> We make our spaces family-friendly and enable parents to fully participate with their children. We dismantle the patriarchal practice that requires mothers to work "double shifts" so that they can mother in private even as they participate in public justice work. We disrupt the Western-prescribed nuclear family structure requirement by supporting each other as extended families and "villages" that collectively care for one another, especially our children, to the degree that mothers, parents, and children are comfortable.

This, plainly, is not a call to sideline the role of parents in raising their children, but it points to relaxation of responsibilities as long understood in American social life, in which the ideal was a two-parent family consisting of a man and woman married to each other and committed to raising their children together. That ideal has not ceased to exist within the Black community, but it has receded drastically from realization. As of 2015, 77.3 percent of children born to native-born Black Americans were born to unmarried mothers, "the highest rate of non-marital births among native Americans."[23] Plainly the "Western-prescribed nuclear family structure" is not available to millions of Black American children, and the BLM call for the intervention of extended families and other "collective" arrangements makes sense as an expedient. The question that BLM raised, however, is whether such an expedient should be treated as a positive alternative. Would the Black community be better served by further "disruption" of the nuclear family?

A wealth of social scientific evidence suggests otherwise. The absence of resident, married fathers to children is a leading indicator of a wide range of social pathologies in children, especially boys, who are more likely to fail in school, to become in involved in street gangs, to engage in drug use, to graduate to street crime, to be arrested, to serve jail time, and to die of violence compared to children raised in two-parent families. Of the various pathologies, however, one in particular bears on the topic of this book. Children raised in these circumstances have poor emotional control. They anger easily, and they tend to act on their anger. They are raised as tinder for the storms of wrath that were on national display in the post–George Floyd riots.

The prevalence of anger among young Black teenagers and men is registered every day by the wildly disproportionate rate at which they commit murder, most often the murder of other Blacks. FBI statistics show that 52.4 percent of homicides in cases where the killer is known are committed by Blacks, though only 13.4 percent of the population is Black.[24] Some 89 percent of the people killed by Black offenders are themselves Black. If this seems overly precise, consider Glenn Loury's mournful summary:

> There are about 17,000 homicides in the United States every year, nearly half of which involve black perpetrators. The vast majority of those have other blacks as victims. For every black killed by the police, more than 25 other black people meet their end because of homicides committed by other blacks.[25]

Homicides spiked in 2020, in what may have been "the largest percentage increase in homicides in American history."[26] In 2019, an estimated 16,425 Americans were murdered; in 2020 the estimated total was greater than 19,000, an overall increase of 16 percent, but the murder rate in cities was much higher – up 37 percent in a sample of 57 cities. "At least 2,000 more Americans, most of them black, were killed in 2020 than in 2019."[27] The perpetrators of this carnage in Black communities were overwhelmingly young Black males.[28]

Do Black lives matter? Of course they do. But if we wish to

save Black lives, we should, among other things, work very hard to restore the once-dominant "Western-prescribed nuclear family structure." BLM, as the organization and not necessarily the movement that employs its name, militates against that family structure and puts yet more Black lives at risk.

Hell You Talmbout

The riots in the summer of 2020 had several proximate causes. I intend not to offer an analysis of the many contributing factors but to treat these events as exemplifying one of the key scripts for progressive anger. The riots were meant, above all, as a political signal sent to both fellow progressives and their Trumpian opponents. The major statements were (1) America is a profoundly unjust society, (2) the police are among the primary enforcers of that injustice, and (3) we will burn down your society unless we prevail in the 2020 presidential election. The riots were not random eruptions of anger over specific injustices. They were organized and orchestrated insurrections meant to frighten and intimidate Americans at large. They succeeded.

The script that BLM provided for the riots focused on the conceit that American police target and kill Black people with impunity. A few days after George Floyd's death, former president Barack Obama and presidential candidate Joe Biden each amplified the idea that Black people are in especial peril from the agents of law enforcement. Obama said:

> *We have to remember that for millions of Americans, being treated differently on account of race is tragically, painfully, maddeningly "normal" – whether it's while dealing with the health care system, or interacting with the criminal justice system, or jogging down the street, or just watching birds in a park.*[29]

Biden said:

> *This is the norm black people in this country deal with. They don't have to imagine it. With our complacency, our silence, we are complicit in perpetuating these cycles of violence. If we simply allow this wound to scab over once more without treating the underlying injury, we'll never truly heal. We need real police reform and to hold cops to a higher standard.*[30]

Among the very few who disputed the validity of the especial peril theme was Heather Mac Donald, bestselling author of *The Diversity Delusion: How Race and Gender Pandering Corrupt the University and Undermine Our Culture* (2018) and *The War on Cops: How the New Attack on Law and Order Makes Everyone Less Safe* (2016). She cited actual data: "In 2019 police officers fatally shot 1,004 people, most of whom were armed or otherwise dangerous. African-Americans were about a quarter of those killed by cops last year (235), a ratio that has remained stable since 2015." Given that Blacks commit a hugely disproportionate amount of the nation's crime ("53% of known homicide offenders in the U.S. and commit about 60% of robberies, though they are 13% of the population"), the proportion of individuals shot by the police who are Black is actually much smaller than might be expected.[31] Examining the actual intersection of violent crime with race in America is generally a thankless task, as few welcome the distressing facts.[32]

In any case, much of America's progressive political class instantly accepted the claim that Black communities are beset by police who deploy violence with little or no excuse and are seldom held to account for even major transgressions.

The riots were one way in which this thesis was deployed, but there were other expressions of the anger and dismay – some in the form of peaceful rallies, and others of a ritual character, as when the names of real and alleged Black victims of police violence were chalked on sidewalks, rhythmically chanted, or posted sequentially on websites.[33] Sometimes the name recital became a form of anger music, as in "Hell You Talmbout." "Talmbout" is Black dialect for "talking about," and "hell you talmbout" translates as the rhetorical question, "What the hell are you talking about?" In 2015, Janelle Monáe and members of her Wondaland artist collective – Deep Cotton, George 2.0, Jidenna, Roman GianArthur, and St. Beauty – recorded "Hell You Talmbout" with lyrics that follow that phrase:

> *Walter Scott say his name*
> *Jermaine Reid say his name*
> *Philip White say his name*
> *Eric Garner say his name*
> *Trayvon Martin say his name*

The list of the names of Black victims of White violence is a flexible device and entered into the protest repertoire as a tool for intensifying rage.[34] It also became a musical platform for protest dance routines.[35] Eventually, it was appropriated by White singer David Byrne for his 2019–2020 Broadway show, *American Utopia*, and produced as a concert film by Spike Lee.[36] (The show is expected to return to Broadway in September 2021).[37]

Janelle Monáe, the originator of the song, not so incidentally, was also the star of the *New York Times'* lavish February TV commercial for its racially goading 1619 Project.

These are important reminders that the ingredients for a summer of riots had been in workshop since at least the killing of Trayvon Martin in February 2012 and had been greatly amplified by the killing of Michael Brown in Ferguson, Missouri, in August 2014. Large-scale protests sometimes spilling over to violent disorder had been part of this history, but it was not until after George Floyd's death that the protest movement turned dramatically violent. What happened? What turned sporadic episodes of angry protest into wrath?

Permission helped. Obama's and Biden's words gave a sense of official endorsement to the idea that American police are the enemy of Black Americans. Senator Kamala Harris, then running for the Democratic nomination, spoke on *The Late Show with Stephen Colbert*, June 22, 2020, and fanned the flames:

> *But they're not going to stop. They're not going to stop. They're not. This is a movement. I'm telling you. They're not going to stop, and everyone beware. Because they're not going to stop. They're not going to stop before Election Day in November, and they are not going to stop after Election Day. And everyone should take note of that on both levels. That they're not going to let up. And they should not, and we should not.*[38]

Harris's "we" in the final sentence was the dramatic conclusion to an interview focused on her lifelong involvement in protests, beginning with her story that she first appeared in a baby stroller when her parents were "marching in the sixties."

Democrats were effectively endorsing the violence – though, prudently, hedging their remarks as sympathy with "protest," not riot. And the liberal media sustained the ruse by repeating thousands of times that the post–George Floyd events were "mostly peaceful protests." Mostly peaceful protests, however, do not cause billions of dollars in property damage or send people to the morgue. The American public registered that the riots were indeed riots.

Frenzy

They were in large part *political* riots. They had something to do, as Senator Harris inadvertently acknowledged, with the impending presidential election. One aim of the rioters was to undermine the Trump administration. This was apparent from the start, when one of the riots (or "violent protests") was staged outside the White House beginning on May 29 and extending to June 7. More than fifty Secret Service agents were injured during the first six nights of clashes.[39] Trump himself was taken to the White House "terror attack" bunker on June 1. The demonstrators' proclaimed purpose was "justice for George Floyd," but opposition to Trump and support for BLM protests were inextricable.[40]

Trump responded to the political challenge embedded in the riots by running a thirty-second reelection ad that displayed images of the rioters, calls for "defunding the police, eliminating cash bail, and letting criminals back out on the street," and burning buildings, and concluding with the words, "You won't be safe in Joe Biden's America" superimposed on an empty police HQ.[41]

This could happen by provoking Trump to overreach by using the National Guard or other federal power to suppress the riots. Or it could happen by making the country look ungovernable on his watch. Or it could serve as a way of extorting the American public by implying that the violence would continue until Trump had been removed from office. (As Harris said, "They are not going to stop after Election Day.")

To say what a riot means, of course, is to interpret. Riots themselves are chaotic events that don't translate into simple declarations of purpose. The riots could be seen as merely spontaneous expressions of outrage among aggrieved Black residents of various cities and towns. That interpretation, however, attracted few supporters on any side of the debate. Ross Douthat, writing in the *New York Times*, argued that the Minneapolis riot, like the 2015 riots in Ferguson and Baltimore, was a mistaken attempt to attract positive public attention to the grievances of the Black community – *mistaken* because it was more likely to inspire a public backlash.[42]

Douthat's view didn't sit unchallenged. Zak Cheney-Rice, a writer for *New York Magazine*, responded two days later that the rioting isn't "strategically imprudent" but often serves as "the vanguard for a range of political and cultural shifts," including "a leftward lurch in public opinion around inequality in the criminal-legal system." Such changes, according to Cheney-Rice, "are far from guaranteed," but they are efforts "to establish an alternative social order." The rioters seek "to upwardly redistribute the contempt that the current order and its guardians have shown towards them."[43]

Douthat and Cheney-Rice can serve as two touchstones of an old and continuing debate. When is it useful to destroy homes and businesses in your own community, many of them owned by the very people whose grievances you seek to represent? The puzzle cannot be resolved if it is examined as though riots are simply an extension of pragmatic calculations about the best ways to rally support, win sympathy, or galvanize discontent. Riots are, above all else, emotional outbursts – more precisely, collective emotional outbursts. They are expressions of wrath, and, like all forms of wrath, they summon others to wrath and they summon counter-wrath from those they attack.

When Molly Ball, the author of *Time*'s "Secret History" of the Democrats' 2020 campaign strategy, addressed the post–George Floyd riots, she took care to assert: "The racial-justice uprising sparked by George Floyd's killing in May was not primarily a political movement. The organizers who helped lead it wanted to harness its momentum for the election without allowing it to be co-opted by politicians." As Tony Thomas, writing in *Quadrant*, immediately pointed out, Ball's two sentences contradict each other: the riot was "not primarily political," but its organizers "wanted to harness its momentum for the election."[44]

The frenzy of a riot is difficult to capture, even on camera. That's because much of it takes place in the minds and bodies of the rioters. The riot takes over. This does not mean that the rioters are typically angry, in the sense of two men squaring off to fight or a husband and wife in the midst of a quarrel. Often rioters act in what seems like a cool and deliberative way. They arm themselves with appropriate gear. They choose particular targets. They coordinate with one another. They plot tactics against the police. Gleefulness and pride are apparent. The riot is an act of transgression in which most, if not all, the norms of social order that ordinarily ensure respect for life and property are thrown out the shattered window.

Perhaps the best accounts we have of riots are those of novelists whose talent is getting inside the minds of people who would not ordinarily unleash their worst impulses on their neighbors. In his novel *Barnaby Rudge*, Dickens imagines his way into the anti-Catholic Gordon Riots in London in 1780, targets of which included Newgate Prison and the Bank of England. His focal point, the simpleton Barnaby, is caught up in the madness with no clear idea of what is happening but with a strong sense of satisfaction. At one point: "After the whirl of noise and riot in which the last two days had been passed, the pleasures of solitude and peace were enhanced a thousand-fold. He felt quite happy; and as he leaned upon his staff and mused, a bright smile overspread his face, and none but cheerful visions floated into his brain." Poor Barnaby is doomed, but he is not alone in feeling that the riots were gratifying. Elsewhere we read of Hugh, a hostler who is a ringleader in the riot, who, though fatigued by "the mischief and destruction" he has achieved, is still full of "boisterous merriment."[45]

London riots in 1780 are a long way from the American mayhem of 2020, but every riot consumes its Barnabys and Hughs. The most astonishing chapter in Ralph Ellison's brilliant novel *Invisible Man* (1952) describes the Harlem race riot of 1943 from the standpoint of the unnamed narrator – who is part instigator, part restrainer, and full participant in the riot, which in turn destroys him, at least psychologically. Ellison himself had covered the riot as a reporter for the *New York Post*. Ellison described getting off the subway in Harlem during the riot and hearing "not only crashing glass, gunfire, and sirens but also the shouting of a great celebration. In fact, a carnival-like atmosphere developed as thousands of Harlemites looted White-owned stores and spared Black ones. White mannequins were torn limb from limb as looters shouted, "I'm doing this for revenge."[46] What caused this? What turns long-endured grievances into a riot? Resentment over high prices, police brutality, and the mistreatment of Black World War II soldiers didn't just crystallize as a riot out of thin air.

In the pages of *Invisible Man*, this sense of jubilant celebration sweeps up the narrator, even as one of the rioters is shot dead in front of him. He joins a band of rioters who carefully equip themselves with flashlights, other gear, and pails of fuel oil at a hardware store they have looted and who proceed to burn down the tenement in which many of them live. The "invisible man" himself helps spread the fuel and light the fire. Later he battles a rival Harlem leader who is intent on using the riot as a cover for killing his Black opponents. The riot summons feelings of terror and disgust, but the dominant notes are excitement, power, and glee.

A riot, to be sure, is an expression of wrath, but wrath is a special form of anger, one that can be experienced as pure pleasure. When we look back on riots, we tend to see them through the lens of what happened before and what happened next. The accepted account of the August 1943 Harlem riot is that a White police officer, James Collins, shot and superficially wounded a Black soldier, Robert Bandy, who had interrupted the arrest of a Black woman, Marjorie Polite, for "disturbing the peace" at the Braddock Hotel in Harlem at the corner of 126th Street and 8th Avenue.[47] A rumor circulated that Bandy, who had been shot in the shoulder, had died. In the ensuing two days of rioting, six people were killed. In the book, the trigger is a White cop who shoots and kills a young Black man in Bryant Park when he resists arrest for peddling paper dolls without a license. According to a biographical film about Ellison, the race riot in *Invisible Man* "foreshadowed a new Black assertiveness, a boldness that would energize the coming civil rights struggle."[48]

Riots, we might say, always draw from the deep well of resentments, mixed with the freshening taste of freedom from all the constraints that normally hold people back. In an instant, those angry resentments can become exuberant delight. It is a flash flame that usually burns itself out quickly, but in the right circumstances it can be organized and sustained. "But they're not going to stop. They're not going to stop. They're not," said Senator Harris. She was right.

Chapter Two

VERY FINE PEOPLE

JACOB ANTHONY CHANSLEY, who also goes by the name Jake Angeli, was one of the people who made their way into the chamber of the U.S. Senate in the Capitol on January 6, 2021, to protest the Senate's impending certification of state electors who would install Joe Biden as the 46th president of the United States. His name may not register, but his image will: he was the fellow bizarrely attired in a coyote-fur hat sprouting black buffalo horns; shirtless, showing his muscular but heavily tattooed torso; sporting black gloves and a red knapsack; face painted in vertical red, white, and blue stripes; and carrying an American flag on a spear.

The disorderly intrusion of several hundred protesters into the Capitol was quickly characterized by the media, and by many politicians, as an "insurrection." Moreover, the accusation of insurrection was applied to the many thousands of Trump supporters in Washington that day who had nothing to do with the intrusion into the Capitol. And that characterization became the basis for the House of Representatives to impeach President Trump for supposedly inciting the "insurrection" and the impetus for President Biden to order 26,000 National Guard troops to defend Washington during his inauguration on January 20. As it happened, there was no insurrection.

Images of Chansley in his costume – arguing with a police officer; posing with other protesters in a foyer; standing behind the Senate dais with his fist raised in triumph; outside holding a sign that declared "Q Sent Me!" and speaking into a microphone while clutching the obverse of the sign, "Hold the Line Patriots God Wins"; and, in several shots, chin raised as he apparently sings – stand out among the handful of photos of the Capitol protest that that have become iconic. They helped cement the reputation of the protesters as crazy extremists.

Chansley was never photographed committing or threatening violence against person or property. In several of the images, he is calm and – if one can see past his strange garb – even dignified. But he was charged with "violent entry and disorderly conduct" on the Capitol grounds. Details of his life soon came spilling out. A thirty-three-year-old from Phoenix, Arizona, who had been living with his mother since January 2019, Chansley refused to eat in jail because he was denied organic food. He had attended other Trump rallies in his odd costume, where he had gained the nickname "the QAnon Shaman."[1]

At least some of his tattoos have esoteric meanings. The rectangular blocks on his arms are said to represent the wall President Trump was building at the Mexican border. "One of his tattoos is said to show the symbol of Wotanism, an acronym for "Will of the Aryan Nation."[2] "Wotan" is the German name for the god known as Odin in Norse mythology. QAnon is a fringe network of believers in a sinister global conspiracy that engages in sex trafficking of children and other heinous crimes. Some of its participants saw Trump as their champion.[3]

From almost any perspective, Chansley must be understood as a strange and disturbed individual. As "the QAnon Shaman," he may have attracted a certain following within this cult-like group, but he stands on the far fringes of Trump's supporters and American politics generally. His elevation by the media and Trump opponents as a symbol of the angry right does deserve attention. But Chansley's depiction in the media as an out-of-control rioter has proven to be a fabrication. In May 2021, video footage of Chansley came to light in which Capitol Hill police officer Keith Robishaw instructs the leaders of the crowd, "Show us no attacking, no assault, remain calm"; Chansley then turns to his followers and loudly declares: "This has to be peaceful. We have the right to peacefully assemble."[4]

The costumes of madmen often reveal something. Chansley offered a mash-up of Wild West frontiersman, Mandan Indian buffalo dancer, and European barbarian. The buffalo horns may have owed something to George Catlin's famous images of the Mandan Buffalo Dance, 1835–1837. The shirtless, spear-carrying look derived from popular images of Germanic tribesmen descending on Roman troops. His facial decoration may have been an homage to the war paint used by the ancient Picts and Celtic tribes – revived (without historical warrant) in the 1995 Mel Gibson movie *Braveheart*, about the fourteenth-century Scottish hero William Wallace. If we consider the pieces, it all makes a crazy kind of sense. Chansley adorned himself in references to heroic rebellion: the man standing apart from the established order to call it to account, ready to invoke mystical powers on behalf of his righteous war.

Chansley was dressed to play his part in a fantasy game, in which he was an angry avenger of injustices against the American people. Dressing the part of a character endowed with extraordinary powers has, of course, gained a degree of ordinariness. It is called "cosplay," short for "costume play," and many thousands of people attend conventions and enter competitions where they can win prizes for their imaginative impersonations of figures from science fiction, fable, and romance. Cosplay has its own magazines, a documentary, a movie or two, and what might be summed up as a subculture, which provides innocent recreation for many and delusional obsession for a few.

"The QAnon Shaman" is a figure from that world of self-delusion, which on occasion intersects reality. Lincoln's assassin, the actor John Wilkes Booth, imagined himself a tyrant-killing hero when he leaped onto the stage at Ford's Theater, held up a knife and proclaimed, "Sic semper tyrannis" – *thus always to tyrants* – legendarily Brutus's words on his participation in the assassination of Julius Caesar. Booth, like Chansley, was filled with political rage. In Booth's case, that eventually took the form of orchestrating a plot to kill not only Lincoln but also General Ulysses Grant, Secretary of State William H. Seward, and Vice President Andrew Johnson. QAnon, or at least some of its members, likewise seemed intent on assassinating several senators and perhaps Vice President Mike Pence. The details are murky, and there is no evidence that Chansley sought to injure anyone. The analogy, however, holds in a crucial way: Chansley, like Booth, saw himself as an agent of wrath against unjust authority, and, like Booth, he invented a persona to embody his desperate design.

Booth will forever remain in history for his contemptible act. Chansley will be remembered, if at all, as a buffoon, but one who was quickly elevated by opponents of President Trump into a defining image of his preposterous supporters. Charged with civil disorder, disorderly conduct, and obstruction of an official proceeding, Chansley offered through his lawyer to testify at the Senate impeachment trial of Trump. He was reportedly upset that Trump had not issued him a presidential pardon.[5]

"The QAnon Shaman" became a figure to reckon with because he summed up the farcical, if still dangerous, side of the angry mob that persisted in denying the legitimacy of Joe Biden's election.

Then and Now

Americans are too angry. Americans aren't angry enough.

Which is it?

In *A Bee in the Mouth: Anger in America Now* (2006), I traced the rise in American culture of a flamboyant style of anger. I argued that we had become addicted to a dangerous kind of self-indulgent anger. The *Bee* was a bit ahead of its time. The self-indulgent anger is incandescently worse today.

A Bee in the Mouth distinguished between, on one hand, those who proudly embraced the new cultural permission to throw aside the old restraints and strut their anger as if it were an accomplishment that others should respect and, on the other hand, those who continued to feel that unloosed anger was embarrassing and a bit shameful. I observed that the former category, the celebrants at the anger festival, generally belonged to the progressive side of the Great Cultural Divide, while the latter, the diffident crowd, represented what remained of traditionalist America. But I also observed that traditionalist America was at the threshold of discovering its own inner Rumpelstiltskin. Show-offy rage was proving contagious. Some figures on the right, including radio talk-show host Rush Limbaugh, had also developed flamboyant "new anger" styles.

What happens when one's side scorn and derision of the other is met with the other side's mockery and contempt? We are in the midst of finding out. I would rather it had not come to this, but, since it has, I would counsel my fellow traditionalists to discover better ways to focus their wrath. "The QAnon Shaman" and his fellow mummers do not exemplify our cause.

No one today would dispute that Americans are profoundly and often bitterly divided and that angry denunciations are now a major part of our cultural currency. But after publishing *A Bee in the Mouth*, I encountered a fair number of critics who disputed that there was anything new in what I called "new anger" and who found the public indignation and private raptures of hate to be merely the ordinary course of human emotion. Hadn't I forgotten the Civil War? My argument, however, demanded that we look at our emotions at a distance and to notice, over the long term, how much they change.

Other forms of cultural change are easier to spot. We can look at movies from the 1930s and notice how much styles of clothing have altered over the decades. Men at that time wore hats; they preferred broad-shouldered suits with thin waists and wide, tapered legs. Zoot suits were favored by some. Women wore calf-length dresses with clean lines and exaggerated shoulders. But as with styles of clothing and other tangible aspects of culture, so too with at least some of the intangibles. Did people in the 1930s love, hate, yearn, anger, or grieve? Yes. With the same intensity as people today? Surely. But did they act on and experience these emotions in the same way?

We might want to say yes to that question too – but, if so, we would miss a great deal. If we flip the calendar back through the decades to, say, any point before 1950, we come to a time in which an ethic of emotional self-control dominated most of American life. Children were taught to restrain their feelings; adults were counseled to bear their disappointments. And Americans learned not to be governed by their anger. This didn't mean those feelings didn't exist or weren't expressed. Rather, it meant their expression was held back or controlled, at least until it could be controlled no longer – and, even then, pulled back as soon as the person mastered himself.

If you doubt that anything has changed, see whether you can find the equivalent of "the QAnon Shaman" playing a role in the electoral politics of the 1930s or any earlier epoch in American life.

My generalizations, even now, aren't likely to persuade readers who are new to the idea that emotions are culturally patterned. The evidence in favor of such patterning filled up much of *A Bee in the Mouth*, chapters of which I have repurposed in this new book. As in that book, my particular focus is how we deal with anger, and my claim that we have developed over the last seventy-some years a new form of anger – *new anger* – remains central. What is new about "new anger" is that it is unashamed of itself. The person possessed by new anger is proud of his fury and eager to show it. New anger is anger on purposeful display, anger that declares "Look at me! I'm angry!!!" The exclamation points multiply. New anger is almost always vituperative. It finds words, and those who are dexterous with angry words win applause. That's because new anger is intensely aware of its audience, and the audience for performative anger encourages the performer to dig deeper and discover still better insults, curses, and screeches of outrage.

The audience for new anger, however, can be fickle. The spectators may like the performance but not the performer, and they may well be indifferent to the actual grievance behind the anger. The anger-performer can sometimes be laughed at even while his performance is considered rather good. The rapper Kanye West and the actor Alec Baldwin exemplify this ambiguity. Both are laughed at for their over-the-top tirades, but they are admired as well for their pyrotechnics.

One of the arguments in *A Bee in the Mouth* is that, although new anger had become part of our national politics, it didn't start out as political anger. We became newly angry with one another before we channeled that anger into political division, and political division remains only one arena in which the relaxation of old taboos on emotional aggression plays out.

In the years since I published that book, the angrification of our politics intensified, and now in this book I give that development a lot more attention. *Wrath* looks at our society as a place starkly divided between two sides, both animated by sharp disdain for each other. New anger, as I've said, is first of all a verbal thing. It expresses itself in flamboyantly harsh words. But new anger has never been merely verbal. It expresses itself in myriad other ways, including songs, music, clothing, the styling of cars, and sports. At its deepest end, it spills over to violence. And as I write this, that possibility – of our mutual wrath turning to riot, injury, and killing – has already been realized on a limited scale.

A Bee in the Mouth was, ultimately, a call to rein it in: to resume control over our anger. I put limited stock in "anger management" but, at the time, hoped for our collective rediscovery of why, for many generations, we sought to control anger rather than license it. My hope for such a restoration has faded. Wrath apparently will have its day, and we will have to learn afterward what our civilization once knew and we have managed to forget.

Donald Trump

Not long after *A Bee in the Mouth* came out, I published a short article, "I Paid for This Microphone," in which I summarized the concept of new anger and alluded to what struck me as a nice example of how new anger was forcing its way onto the public stage:

> *The sort of sneer-fest that we saw earlier this year with [comedienne] Rosie O'Donnell and Donald Trump had no equivalent in the Reagan years. Reagan himself could stage an angry moment, as in 1980 when he told debate moderator Jon Breen, who had tried to get a techie to turn off Reagan's microphone, "I paid for this microphone, Mr. Green." The quip, which Reagan took from the 1948 Spencer Tracy movie,* State of the Union, *left his opponent, George H. W. Bush, looking lame.*[6]

As far as I can remember, that was the first time I ever mentioned Trump in print. The second time was in August 2015, when I wrote an essay taking disapproving notice of his "bursting the confines of civility to say aggressively rude and obnoxious things." My views of Trump's presidency were transformed by his time in office, but my views of his temperament were not. I noted that Trump was among those who put "authenticity to oneself" above "respect for others" and that he played to the public's love of "the spectacle of other people's anger." In so doing, he "found a responsive chord in a significant segment of Republican primary voters." I concluded that "new anger is a performance, and for every performance there is eventually a curtain, if not a final bow."[7]

I returned to the topic of Trump's anger again in October 2019, but this time weighing his new anger against that of his foes. When did Americans lose their cool?

> *The two most popular answers are Donald Trump and "the Resistance." Both are superficially plausible. The Tweeter-in-Chief has made a performance art of his own anger and enjoys publicly humiliating his foes. His pussyhat wearing, impeachment-obsessed, and Antifa-admiring antagonists, however, have sustained an equally long display of indignation.*

In that article, I also went back to the Rosie O'Donnell saga and recounted it in more detail:

> *One of the swiftest paths to celebrity these days is a public spat in which the parties attempt to top each other in calumny. Part of Trump's rise to national prominence was his insult-slinging feud with the comedienne Rosie O'Donnell, 2006–07. After Trump had decided not to fire Miss USA for drug use, O'Donnell, speaking on* The View, *described him as a "snake-oil salesman on* Little House on the Prairie." *Trump responded by calling O'Donnell a "real loser" and "a woman out of control." In the years that followed the two continued at intervals to revile one another, often gleefully. In 2014, Trump tweeted, "Rosie is crude, rude, obnoxious and dumb – other than that I like her very much!"*
>
> *O'Donnell probably got the worst of this long-term feud because she ended up appealing for public sympathy. In 2014, she declared, "Probably the Trump stuff was the most*

bullying I ever experienced in my life, including as a child. It was national, and it was sanctioned societally. Whether I deserved it is up to your own interpretation." And after Trump had derided her in an August 2015 presidential debate, O'Donnell tweeted: "Try explaining that 2 ur kids."

The contretemps continues, each side showering contempt on the other. But is this really anger? It is performative anger: a show meant to entertain, not all that different from a World Wrestling Entertainment match, which not so incidentally has its own Trump connection going back to 1998 when he hosted Wrestlemania in Atlantic City. In 2006, wrestlers wearing Trump and O'Donnell disguises faced off in a WWE match.[8]

Curiously, I addressed the question of who Trump's core opponents and supporters really were, and I noted that their reciprocal anger seemed "to answer the question 'Who am I?' with 'I'm someone enraged at Trump and everything he stands for,' or 'I'm enraged at the criminals who have undermined our democracy by trying to undermine a duly elected president."

It took the 2020 presidential election for me to put aside, for once and all, my ambivalence about Trump and about the seeming equivalence of the rage of his critics and rage of his supporters. I didn't approve the self-indulgent anger of either side, but I judge the behavior of Trump's opponents in that election to be unconscionable at a level far beyond Trump's faults as an individual and as a president. This book is not about how the election was decided. I acknowledge my own stand only because not to do so would be to handicap readers for whom the decisive question is "Whose side are you on?" I am on Trump's side – but, more importantly, I am on the side of traditional American values for which Trump is an imperfect but important advocate. In these pages, I fault one and all who have led our nation into the often exciting but ultimately dispiriting and destructive sport of histrionic anger.

Civility?

As Jacob Chansley, "the QAnon Shaman," understands, anger *feels* empowering. As he may also realize, anger can prompt some poor choices that turn out to be significantly disempowering. Anger provokes reprisal, which of course provokes more reprisals, until we reach a point at which outrage leaps out in every direction. In such a situation, calls for unity and pleas for civility seem hapless. I don't want to make light of those calls. Groups such as Braver Angels and the Institute for Civility in Government articulate commendable ideals, and there is perhaps no better time to give those ideals voice than when we are in the midst of strife. Yet to summon people to listen to one another respectfully assumes that mutual trust is possible and mutual tolerance is desirable.

Those are not safe assumptions in America right now. Trust and tolerance do not thrive in the midst of wrath. In the spheres of culture and politics, trust has been displaced by deep suspicion of the other side's motives. And why should you think it worthwhile to tolerate an enemy who means to destroy you? If he says he doesn't mean to destroy you, you distrust what he says. If he tolerates you for the moment, is it not because he is waiting for a better opportunity to attack? This is the psychology of wrath, compounded of hatred and doubt, and not especially amenable to the balm of "communicating across political differences."[9]

When wrath has exhausted itself, the counsels of unity and civility may prevail – but, until then, we should expect to be immersed in vitriolic denunciation and worse. How much worse is not clear – but, plainly, illegal violence, the deployment of military force, wanton riot, and occasional murder are already part of the picture, as are efforts by the progressive side to deny the populist side access to the means of mass communication. Those efforts to silence the populists are, more than anything else, the obstacle to any rapprochement.

The Age of Rage

But not the only obstacle. "The QAnon Shaman" was pushed forward as the personification of pro-Trump lawlessness and sedition. But long before Chansley donned his horns and climbed the Capitol steps, Americans who liked Trump were faced with provocations for which they had no recourse. Where was "civility" on February 4, 2020, when House Speaker Nancy Pelosi stood up at the end of Trump's State of the Union speech and tore her printed copy of it in half? Where was "unity" when, with violent riots raging in towns and cities across the country in the summer of 2020, the national media in chorus described the events as "mostly peaceful protests?"[10]

How were Trump supporters to deal with the manufacture and endless repetition in the mass media of false stories about Trump? The claim that Trump colluded with Russian president Vladimir Putin in the 2016 presidential election turned out to be baseless, but for more than three years it was treated as an article of faith by his opponents. When Trump spoke publicly about the riots in Charlottesville, Virginia, on August 15, 2017, he praised the restraint of parties who peacefully disagree with one another ("very fine people on both sides") and condemned the rioters: "I'm not talking about the neo-Nazis and White nationalists, because they should be condemned totally." With dishonest editing, news outlets made it appear that Trump had called neo-Nazis "very fine people." This has sufficient durability that Joe Biden referred to it when he announced his presidential candidacy, saying that Trump had "assigned a moral equivalence between those spreading hate and those with the courage to stand against it."[11] The slander continues to be repeated *ad nauseam* by journalists, politicians, and ordinary people who are unlikely ever to check the actual video.

Adjectives intended to leapfrog the facts and impose a biased

33

judgment on events have become standard practice in journalism. Claims about voter fraud were nearly always described without further ado as "false" or "baseless" – presumably because, in the minds of the journalists, any possibility that such a claim was factual or supported by strong evidence had to be extinguished. The same automatic negation is applied to any mention of doubts about the prevailing theory of global warming; assertions that humans have only two sexes; ideas that COVID-19 was only a little more deadly than the flu; arguments that women are treated advantageously in the workforce; and demonstrations that police, in general, treat Blacks with dignity and respect. Such views are seldom mentioned – but, when they are mentioned, they are reliably accompanied by an editorializing adjective that asserts they are patently untrue.

When Trump was still protesting the results of the election in January, the *Washington Post* ran a major story, based on an anonymous source, claiming that Trump had told Georgia's lead elections investigator to "find the fraud" and that she would be "a national hero" if she did. The story received widespread attention, and its claims – that Trump was illegally interfering with the election – were widely repeated. In March, the *Post* ran a correction, based on a recording of Trump's actual conversation with the investigator. The paper acknowledged that important claims made in the original article were false:

> *Instead, Trump urged the investigator to scrutinize ballots in Fulton County, Ga., asserting she would find "dishonesty" there. He also told her that she had "the most important job in the country right now."* [12]

Trump supporters were, once again, confronted with a damaging falsehood retracted only at the point where the retraction could make no material difference.

Epithets of a different kind are written into stories favored by the left. Riots by BLM or Antifa remained in the category of "mostly peaceful protest" no matter the level of destruction, while the Capitol riot by Trump supporters was "domestic terrorism" and "insurrection," no matter the absence of firearms among the protesters and significant injuries to law enforcement. The one-sided vocabulary is buttressed by the silencing of those who objected. Ordinary citizens who disputed the tendentious terms could find themselves banned from Twitter, Facebook, and other social media.

By the time you are reading this, some of these examples will surely have faded from memory, but the stoking of public anger by the media will just as surely continue. That's because the media have transformed themselves from their old configuration as a source of news, information, argument, and entertainment into a device for affirming identity-group solidarity. That's the thesis of a recent book by Andrey Mir (Andrey Miroshnichenko), *Post-journalism and the Death of Newspapers: The Media after Trump: Manufacturing Anger and Polarization*.[13] Mir argues that newspapers, having lost their monopoly over determining what events count as "news" and therefore deserve in-depth reporting, have flipped to a new kind of product. They now focus on stoking the prejudices of a core readership who are willing to pay to have their favored opinions validated, day after day. Mir's book caught the attention of Martin Gurri, who amplified Mir's thesis in a widely read article in *City Journal*, in which he observed, "The old media had needed happy customers. The goal of post-journalism, according to Mir, is to 'produce angry citizens.'" Gurri added that the exemplar of this new type of journalism is the *New York Times*, which serves as "the Vatican of liberal political furor."[14]

That the media strive to intensify anger as a way of securing a market niche seems likely enough, but it is important to add that the public addiction to anger and the angrification of identity groups began long before newspapers and network TV threw objective journalism overboard. My 2003 book, *Diversity: The Invention of a Concept*, dealt with the roots of identitarianism in the United States, and my 2020 book, *1620: A Critical Response to the 1619 Project*, tracked the descent of *diversity* into a world of historical fantasy and contrivance. Rallying people to hate Trump, or rallying people who hate Trump's supporters, add up to only a fraction of the fervor that now grips the progressive left. Another substantial fraction is racial animus. The 1619 Project, the post–George Floyd riots, and the pervasive idea that Blacks are only victims and Whites are only oppressors are the staple diet of the anti-American wrath of the left. Other dishes are served as well – among them climate change, transphobia, and immigration. But the angry tribalism of our time is based primarily on the vaporous idea that America is systemically racist.[15]

If, Then, and In Between

Wrath entails more than a sense of deep alienation, at least if it is to go beyond a single act of self-destructive madness. To be more than that, it needs the endorsement of others. It has to have its own mob, a crowd of people who share a sense of outrage. And, for it to become true wrath, that crowd must believe that all of its ordinary avenues of redress have been barricaded: it has a just grievance and no place to turn for justice. Wrath is a matter of the crowd taking things into its own hands. It might do that by stealing an election, or it might do that by marching on the Capitol. Whichever direction it goes, it will do so in a spirit that, in the interests of true justice, the old rules have to be discarded. A higher justice calls for action that would ordinarily be out of bounds.

If Donald Trump were a tyrant about to impose his personal dictatorship on the United States, or install a fascist regime, or destroy the world via the unbridled use of fossil fuels, or destroy the Constitution via his defiance of the rule of law, or unleash vicious racism into our national life, or bring an end to all sense of dignity and decency in America, or do all these things, *then* launching FBI investigations on spurious evidence, staging riots, suppressing news stories, conjuring impeachments, and manipulating elections would be fair and honorable. *We've got to do something,* say the proponents of these measures. *Otherwise, this terrible man and his army of deluded deplorables will destroy our country.* This is war, and the only rule is *we must win.* Thus, it is not enough to remove Trump from office. He must be obliterated. The latest step, as I write, is a congressional bill, HR 484, the "No Glory for Hate Act," which would prohibit the burial of Trump's body in Arlington National Cemetery or the erecting of other memorials in his honor.[16]

But *if* Donald Trump were a tribune of the people who was successfully empowering ordinary Americans who had been marginalized by the "deep state"; or restoring jobs and prosperity to Americans who had lost ground because the government had colluded with global business; or standing against a tide of illegal immigrants who undercut wages and usurped job opportunities; or opposing the race hustlers and their efforts to impose racial propaganda, such as critical race theory, on students; or standing up to the bullies who manufacture fake news, or who corrupt elections and steal votes; *then* gathering in mass protests, questioning the validity of the electoral results, and marching on the Capitol would be entirely warranted (and perhaps too little). *We've got to do something,* is what the people on this side also say. *Otherwise, this terrible band of progressive authoritarians will destroy our country, our freedom, and our future.* This is war, and unless we learn how to fight back against a ruthless and unscrupulous enemy, *we will certainly be crushed.*

While there are those who reject this stark set of alternatives, I believe they have thin popular support. The moderates – if that is a fair label for those who fear and reject both extremes – have no grip on public sentiment, and they are shunned by both sides, who see them as unprincipled, self-serving, or oblivious to the real dangers ahead. They have escaped the winepress of wrath only to end up as withered grapes. Most of them are Republicans who reject Trump but who have only a sliver of support in their own party. The turncoat members of the Lincoln Project, formed in 2019, came apart after its cofounder John Weaver was revealed to have used his position to extract sexual favors from young men hoping to advance their careers. The Never-Trumper news network, the Bulwark, founded in 2018 by Charlie Sykes, simply made it easier for conservatives to recognize the media figures who had detached themselves from the common interest of ordinary Americans. Whatever else the Lincoln Project and the Bulwark accomplished, they both made clear that the histrionics of new anger were not limited to Trump and his supporters or to the increasingly hysterical progressive left. "Moderates," too, could engage in wild accusation and vitriolic denunciation. The middle did not hold.

What then? One side or the other will have to prevail. President Biden's call for "unity" is spurious. He may like the sound of the word, but he has no intention of reaching out seriously to his opponents and no policy that moves an inch in their direction. If we have a President Harris by the time you are reading this, we will have even more of the same antagonism toward traditional Americans. The progressive left, hurriedly institutionalizing its programs and seeking to lock in place the devious means by which it prevailed in the 2020 election, may well prevail further. Jacob Chansley and his compatriots will definitely lose. What we need is the righteous wrath of patriots who will not let their freedoms slip away.

On December 19, 1776, Thomas Paine published "The American Crisis." General George Washington was on the verge of losing the Revolutionary War, as more than 11,000 of his volunteer troops had given up and left after a string of defeats. Paine rallied the remainder with his oft-quoted lines:

These are the times that try men's souls; the summer soldier and the sunshine patriot will, in this crisis, shrink from the service of his country; but he that stands it now, deserves the love and thanks of man and woman. Tyranny, like hell, is not easily conquered.[17]

"Try," in that sentence, is in the original meaning of "sift, examine, test, or scrutinize." It survives when we say "He was tried for high crimes and misdemeanors," and it is why we have "trials." These are the times that try men's souls. Some will be found wanting. Others will come through with a pure and noble wrath.

Chapter Three

BEES

"A BEE IN THE MOUTH is always bad." I was walking down Bay State Road in Boston in summer 2004 when I heard a workman say this to his partner.

The two men were struggling to carry a wobbly Plexiglas shower stall out of a townhouse. But when they got outside, their driver had taken off with the truck. One of them began to curse the truant driver; his partner responded by warning about entertaining bees in his mouth.

I took his arresting way of referring to his partner's over-the-top vocal anger as the title of my 2006 book on anger in America. What I especially liked was the suggestion that extravagant cursing is harmful to the man who gives full cry to his vexation. That idea was drastically out of tune with the times, in which letting loose with vituperation seemed more likely to be applauded than reproved.

Who was the cautionary workman? I never found out, but over the years I've continued to look for the origins of that particular phrase. I may have been looking in the wrong places. I found an improbably large number of cases in which people have had the unfortunate experience of being stung in the mouth.[1] (One lesson is to look at that picnic sandwich before you bite.) I thought I might be in search of a proverb, perhaps from a culture that cautions people against letting anger turn into rant, but I found nothing in that vein.

But I did eventually find a celebrated ten-second moment in the 138th episode (December 3, 1995) of the cartoon *The Simpsons*, in which Homer Simpson faces his boss, Mr. Burns, who has arrogantly appropriated Homer's son Bart. Burns, the high-handed plutocrat, tells Homer, "May I suggest you leave immediately?" Homer defies him:

> *Or what? You'll release the dogs, or the bees, or the dogs with bees in their mouth, and when they bark, they shoot bees at you? Well, go ahead. Do your worst!*[2]

That moment in *The Simpsons* may have had nothing to do with what the workman said, but it does fill in a space in this story. *The Simpsons*, which debuted on Fox TV in December 1989 and became the longest-running prime-time TV series in history, began as a satire of the saccharine family comedies of the 1980s, such as *Diff'rent Strokes, ALF*, and *Family Ties*. As one commentator put it:

> *Each of these big shows centered around instilling the virtues of the American family unit with smart aleck but well-meaning kids, and wise and loving parents. The families being shown on TV were safe and comfortable depictions of the staunchly middle-upper class, rich enough to be aspirational while not so wealthy that they become unrelatable ... TV at its softest and most docile.*[3]

The Simpsons burst into this banality with a wildly dysfunctional family, clinging to the lower blue-collar edge of the small-town American middle class. The smart-aleck kids were now junior anarchists, and the parents, especially Homer, anything but wise. Homer is lazy, ignorant, wantonly aggressive, self-centered, gluttonous, and incapable of giving good counsel to his children.

For all that, he fiercely protects his family. When they are threatened, he gets really angry.

The show was at its most subversive in its early years, when it depicted the unraveling of once-taken-for-granted standards of American family life. And it was during that period that its writers gave Homer the inspired lunacy of his weaponized "dogs with bees in their mouths" speech. Homer's speech somehow ties up anger, aggression, and class envy with virtuoso verbal performance. It is an example of what I soon came to call "new anger." New anger is not just performed, but performance-oriented. It assumes an appreciative audience that recognizes and applauds the verbal creativity and the emotional position of the performer, who is, in principle, standing up to injustice.

New anger long predates *The Simpsons,* although the show can be taken as one milestone on new anger's career toward cultural dominance. In this and following chapters, I am going to trace that career as the foundation of the wrath we face today. But I'll start with a small but interesting early example.

In a scene in the 1967 comedy-drama *Guess Who's Coming to Dinner?* Matt Drayton, a crotchety character played by Spencer Tracy, has just purchased some Oregon boysenberry sherbet from Mel's Drive-In ice cream stand and is back in his car. Paying little attention, Drayton backs his Plymouth Valiant into the side of a hot rod, a '32 Deuce Roadster, whose owner is rightly incensed. Drayton is the wealthy White publisher of San Francisco's leading newspaper, and an outspoken liberal, whose enthusiasms include his ardent support for racial equality. The roadster's owner is a young Black man of whom we learn little except that he has just spent some money fixing up his hot rod.

Drayton apologizes perfunctorily, asks the owner what it will cost to fix the car ($40), hands him $50, and drives off. The car's owner, still enraged, yells after the departing Drayton. What's most arresting about the scene is that as the young man expresses his outrage, the bystanders at the ice-cream stand cheer.

Guess Who's Coming to Dinner? is a movie about racial relations, centered on Drayton's daughter Joey's surprise announcement that she intends to wed Dr. John Prentice (played by Sidney Poitier). Liberal Drayton is thrust into the uncomfortable position of having to live up to his professed principles. While this main drama unfolds, the movie runs through a series of other interactions between Black and White characters that reveal their hidden or not-so-hidden prejudices. Drayton shows himself to be thoughtlessly privileged and self-indulgent. The crowd at the ice-cream stand shows itself alert to the status difference between Drayton and the man whose car he has dented, and they are clearly on the side of the victim when he loudly and angrily stands up for himself. It is 1967 in San Francisco, after all, and the righteous anger of the oppressed is something to celebrate.

Malice

It wasn't always that way. When I wrote *A Bee in the Mouth,* a lot of Americans still had some memory of a time when public expressions of anger were pretty rare – or, at least, rare enough to deserve comment when they occurred. Moreover, cultural observers had made a small industry of lamenting the decline in "civility." For instance, in 1997, Nicolaus Mills, a professor of American studies at Sarah Lawrence College, published *The Triumph of Meanness: America's War against Its Better Self.* Mills's book discovered a "new meanness" where a decade later I found "new anger." The difference was that the "new meanness" was the uncharitable spirit of conservatives, such as those who ordered the removal of benches in New York City subway stops to prevent "homeless people" sleeping on them. Meanness to Mills meant the income gap between rich and poor, the unwillingness of the affluent to pay higher taxes for social services to the less well off, resistance to mass immigration, the popularity of bare-knuckle fighting, and a thousand other ways in which "cruelty wins out over compassion." Mills defined "meanness" as "a politics of spite and cruelty that targets the vulnerable."[4]

I have limited sympathy for Mills's political views, but his book did capture something real. In a chapter titled "The New Savagery," Mills surveyed the seamy underside of popular culture in the 1990s, mentioning cockfighting; high-stakes dogfights; the rise of mixed martial arts matches; "True Crime Cards" (like baseball cards but featuring gangsters and serial killers);[5] violent video games, such as *Mortal Kombat*; TV shows, such as *The Jane Whitney Show* and *The Geraldo Rivera Show*, that staged confrontations between guests; a vigilante group in Dallas called Dead Serious that offered $5,000 rewards to members who killed someone who was committing a felony; and more. He cited the 1994 trial of Lorena Bobbitt for cutting off her husband's penis, attended by supporters with signs such as "Lorena Bobbitt for Surgeon General," and the rise of musical genres that celebrated "hate and violence." He mentioned Guns N' Roses' misogynist lyrics and Ice-T's encomium to murdering police, "Cop Killer." We are reminded that Quentin Tarantino's Academy Award–winning (and blood-soaked) *Pulp Fiction* was released in 1994.

Mills's catalog is a litany of real and imaginary violence that fostered a moral callousness in the public. This willingness to commit acts of cruelty or to consume them vicariously surely tells us something about the changing character of Americans during this period, and Mills's words "meanness" and "savagery" are apt – up to a point. They describe what was happening, however, from an emotional distance. Mills says nothing about the emotional incitements that brought these sorts of degradation into our common life.

The "meanness" that Mills found in these materials is merely the manifestation of the new kind of anger that had begun to settle, bone-deep, in the American soul. It was an anger directed at no one in particular and everyone at once. A lonely and isolated self was demanding attention and recognition. Violence, both real and pretended, was used to shock and offend but, most important, to define the individual as fully present. Anger was a way to become visible to oneself and others. Theatrical violence was one of the ways to focus that anger.

How we became so angry is another question.

Electing Anger

Was it the consequence of several bitterly fought presidential elections? Were the news media to blame? Did we just endure a slow erosion in civility that has finally exposed the raw feelings underneath? Did we develop a hair-trigger intolerance for one another?

Some scholars assure us that this profusion of anger isn't really new. Americans, say these scholars, were always angry. We had an uncivil Boston Tea Party and an eight-year Revolutionary War. The presidential election in 1800 – Adams vs. Jefferson – was at least as nasty as Bush vs. Gore or Bush vs. Kerry. (Though being more recent and therefore more vivid, Obama vs. McCain, Obama vs. Romney, and Clinton vs. Trump were actually tamer affairs. Trump vs. Biden is another matter altogether.) We fought a bloody Civil War with over a million casualties. The late nineteenth and the first half of the twentieth centuries were replete with bloody labor and race riots. And the 1960s unleased mass protests, riots, tear gas, and more protests on a new scale.

For a while, some scholars argued that the angry culture war of recent years ("red states" vs. "blue states") is an illusion. We are, they say, mostly in agreement on the important matters, and it is merely political elites and the controversy-hungry media that conjure up the so-called culture war. These views are mistaken, and, in light of the 2016 election of Donald Trump and the bitter aftermath of the 2020 election, the proponents of this no-culture-war theory have fallen silent. The new line is that the Trumpian side of the culture war is profoundly illegitimate and deserves to be stigmatized and prevented from any further involvement in public life. That approach primes the "deplorables" for a wrathful response, which may be exactly what the dominant progressive left hopes will happen. An actual rebellion would provide an excuse for a decisive use of force against these enemies of the "woke state."

Which is to say, the anger we see and hear around us differs in character from the anger of previous epochs, and it is no illusion. The anger of the present is, among other things, more flamboyant, more self-righteous, and more theatrical than anger at other times in our history. It often has the look-at-me character of performance art. And it is readier to tip into outright war.

I have said enough about that in previous chapters. Here I turn back to examples from *A Bee in the Mouth* to provide such historical depth.

For instance, in mid-July 2004, Ben Cohen, the cofounder of Ben & Jerry's Ice Cream, launched his Pants on Fire Tour in Spokane, Washington. Cohen planned to tour the country, as an Associated Press writer put it, "towing a 12-foot-tall effigy of President Bush with fake flames shooting out of the pants,"[6] alluding to the children's rhyme, "Liar, liar, / Pants on fire." What was Bush accused of lying about? Iraq's involvement in the 9/11 attacks? Its possession of weapons of mass destruction? What matters for my purposes is the theatricality of Cohen's anger.

The anger in America today differs from earlier epochs in that many people seem proud of their anger. It has become a badge of authenticity, and holding back or repressing anger is often depicted as a weakness or failure of self-assertion rather than a worthy form of self-control. We have elaborated this view into several popular theories that encourage the expression of anger as a way for members of ethnic groups, women, political parties, children, or people in general to "empower" themselves. This is new. However angry Americans were in 1776, 1800, 1860, or 1963, they were not congratulating themselves for getting angry.

The people and situations that evoke our anger today also differ in some interesting ways from angers past. Today we don't pick too many fights over family honor, and we don't seem to get especially worked up by people who defy our authority. We can be calm in the face of insults that not so long ago would have led to armed duels. But then we flare into livid fury for reasons that would have baffled our ancestors. What was the nineteenth-century equivalent of road rage on the Los Angeles freeways? Something has happened to us that allows hugely disproportionate responses to what are, after all, small provocations. We also can get furious if we feel disrespect aimed at our self-definition. "Take me seriously" is the message of much of our anger, where, in another time and place, a self-reliant American would have shrugged and walked away. Some of the contemporary rhetoric of anger is based on claims that our rights have been violated. Rights-based grievances are old, but our sense of what those rights are has ballooned beyond anything Jefferson, Lincoln, W. E. B. DuBois, or even Justice Earl Warren might have imagined.

And our anger is especially sharp at those who pretend to be one thing and really are another. A characteristic anger of our times enunciates outrage at the phony, the hypocrite, the liar, and the fake – so much so that we often reframe anger caused by something else into an accusation of phoniness, hypocrisy, lying, and fakery. They are the trump cards in our anger deck. Think of the anger provoked by Rachel Dolezal, the NAACP chapter president in Spokane who was revealed in 2015 to be a White woman pretending to be Black. The anger Dolezal provoked, however, is less interesting than her own anger. A reviewer noted that when Ijeoma Oluo, "an actual black woman," interviewed Dolezal, the "simple presence of Oluo . . . appears to make Dolezal seethe."[7] Dolezal turned out to be only one of several White women to have pursued this ruse. Jessica Krug, aka "Jessica La Bombalera," a professor of African American history at George Washington University, also passed herself off as Black and also profited from her disguise. In Krug's case, she took grants intended for Black scholars. Krug confessed that her career was rooted in "a toxic soil of lies."[8] Krug was especially known for her "rage." As one commentator observed, she busied herself angrily policing "who was 'Black enough' or 'down enough' to engage" with Black subjects.[9] In September 2020, yet another woman, CV Vitolo-Haddad, a graduate student at the University of Wisconsin at Madison, resigned from a teaching position after she was outed as a White person pretending to be Black.[10] Vitolo-Haddad stayed true to the pattern through her angry disparagement of others for racial-identity transgressions, including Krug, whom she called a "Kansas cracker" who got her PhD "performing blackface." She "also described 'transraciality' as 'violence.'"[11]

The performance-art aspect of anger; its merit-badge "I'm angry, therefore I'm real" quality; its road-rage "respect-me" style; its rights assertions; and its furious judgments of others are not the only characteristics of new anger. But they will do for a start, as we examine the emotional terrain in which anger has achieved prestige and celebrity. We have become, without really noticing it, a culture that celebrates anger.

Early in 2006, a small political ruckus broke out over a remark by Ken Mehlman, chairman of the Republican National Committee. Speaking on ABC's *This Week* (February 5), Mehlman said that Senator Hillary Clinton "seems to have a lot of anger," and he added, "voters do not send angry candidates to the White House." Within a few days, Democrats and left-leaning pundits responded by attacking Republicans for running an "anger strategy." They countered the depiction of Hillary with the claim that it was Republicans, including Mehlman, who really were angry. George Lakoff, a University of California at Berkeley linguistics professor who frequently advised Democrats about how issues were rhetorically framed, accused Mehlman of deploying a sexist stereotype, "the crone – angry, nasty, but powerful."

Hillary Clinton, however, never escaped that judgment of her temperament, and the episode helped bring the peculiar dynamic of contemporary political anger out in the open. In 2007 and again in 2016, Clinton's angry persona cut against her with voters, many millions of whom no doubt regarded their own anger as empowering but hers as off-putting. Plainly, all anger is not created equal. If anger is a performance, it can be judged. If the person is seen as controlled by rather than controlling the anger, the judgment can be decisively negative. Trump frequently performed anger but was never seen by his supporters as temperamentally angry.

Hillary Clinton provided many occasions for her supporters to repeat the feminist cliché that men are honored for their anger while women are castigated for theirs. The truth is considerably more complicated, but the reminder that men and women get angry in different ways and often about different things is worth bearing in mind.

A story is told of both Plato and Saint Ambrose that when they were infants, a swarm of bees flew in and out of their mouths, presaging their future eloquence. A bee in the mouth, apparently, isn't always bad. Ambrose, as it happened, grew up to have special wisdom about anger, counseling his followers that when confronted by anger, they should keep their mouths shut. But verbal expression isn't the only way we might show anger.

Going Postal

On December 2, 1983, a postal worker named James Brooks opened fire on his manager, the postmaster of Anniston, Alabama, killing him and wounding another supervisor. In the following decade, ten more post-office shootings around the nation left thirty-five people dead and inspired the term "going postal" for that boil of frustration that results in murderous rage.

Anger that triggers a man (it's almost always a man) to pack a gun to work and shoot people is rare and, of course, not culturally sanctioned. It does, however, occupy a place in our collective imagination. Most of the time, when we use the phrase "going postal," we don't mean a murderous rampage. We mean, instead, a noisy, dramatic outburst against someone – usually a bureaucrat – who has exhausted someone's patience. The metaphor of going postal, not James Brooks and his flesh-and-blood imitators, says something about the sardonic, darkly self-pleased way in which many Americans regard expressions of anger.

The symbolic representation of anger has, in fact, become ubiquitous in American life and, like other stuff we see every day, has ceased to be especially noticeable. By way of experiment, one day back in 2004, notebook in hand, I took a fifteen-minute walk through Boston's Kenmore Square, in the shadow of Fenway Park. My goal was to press the question: how many symbolic expressions of anger would I find in those few minutes?

Naturally, I started at the post office. "I see dumb people," read a bumper sticker on a car parked in front, declaring the driver's notional contempt for whatever portion of humanity crossed his path. The small-time misanthrope was apparently inside dealing with the clerks. "I see dumb people" played off the catchphrase for the movie *The Sixth Sense* (1999), in which the psychic child, Cole Sear, says, "I see dead people." The twist in the movie is that the dead people didn't know they were dead. The bumper sticker thus coyly abused other drivers who presumably didn't realize their own lack of mental agility. The bumper sticker thus presented the owner's hauteur and offered a general insult to fellow drivers. But was it angry?

A young man swaggered past in baggy jeans and a black sweatshirt, the hood – fringed with silver spikes, a corona of malice – thrown back, taunting passersby. Nearby, a young red-toenailed woman sat on some steps lapping an ice cream, unperturbed for the moment by whatever demon of self-loathing caused her to sew her own face and leave the needles in. Perhaps both the boy and the girl were better understood as making fashion statements.

But then the question becomes, why the popularity of fashions that represent hostility and self-loathing?

Not much is left today of the punk fashion that was already passé in 2004, but other forms of angri-fashion can be spotted. The all-black and masked Antifa style has its epigones. On October 11, 2020, I snapped a picture of a window display in Saks Fifth Avenue, across 50th Street from Saint Patrick's Cathedral. On show was the work of a Brazilian fashion designer Guilherme Licurgo, whose "Manifesto" line of clothing, as helpfully explained by a sign, "questions the current state of affairs and invites transformative action." The three manikins were dressed in black militaristic garb that would have done Mussolini's fascist thugs proud. What made the display even more interesting is that four months earlier this part of midtown Manhattan had been visited by post–George Floyd rioters, who vandalized Saint Patrick's Cathedral and who spared Saks Fifth Avenue only because the department store had preemptively boarded up its windows and hired dozens of guards to stand vigil. I took pictures of that too. The anger of the mob is to be feared, but, when the fear fades, it is time to merchandize it.

I didn't judge the boy or the girl in Boston to have been angry when I saw them – not angry as physiologists describe the state. Their pulses didn't drag; their temperatures weren't rising or falling. They weren't scowling; they didn't glare. They neither flushed red nor turned pale. They weren't twitching; they didn't clench their fists. They looked relaxed, rather than tensed. They weren't sweating. If I had sent drops of their blood to a laboratory, I would have expected to find that neither had been secreting noradrenaline, the chemical trigger to the bodily signs of anger. They were just two people mindful of a fine afternoon.

Nor do I imagine that the window dressers or the purchasing agents of Saks Fifth Avenue, or their customers, were actually angry. Dressing up angry isn't anger, but what exactly is it? What does it mean?

In Boston in 2004, while neither of the people I described was literally angry, both were adorned with the insignia of anger that harmonized with their environment. Like the bumper sticker, the boy's baggy jeans and hood with silver spikes and the girl's face mutilated with an assortment of needles and pins summed up a general attitude. These were not just private, wholly individual statements. Rather, they were choices from the wardrobe of American culture as it then stood. The bumper sticker played on a tagline from a mass-market movie. The baggy jeans announced identification with hip-hop, and, along with the hooded sweatshirt, they suggested a young man who took his bearings from gangsta rap. The girl's self-mutilations announced that she saw herself in the post-punk scene. The driver, the boy, and the girl all sported an implied message: "Don't mess with me."

New anger is not a set of isolated events. It may flare up at times, like the Senate confirmation hearings for Supreme Court nominee Brett Kavanaugh in September 2018, but the spectacular examples are misleading. They wouldn't happen if anger had not become an accepted part of everyday life. New anger, in this sense, is all around us all the time, invisible to the eye, though we breathe it in like air pollution. On a particularly bad day, we may notice it: people around us seem especially rude and unpleasant; we encounter road rage (or worse, commit it); or we unexpectedly run into an anger exhibitionist. But generally the smog stays just below the threshold of what we notice. We've grown used to it, and, having breathed it for so long, we've made it part of ourselves.

Across the street from the young man and woman, near Fenway Park, a man was selling "Yankees Suck" ball caps.

Nearby, a car-stereo system was humping the rhythms of the rapper 50 Cent:

> . . . control your jealousy
> 'Cause I can't control my temper, I'm fittin' to catch
> a felony

52

Pistol in hand homie, I'm down to get it poppin'
Once I squeeze the first shot [gun shot], you know
          I ain't stoppin'
Till my clip is empty, I'm simply
Not that nigga you should try your luck with, or fuck with
Hollow-tip shells struck you with your bones broken,
          gun smokin', still locin'... [12]

Headphones Required

Hip-hop was then the music of self-aggrandizement and power and sex, but it was mostly anger music. The genre has moved on. But we have plenty of other anger music. In *A Bee in the Mouth*, I devoted a whole chapter to anger music, not least because popular song is one of the nurseries of adolescent emotion. In this book, I touch on the topic in several places. That's because the songs that teenagers and young adults listen to become the playlist or soundtrack of their adult lives, teaching them how to feel, especially toward romance and sex. They are a major part of that "sentimental education" I referred to in the preface. But they are also very difficult to capture on the page. Transcribing lyrics doesn't come close to capturing the sound, the performance, or the presence of the performer. And in the case of anger music, the angriness of the performer is crucial.

In 2006, I referred to old thrashers such as Metallica's "St. Anger," Ablaze My Sorrow's "Anger Hate and Fury" (AMS's anger seemingly extends to commas), Flake's "Wild Cool Anger," the Anger Brothers pop act, and the Ministers of Anger. I mentioned the advice of Matisyahu, a Jewish rapper from Brooklyn's Crown Heights: "Slam your fist on the table and make your demand." I am willing to go only so far for the purpose of research. In this case, I've found a website that offers "11 Rage Anthems to Listen to When You're Angry." [13] It is telling that websites like this exist.

53

suspect that in the age of ragtime, or in the era of Glenn Miller and the big bands, rage anthems were not a thing. Here is the list:

1. *Kelis, "I Hate You So Much Right Now" (1999)*
2. *Eminem, "The Way I Am" (2000)*
3. *Linkin Park, "In the End" (2000)*
4. *Taylor Swift, "We Are Never Ever Getting Back Together" (2012)*
5. *Kanye West, "Black Skinhead" (2013)*
6. *Pink, "So What" (2008)*
7. *30 Seconds to Mars, "The Kill" (2006)*
8. *Rage against the Machine, "Killing in the Name" (1992)*
9. *Nirvana, "Smells Like Teen Spirit" (1991)*
10. *Limp Bizkit, "Break Stuff" (2000)*
11. *Skrillex, "First of the Year (Equinox)" (2011)*

In some cases, I would never have recognized the song as having anything to do with anger – Skrillex's "First of the Year" starts out as a jaunty tune eventually joined by a falsetto voice, which the lyric transcribers tell me is reciting over and over again, "Baby you've got a nightmare." The accompanying video depicts an encounter between a would-be child molester and a witch child who turns the tables. Pink roars, "na-na-na-NA-na I want to get in trouble / I want to start a fight."[14] That's more like it. But I leave this collection of audio anger as a homework assignment for the reader. Put your headphones on.

Philadelphia radio and podcasting company Audacy (which formerly used the brand Radio.com) maintains a constantly updated "Angry Playlist," devoted to "Angry. Classic. Rock."[15] I suspect the periods represent that emphatic drumbeat in Twisted

Sister's "We're Not Going to Take It" or a song like it. Anger music, of course, is one genre among many. Audacy also offers playlists for pop, alternative, Latino, country, hip-hop, rock, and classic rock. The point is not that anger music prevents other kinds of music from thriving but that anger music is recognized as a distinctive category, with enough recordings to fill in weeks of continuous play. No other "emotion" gets such a treatment from Audacy or other music providers as far as I can tell.

When I ask younger acquaintances today about music that depicts anger, Billie Eilish ("Bad Guy;" "When the Party's Over") comes up fairly often, as does Taylor Swift. Swift specializes in what might be called "happily angry" songs in which she revels in revenge fantasies ("Mean": "Someday I'll be living in a big old city, and all you are ever going to be is mean"; "Bad Blood"; "Picture to Burn": "'Cause coming back around here would be bad for your health"; "Look What You Made Me Do"; "Better Than Revenge": "There is nothing I do better than revenge.") Ariana Grande has a reputation not only for angry songs ("Good as Hell;" "No Tears Left to Cry"), but also for angry interviews. Halsey, the professional name of the singer Ashley Nicolette Frangipane, ("Nightmare": "I've tasted blood and it is sweet," "No, I won't smile but I'll show you my teeth") is another of the "female pop rebels" who generally occupies a realm of tortured souls who croon their anger.[16]

Perhaps there are as many angry songs by male singers as by women, but the genre seems to be dominated by female singer/songwriters at the moment.

Back to Boston

My fifteen-minute excursion to Kenmore Square in 2004 is almost over, but not quite. A bus rumbled by, its side emblazoned with an ad for FCUK – which stands for "French Connection United Kingdom," the hip purveyor of clothing, cosmetics, and accessories to those whose taste in acronyms runs to the puerile. FCUK's website at the time offered games as well as merchandise. In "Not Idol," for example, the player could use "FCUK's instruments of torture" to eliminate "Barry," a cartoon character who auditions for the popular TV show *American Idol* even though "his voice sucks big time." The theme seemed to be that buyers of FCUK merchandise were the folks cool enough to humiliate those who, though lacking talent, had the audacity to seek attention. Anger at attention seekers in those who themselves seek attention by wearing FCUK-emblazoned clothes may seem perilously close to home, but French Connection United Kingdom calculates that teenagers draw fine distinctions among forms of self-advertisement. (In the years since, FCUK has grown up. The website games are gone. Its models look like grown-ups, mostly wearing casual grown-up clothes. It sells home furnishings that look a bit rustic. But one can still purchase a FCUK black hoodie or a "fcuk negativity" black T-shirt.)

At the corner was a row of plastic news boxes with the week's supply of free tabloids. Here, for sure, was a distillation of fashionable attitudes. The *Weekly Dig* commenced with Ted Rall's cartoon depicting Americans torturing Iraqis; plugged an anti-Bush product, "National EmbarrassMints"; and reviewed local music and art. In her column, "Screaming from the Gallery," Kate Ledogar framed her review of a photography show by grousing that her car had been towed because she hadn't paid her tickets. One of the photographs praising Snow White's evil stepmother as "beautiful, assertive, and constantly asking questions" prompted Ledogar to reflect, "There it is! It's all those fairy tales that poisoned me into passivity, made me think that some big, shiny man would come and rescue me from my predicaments. That's why I've been getting all these parking tickets."

Ledogar's tone was not anger but ironic helplessness. That theme tied together the culture reviews, the sex ads ("I'm temporarily yours"), the comics page (Bush feeding American soldiers into a giant meat grinder), and the personals ("I'm not angry! Just wanna have fun!"). If these folks were not exactly angry, anger was the sun they orbited, and in its heat they felt their own torpor, self-contempt, disdain for others, and longing for escape.

The newspaper vending machines themselves had been defaced and the original defacements themselves defaced with stickers for alternative rock bands and the scrawled initials of kids desperate to make a mark somewhere. But perhaps it is too much to read "anger" into www.copperpmine.com's attempt to snag a little free attention with its sticker on the vending machine. The stealing of a few square inches of public space felt to me like an act of aggression, but was it?

On that particular day, I saw no road-raging drivers, no pushing matches, and no lovers' jagged quarrels in Kenmore Square. If anger was present, it was only in the small texture of things, where lives and artifacts mingled, for the moment unnoticed, except by someone bent on noticing. This sub-texture of the world that humans create for themselves is one of the meanings we anthropologists give to the word "culture."

I could, in principle, repeat this experiment today, as I write this from my office in midtown Manhattan. But not only is there no need to replicate it, I fear that doing so would be an unnecessary risk. In Manhattan today, unlike Boston in 2004, there is nothing subtle about the anger in the air. In the wake of "de-fund the police" campaigns; actions by the mayor and the city council to curtail law enforcement; the abandonment of efforts by city authorities to control vagrancy, public drug use, fare evasion, and other "lifestyle" offenses; and the rise of random attacks that range from punching and stabbing strangers to hurling people onto the subway tracks, the city has become a far more dangerous place. The Wuhan Flu–inspired shutdown drastically thinned the numbers of people who are out and about even in areas like Times Square. Those of us who still live and work in the city have learned to move about quickly and cautiously. This is no place to stand idly and contemplate the ambience. But I can testify that the boarded-up storefronts and "space for rent" signs that fill up the street-level view, and the largely empty skyscrapers, have an angry tone all their own.

Ambient Anger circa 2005

Culture, in the sense of the emotional background, may not intrude into our conscious thought very often. It is, rather, a context that we take for granted, save when we deliberately place it on display to affirm it, or on those infrequent occasions when it erupts by itself. Angri-culture, however, surrounds contemporary Americans. It is, of course, most visible in our politics. Back when I wrote *A Bee in the Mouth*, the icon of political anger was former presidential candidate and Vermont governor Howard Dean, brows arched, eyes aflame, veins bulging, and maxillary muscles stretched to their extremes in a rictus of rage. Dean had crossed some invisible line: anger is OK up to the point where it becomes genuinely scary – and just there the angri-culture draws its limits. Who would today stand in Dean's place as our angriest public figure? Many candidates come to mind but no clear winner. I will place in nomination, however, Greta Thunberg, the Swedish global-warming fanatic, who in the absence of any informed understanding of a complex issue has made herself an international celebrity on the basis of nothing other than sheer anger.

The Dean-style rage and the Thunberg-style contempt assume an audience of people who respond positively to the histrionics of extreme anger, but the example of a public figure abandoning himself or herself so completely, in turn, gives everyday anger a lift. It says, in effect: "Society is run by conniving people who are in it for themselves. You are being screwed. Your anger is justified." Then, if we are not actually feeling angry, we can at least pay homage to the emotion with the little flags of anger pasted to our cars or stitched into our skin.

Is this ambient anger really justified? Anger, in a certain sense, is always hanging around waiting for the opportunity to take charge. Often all that is needed to turn an underlying frustration into an outbreak of real anger is someone to enunciate the grievance. A key difference between new anger and old anger, however, is the vagueness and elasticity of the grievances. Angri-culture issues an extremely broad warrant for getting angry and a still broader one for striking angry poses even when we are not actually angry. The angri-culture is more a pervasive attitude than a specific grievance. Indeed, the word "attitude" has recently emerged as a synonym for a generally surly disposition – for example, "That girl has attitude."

Consider the contrast between "that girl" and the six-foot Carrie Nation, dressed in crepe, chopping her impressions into the saloons of the 1890s with her trademark hatchet. Nation was an angry woman, and her hymn-singing female vanguard conveyed a righteous contempt for men who drank, whether a shot of whiskey or a growler of beer. But the anger of the Prohibitionists was focused and specific. Can we say the same of Rage against the Machine? We now live in a society in which a great many people seem angry for trivial reasons or no reason at all.

In the winter of 2003–2004, Dean became the political face of some of this anger. He took hold of a particular theme, opposition to the war in Iraq, and fused it with what had been until that moment the inchoate contempt that many Democrats felt toward President Bush. As a candidate, however, Dean proved maladroit, stumbling for an untimely consistency, for example, when he responded dismissively to the capture of Saddam Hussein. Dean summoned the sea monster of anger into a presidential campaign, but he had no ability to control the beast. His loss in the primaries came as Democrats worried that a candidate whose main talent was for galvanizing the wrathful would not be able to win the votes of calmer, more pragmatic centrists.

The Dean campaign was, thus, one of those instances in which widespread but typically invisible attitudes suddenly emerge in spectacular form. Dean didn't invent contemporary angri-culture; he just gave it political salience. But if the good doctor from Vermont was only channeling an anger that already existed, where did that anger start? The two most direct sources were opposition to the wars in Afghanistan and Iraq, along with the domestic security policies enacted after 9/11; and the resentments of Gore supporters over the U.S. Supreme Court's intervention in the 2000 presidential election. Dean, however, supported the Afghan war, only later taking issue with the follow-up. In a 2003 interview, he said that the best policy for the United States in Afghanistan would be to build a middle class "where women fully participate in the government." In December 2005, Dean called for an additional twenty thousand American troops to be sent to Afghanistan. These views sometimes irritated Dean's own supporters. So Dean did not rise as the personification of the Angry Left by identifying himself with its whole agenda at the time.

These two grievances were well-articulated and lodged like a bone in the throats of some political partisans by the summer of 2003, but they had yet to become themes that defined a broader political movement. That was Dean's accomplishment in winter 2003–2004, and it was all the more remarkable in light of his ignoring all the actual grievances (with the exception of Iraq) in favor of simply channeling the anger.

Anger over the 2000 presidential election had not really settled into a longing for Al Gore as president. Democrats regretted no longer holding the White House, but it was hard to detect nostalgia for the scandal-ridden Clinton administration. Opposition to the wars in Afghanistan and Iraq likewise had an elusive quality: the anger was far more apparent than its source. No one wished to defend the regimes of the Taliban and Saddam Hussein, and very few held that "the War on Terror" was itself a mistake. The denunciation of the Department of Homeland Security and the actions of Attorney General John Ashcroft as present dangers to domestic civil rights similarly seemed far angrier than could be justified by a list of specific abuses.

The Patriot Act, passed in the weeks following 9/11, gradually emerged as the left's symbol of the supposed erosion of American rights and freedom under the Bush administration. But frequently people became angry about the Patriot Act without being able to give any instance of how it had damaged civil rights. The consequences were occasionally peculiar. In mid-December 2005, for example, a University of Massachusetts at Dartmouth professor told a local reporter that one of his students had been interrogated by federal agents after trying to borrow a copy of a book by Mao Tse-tung.[17] The story spread quickly and was repeated by Senator Edward Kennedy (D-MA) in an anti-Bush op-ed in the *Boston Globe*, just before the student confessed that the whole matter was a hoax. Before the hoax was revealed, the story had already spread through the national media and an account had been posted on the American Library Association website. Why the readiness to believe a story that didn't even pass muster with the *Boston Globe*'s editors? Perhaps there was a thirst for evidence to substantiate a strongly held but weakly supported suspicion that the federal government was abusing its powers under the Patriot Act.

To explain the electoral anger that Dean tapped as the reservoir of bad feeling among opponents to the War on Terror and as lingering resentment over the 2000 Florida recount failed to register the eagerness with which some Americans moved from disappointment and disagreement to a caustic and often aggressive form of anger.

If I were to start fresh on this topic in 2021, whom would I put in the place of Dean as a political figure conspicuous for belligerent anger? It is easy to think of ostentatiously angry movements, such as Antifa and Black Lives Matter, and angry practices, such as canceling people and attacking them as "racist." But most of our prominent political figures seem to have retreated to a style of provoking anger among their followers rather than expressing it themselves. Donald Trump may be the major exception as a man who can give full vent to his anger, but his is a complicated case that I leave for the last chapter of this book. Anger is still our cultural currency, but these days we are spending it in new ways.

But just how did we become so infatuated with anger?

I have mentioned anger's sub-texture (its all-but-invisible background in our everyday lives); the feedback loop between public exemplars of new anger and ordinary folks foregoing patience for petulance; the vagueness and elasticity of new-anger grievances; and its disproportionate quality. We need to look also at cultural changes in the assessment of angry people; a flattening of the American emotional range; the therapeutic rationales for anger – and the newer therapeutic "anger management's" ambiguous repudiation of some of those rationales; the "liberating" quality now assigned to anger, along with its exhibitionist and theatrical forms; the notion of anger as authenticating, and its related roles as a badge of identity and a credential for group membership. As the angri-culture has risen to a national ideal, it has also connected to and partially transformed old fantasies of righteous revenge. And all these factors play into the delight that the true embracers of new anger feel with their uninhibited rage. The angri-culture is, in this sense, an overthrow of older ideals of temperance and self-control.

Chapter Four

POLLYANNA MEETS TAR-BABY

ANGER IS SEEN, heard, described, performed, and represented in myriad ways in popular culture. These representations, especially in times past, were often cautionary. Today they are more often, but not exclusively, celebratory. As America now finds itself reaching a point of anger-driven social breakdown, it will be helpful to have some touchstones of these changing representations.

In 1913, on the eve of World War I, an American novelist named Eleanor Porter published a children's book about the orphaned daughter of a missionary who goes to live with her crabby but well-off aunt in Vermont. The child, dressed in donated clothes and sent on her way by the Ladies' Aid Society, has endured a lot, but she is surprisingly cheerful. Consigned to a bare garret in her aunt's house, she exults in the view from its window. Assigned as punishment to read a pamphlet on the filthiness of flies, she declares, "I love to read!" Her secret? She confides to the housemaid, Nancy, that her father taught her a game: "to just find something about everything to be glad about – no matter what 'twas."[1]

The name of Porter's heroine, Pollyanna, has long since become a byword for naïve optimism in the face of grim facts. Pollyanna's aunt and partial namesake, Polly – austere, punctual, and perhaps a bit too concerned with houseflies – may not be entirely to our taste either, but at least she is angry. Pollyanna cannot seem to rise to life's provocations with anything more extreme than a tearful smile. As conceived by Porter, however, Pollyanna is not the simpleton of our catchphrase, "Don't be a Pollyanna." She is, rather, a strong-willed child who succeeds in bringing adults, including Aunt Polly, around to her side. Steadfast, tough-minded optimism proves more potent than self-pity or angry complaint.

Our ancestors were not oblivious to the seductions of anger. They understood that some people get accustomed to expressing harsh feelings and enjoy the petty tyranny that this gives them over meeker people, whether members of their family or employees. The angry husband or wife, the angry parent, and the angry boss were familiar figures in life and in fiction. Dickens's Scrooge is a man driven much more by anger than by greed. Milton's Satan is a figure in which anger is built on a foundation of envy and pride. Shakespeare gives us a whole gallery of angry characters. Hotspur, in Shakespeare's *Henry IV, Part I*, enters a scene reading a letter from a lord who declines to join his plot. Muttering, "He shows in this he loves his own barn better than he loves our house," Hotspur listens with half an ear as his wife, Lady Percy, complains about his sleepless preoccupation with battle, which diverts him even from the marriage bed. As she realizes he isn't listening because of his angry fixation, she too gets (mock) angry:

> *Out, you mad-headed ape!*
> *A weasel hath not such a deal of spleen*
> *As you are tossed with.* (Act 2, scene 3, lines 81–83)

And he replies in banter that mixes his euphoria over the coming battle with his affection for her. What we see in Hotspur is a man in whom anger is a tonic. It makes him sparkle with energy and wit. He likes his anger.

64

Another of Shakespeare's history plays, *King Richard the Second*, opens with the king hearing two angry young men, Bolingbroke and Mowbray, accuse each other of lying and treason. As King Richard puts it, they are "full of ire, / In rage deaf as the sea, hasty as fire." He orders the pair of "wrath-kindled gentlemen" to forgo a duel and to forgive each other. Mowbray, however, says he can't forgive Bolingbroke's insult, which "no balm can cure but his heart-blood," and, hearing this, Bolingbroke won't back down either. The king then agrees to their settling the matter by combat – though he later exiles them instead. Anger seems to give both young men a force that King Richard does not know properly how to deal with.

It might be possible to create a taxonomy of anger using Shakespeare's characters – Titus, Timon, Coriolanus, Lear, Antony over Caesar's body, Othello, Shylock, Caliban – but, despite the variety, anger in Shakespeare's characters always seems a dangerous intoxicant that variously blights good judgment, stirs destructive passions, and gives a false clarity to the world. Shakespeare, of course, drew on the medieval theory of the humors, in which anger was traced to an excess of "choler." An angry person was literally "out of balance."

The rewards of anger for the person who indulges it were the same then as now: a feeling of domination, at least for the passing moment; frustration giving way to a sense of power; and a surge of clarity. The angry person is decisive. He knows what is to be done and who is to blame. Anger makes things happen.

But the habitually angry person was also seen as weak and unhappy, as well as troublesome to others. The heroic figures in the eyes of Americans from the eighteenth through much of the twentieth century generally were not angry men. Although they may have been men who had good grounds for grievance, most kept their wrath from getting the better of them. Dignity, manliness, and wisdom called for self-control and coolness of temper. Exceptions, such as Aaron Burr and John Brown, come to mind –

but they stood out to their contemporaries as exceptions. Burr was a man whose frustrated ambitions led him angrily into disloyalty to the country he had served as vice president. John Brown was maddened with divine fury against slavery, but such frenzy was its own lesson: Brown destroyed his family and himself. As Hawthorne said of him, "Nobody was ever more justly hanged."[2] Better to consult Teddy Roosevelt's mantra of national self-control, "Speak softly and carry a big stick." In Owen Wister's novel *The Virginian*, the hero offers what became classic advice to those who test the limits of familiarity. A fellow addresses him "you son-of-a-[bitch]," to which the Virginian answers, "When you call me that, *smile*."[3] Anger is ready and waiting in that answer, but quiet strength comes first.

America has its own history of anger as yet largely unwritten, but it is woven into our politics, sermons, literature, and behavior. John Wise was a Puritan cleric born in Roxbury, Massachusetts, in 1652. He was imprisoned for a time for agitating against the royal governor, Sir Edmund Andros, whom the king imposed on Massachusetts Bay Colony. Later, Wise wrote a pamphlet defending "The Churches' Quarrel" with the monarchy. Even the idea of arbitrary government, he said in 1710, puts "an Englishman's blood into a fermentation." But when such a government actually comes along and "shakes its whip over their ears, and tells them it is their master, it makes them stark mad." The "Englishmen" that Wise refers to are Americans, and he warns that they have a "memical genius" that will lead them, angrily, to respond to arbitrary government by turning "arbitrary too." Sixty-six years before the Revolution, Wise provided a pretty precise account of what makes Americans angry.

Wise's text ought to be better known than it is, but we do have a national fable known to almost all Americans that encodes our best wisdom about anger. It is Joel Chandler Harris's retelling of an African American folk tale, "Brer Rabbit and Tar-Baby." Brer Fox "fix up a contrapshun w'at he call a Tar-Baby" and puts Tar-

Baby on the side of the road. Brer Rabbit comes pacing down the road and is astonished to see Tar-Baby, but he shows his good manners:

> *"Mawnin'!" sez Brer Rabbit, sezee – "nice wedder dis mawnin,"*
> *sezee.*
> *Tar-Baby ain't sayin' nothin', and Brer Fox, he lay low.*

Brer Rabbit grows exasperated in trying to make conversation with Tar-Baby; Brer Fox continues to lie low; and Brer Rabbit, losing his temper, punches Tar-Baby:

> *Present'y Brer Rabbit draw back wid his fis', he did, en blip*
> *he tuck 'er side er de head. Right dar's whar he broke his*
> *merlasses jug. His fis' stuck, en he can't pull loose. De tar hilt*
> *'im. But Tar-Baby, she stay still, en Brer Fox, he lay low.*

Brer Rabbit, enmired in his own anger, becomes angrier still, kicks Tar-Baby, and becomes completely trapped.

"Did the Fox eat the Rabbit?" asked the little boy to whom Uncle Remus has told the story. "Dat's all de fur de tale goes," replied the old man.[4]

American popular literature offers many other fables that give instruction about anger, but one more that is certainly still alive in popular memory is the closing scene of Dashiell Hammett's *Maltese Falcon* (1929).

> *Spade pulled his hand out of hers [Brigid O'Shaughnessy's].*
> *He no longer either smiled or grimaced. His wet yellow face*
> *was hard set and deeply lined. His eyes burned madly. He*
> *said, "Listen. This isn't a damned bit of good. You'll never*
> *understand me, but I'll try once more and then we'll give it*
> *up. Listen. When a man's partner is killed he's supposed to*
> *do something about it. It doesn't make any difference what*

67

*you thought of him. He was your partner and you're sup-
posed to do something about it."*[5]

The 1941 movie version, with Sam Spade played by Humphrey
Bogart, is completely faithful to Hammett's text, which continues
with Spade's reasons why he intends to hand over O'Shaughnessy
to the police.

Spade's monologue isn't angry, but that's the point: he is sub-
duing his passions to his code. The proper response to the murder
of his partner isn't anger but "to do something about it." The skein
of betrayals that have led to this crisis in his life might prompt
him to be furious – and he may love the murderess, though Hammett hasn't been very convincing on that point. But, instead of
declaring his feelings, he almost desperately spins out his analysis
of why he must act as he does.

Brer Rabbit traps himself in anger; Brer Spade steels himself
against it and becomes the original of the hard-boiled detective.
We still have this archetype who refuses to indulge anger, but he
is increasingly giving way to the Hulk, the Punisher, and a myriad
of other characters for whom, to the contrary, the anger just can't
be controlled.

If we want to understand today's angri-culture, we need to
develop this sense of how different it is from views that prevailed
in the past. Anger has always been part of both private and public
life, but in our time it has gained a wholly new status.

Don't Forgive My Anger

In the opening chapters, I examined the anger that burst into our
national life with the 2020 post–George Floyd riots and the 2020
presidential election and its aftermath. Political anger now is
escalating into wrath. But we arrived at this point by ascending a
ladder of rhetorical abuse. Let's recall some of the lower rungs.

The 2004 presidential election turned anger into a topic of political debate in the United States. The "Angry Left" attacked President Bush with a vitriolic gusto not seen since the far-off days when demonstrators chanted, "Hey, hey, LBJ, how many kids did you kill today?" After the election, the mood on the left only darkened. The senior managing editor of the *Boston Phoenix*, Clif Garboden, summed up his view of Bush's victory under the headline, "Screw You America: Sometimes the Fish in the Barrel Deserve to Die." Garboden began his screed, "Don't forgive my anger."[6]

In 2004, domestic politics wasn't the only venue for bruised and bruising feelings. Anger bubbled up in nearly all contexts of American life. When Indiana Pacers All-Star forward Ron Artest leapt into the stands at the basketball game with the Detroit Pistons on November 19, 2004, to pummel a spectator he wrongly believed had thrown a plastic cup of beer at him, he lived up to his reputation for hot-headedness. Artest was known for confrontations on and off the court; on a previous occasion, after his team had lost, he smashed a $100,000 TV camera. But the brawl he started that November night was more than just the antics of one player lacking self-control. Rather, it reflected a deeper change in one of America's most popular sports.

The National Basketball Association in those years shed its image of graceful teamwork and players with nicknames like "Magic" and sunny smiles in favor of what many call a "thug league." One sportswriter called it "gangstaball."[7] Games featured hip-hop music and tattooed players who exhibited tough-guy attitudes. An investigative journalist, Jeff Benedict, reported that "40 percent of the players in the NBA during the 2001–02 season have had a formal criminal complaint for a serious crime filed against them."[8] The mood of spectators at basketball games had likewise shifted to coarser expressions of antagonism – such as hurling cups of beer.

Basketball is, plainly, not the only sport in which unsportsmanlike anger gained a footing, but let's stick with it for a moment.

Has the angry basketball of 2004 cooled off? Not much. On October 30, 2019, two of the NBA's star players – Joel Embiid, the center for the Philadelphia 76ers, and Karl-Anthony Towns, who plays for the Minnesota Timberwolves – began a mid-court brawl which became a lead feature of highlight rolls of basketball players slugging it out. The highlights are celebrated under the title "When the Anger FINALLY Comes Out." Plenty of other players have their featured moments, but one incident can stand for the rest. After the referees manage to get the combatants off the court, Embiid turns to the spectators and raises his arms in triumph, squints his eyes, and mouths curses. The announcer, laughing, says, "And Embiid is going to make a curtain call."[9] The announcer is not alone in enjoying the spectacle. Elsewhere a commentator wrote, "The Joel Embiid vs. Karl-Anthony Towns fight is pretty funny, actually."

Others pointed to a long-standing attempt by Embiid to mock Towns. "[The] Sixers are the villains of the league and omg we're here," tweeted one fan.[10] And Embiid explained himself after the game, "That's what I'm good at. I like to get in peoples mind,"[11] and "I was built for this city and they were built for me… you gotta be a Broad Street bully."[12]

What deserves attention here is not just the escalation of taunting an opponent into physical confrontation, but the gleeful pride of the instigator. Anger not only empowers Embiid; it fills him with pleasure and confers social standing.

I will, later on, say a little more about sports, but for now I will leave Embiid to stand for the whole category of sports professionals who make ostentatious anger part of their public personae. And we must keep in mind that this performative anger works because a substantial portion of the audience embraces it.

Angry sports fans, of course, are not limited to America. Foul-mouthed, bumptious, and angry fans have turned some European soccer games into melees. But the resemblance may be misleading. What's happening in the United States is a generational change that has made open displays of anger stylish. The NBA is only one organization that has attempted to keep up with the times by exploiting the new style.

Anger on the Big Screen

Anger in America also has flavors besides that of stale, airborne beer. Americans have mastered a kind of exuberant show-off anger. It is as if the sunnier side of our national disposition got in the way of the grimmer forms of crankiness. Hollywood discovered the humorous potential of the emotion in such films as *Anger Management* (2003) and *The Upside of Anger* (2005). The latter presents Terry (played by Joan Allen) as a wife deserted by her husband and left with four daughters. The trailer begins with the line, "Terry is mad at the world," but her anger leads to romance with her ex-ballplayer neighbor Denny (played by Kevin Costner). Another 2005 movie took the romance of domestic anger up several notches. In *Mr. and Mrs. Smith*, husband-and-wife professional assassins played by Brad Pitt and Angelina Jolie rekindle the spark in their marriage by attempting to kill each other with weapons ranging from a bazooka to an exploding elevator. It's played for laughs, but part of the joke is that the characters indeed come alive – and feel sexual attraction – only after becoming murderously enraged. If we can make light of it, how mad at the world and at each other can we really be? Is American anger real, or is it a pretense?

Anger, being one of the basic human emotions and among the most dramatic, is a perennial theme for theater and movies. It isn't the mere depiction of anger that merits attention but what the story, the actors, and the director want the audience to make of the anger on display. Is it warranted? Are the angry characters enhanced or diminished by their anger? Do we admire their anger or feel sorry for them?

Sometimes the celebration of anger is the whole point. *Mad Max: Fury Road* (2015) is a revenge extravaganza, where the audience is positioned to side with the angry, oppressed women escaping a tyrant in post-apocalyptic Australia. *Unhinged* (2020) is a revenge extravaganza in which the audience is on the other side: rooting for the woman trying to escape an enraged psychopath in contemporary Los Angeles. Anger, in both cases, translates fluently into cinematic mayhem and killing, but these are plainly stories in which anger drives everything, and the driving is literal. Road rage and vehicular homicide are the idiom.

The 2019 hit *Joker* treats anger as part of a character's descent into madness. The protagonist, Arthur Fleck, is a well-meaning but hapless and impoverished clown who, after repeated humiliations, angrily turns on his tormentors. Joaquin Phoenix, in the title role, was nominated for an Academy Award for best actor, but his disturbing portrait of an angry, homicidal madman was too much for some critics.

Pixar gave us the animated movie *Inside Out* (2015), in which a young girl, Riley, encounters obstacles typical for an eleven-year-old. But her emotions (and those of her parents) are represented as committees of personified Joy, Sadness, Fear, Disgust, and Anger. Anger reliably has all the most dramatic moments and prompts all the worst decisions. Anger prompts Riley to run away from San Francisco to Minnesota, and later it dampens all the other emotions to leave Riley apathetic. Riley recovers only when Joy reunites with Sadness and restores memory. The heavy-handed allegory is saved by both the comic visualizations and the buoyant voiceover acting. It is notable that this children's movie is counter-cultural in its treatment of anger, which is presented as Shakespeare presented Hotspur: impetuous and apt to give exactly the wrong counsel.

Ma Rainey's Black Bottom (2020) is the movie version of August Wilson's 1982 play. It deals with a hot-headed trumpet player, Levee, in the 1920s trying to make a name for himself while the famous blues singer Ma Rainey is trying to record a record. Levee quarrels with his bandmates Cutler, Toledo, and Slow Drag, who are determined to stick to a musical style they know. Ma Rainey ends up firing Levee; the record producer also dismisses him; and, in a rage, Levee stabs Toledo to death. The White record producer appropriates Levee's original music but has it performed by an all-White band. Levee, played by Chadwick Boseman, is a powerful presence, full of creative energy and burning with frustration that no one will listen to his ideas. His anger is part ambition, part impatience, and – a very large part – arrogance. He brings disaster on himself as well as Toledo.

The Way Back (2020) is a movie about an alcoholic ironworker, Jack, who gets a chance to coach a high school basketball team on which he was once a star player. The plot is a rendition of a standard Hollywood story about a losing team that is galvanized to a degree of success. Jack succeeds partly because he takes angry command of the not-very-talented kids, but the real anger theme in the movie is Jack's slowly revealed backstory. He was a star basketball player in high school but gave up the game because he was angry at his father for loving his skill on the court rather than the boy himself. Fired from his coaching job, drunk, and reckless, he ends up in the hospital, where he admits his faults and starts on his "way back." The story verges on sentimentality but presents Jack's anger in a modern therapeutic light. Jack's problem was not that he was angry with his father but that he bottled it up and turned it into self-destructive behavior.

I've picked out these movies only as illustrations. They don't begin to exhaust the range and variety of contemporary American movies that represent and interpret anger, but it is helpful to have a few explicit examples. Cinema reflects our cultural conversation back on us in a way that invites further reflection. *Godzilla vs. Kong* (2021) may not stand out as a work inviting much philosophical meditation, but at least it embodies our moment of rapt attention to the angry confrontation of two elemental forces, heedless of the destruction they leave in their wake. Their cinematic battles are pure spectacle, but some of the ways in which we represent anger to ourselves pass almost unnoticed.

Anger of Wheels

The anger that now plays such a large role in our public life, our sports and entertainment, our work, and our domestic lives is in fact a mix of irritation and swagger. While people have always gotten angry and expressed their anger (take John Wise's 1710 tract, Aaron Burr's 1804 duel with Hamilton, and John Brown's 1859 raid on Harpers Ferry), something about today's expressions of anger is new: anger has been transformed from a suspect emotion that most people struggled to keep under control to a fashionable attitude that many people strive to "get in touch with" and exhibit in public. The imaginary Vermonter Pollyanna has been replaced with the incendiary Vermonter Bernie Sanders.

This transformation enters into our culture in all sorts of ways. In 2006, the *Wall Street Journal* took notice of one unexpected outlet for our new fascination with all things angry. In "Why Cars Got Angry," Jonathan Welsh explained, "Car makers used to strive for an inviting face, but lately they're pushing an edgier look: Car faces that look meaner, angrier and, at times, even downright evil." Accompanying photos show model years of the BMW 3 Series sports sedan beginning in 1968, getting meaner and meaner over time. Welsh quoted Kirk Perry, a business owner in Lake Owassa, New Jersey, professing his attraction to the "wide, snarling look" of the Audi Q7. The Hyundai HCD9, the 2005 Dodge Charger, and the Chrysler 300 sedan (with "gaping grille and headlights that seem to scowl") also made the grade. Of course, anger isn't for everybody. Mini Coopers and Volvos, according to Welsh, were resisting the trend.[13]

I came across that observation when writing *A Bee in the*

Mouth, and, uncertain whether it has stood the test of time, I went looking and found a plethora of complaints, including a 2012 article in *Smithsonian Magazine*, "For Experts, Cars Really Do Have Faces," which cites a National Academy of Sciences study to the effect that "the fronts of cars" activate the portion of the brain (the "fusiform face area") that lights up in human facial recognition. Some cars are deliberately designed to have "an aggressive steely stare." That's because "buyers tend to prefer cars with more aggressive, angry faces."[14] That glare seems to catch the attention of new observers every other year. "Why are new cars angry-looking, and what does that say about us?" asked Jack Baruth in 2014:

> *Disagree if you like, but I believe that every car has a face, and I'm right about this. The faces can be froggy friendly, as was the case with the old Porsche 911 or its VW Bug ancestor. They can be reserved and serious, in the vein of the 1980s-era Rolls-Royce Silver Spirit. But when you look behind you on the freeway today, all you'll see is anger.*[15]

"Why Do Modern Cars Look Angry?" asked Clemsie McKensie in 2018.[16] "Why Are Cars Looking So Angry?" asked yet another writer, Renee Nelson, in 2020.[17] The writers sometimes conclude it is an accident of aerodynamic design or safety, but plainly cars can be made to look benign. The real reason we fill our highways with snarling vehicles is the same reason we applaud displays of anger and aggression in many other contexts. We are saying *Look out! Look at me! You don't want to piss me off!*"

Breaking Out

Not so long ago – a matter of a few decades – a person giving free vent to anger was seen as weak and rather pathetic. The anger-prone who did not control their wrath were disdained as having a character flaw. Religions – Protestantism, Catholicism, and Judaism – taught that most anger was a sin; and the secular world pronounced intemperate anger as a sign of immaturity or, sometimes, an illness. The heroes of America, from George Washington to Jackie Robinson, were self-controlled individuals who, if roused to anger, kept it in its place and outsmarted or outplayed their foes. Should it light, the bee of anger was crushed, not cosseted.

Today, many Americans have adopted an entirely different view of anger. We feel entitled to express that emotion. Perhaps more important, we feel justified in feeling it in the first place in contexts in which earlier generations would have felt ashamed. Clif Garboden ("Don't forgive my anger"), in responding to President Bush's electoral victory in 2004, gloated in having feelings that better men would be ashamed of. Today there are many millions of Clif Garbodens in America. (Clif himself passed away in 2011, presumably to manage an "alternative press" in a warmer place.) We have turned a corner after which rude and unruly anger is not just tolerated but generally expected. The only question is whether it will be accompanied by broken glass or other forms of assault on property or person.

We have begun to go beyond feeling and verbal expression to outright acts of angry aggression. The bee in the mouth, rather than the gun in the hand, is the most conspicuous sign of the newness of new anger. The anger we speak (and write, gesture, sing, growl, and shout) in both private and public now comes in many flavors: multicultural righteous; leftist sneer; right-wing snivel; patriotic rage; ironic cooler-than-thou; and designer flavors in the names of most of the syndicated columnists and cable TV anchors.

New anger tends more to the political left than to the political right, though there is plenty on both sides. I will take up the preponderance of anger on the left in a later chapter.

Is the political polarization of the United States the root cause of new anger that is just spilling over into nonpolitical domains of life? Did politics make our cars look angry? I think not. Our new anger commenced before the political inflammations in which it is most conspicuous, and that new anger is broader and more pervasive than politics.

My view runs squarely against what many political observers have been saying for a generation. They think this national epidemic of anger is mainly the creation of political elites and their ratings-conscious friends in the national media. But new anger was preening itself in many contexts before it ran for office or auditioned for prime time.

This is not to minimize the political aspect of new anger. Our politics are now angrified to an extraordinary degree and in a new and dangerous way. Wrath is brewing. New anger in politics does mean that we have discovered a new kind of political satisfaction: deriding an opponent for the sheer pleasure of expressing contempt for other people. In the 2016 election, both Hillary Clinton and Donald Trump indulged in this kind of anger, and it has only intensified.

As a nation, we have had many previous occasions of public rancor. The most rancorous, in the estimate of many historians, was the period leading up to and following the presidential election of 1800 between John Adams and Thomas Jefferson. Adams's commercially minded, mainly Northern supporters viewed Jefferson as a would-be tyrant, a man of low morals, and a closet atheist. Jefferson's agrarian, mainly Southern supporters viewed Adams as a hypocritical betrayer of the Revolution, ready to sell the nation back to the British. The two candidates tied in the electoral college, and the tie was broken only by a secret deal that got one of Adams's supporters to switch his vote. The bitterness endured for years. Can today's anger top this?

I suspect the answer is yes, but, in truth, there is no way of knowing. We can't count units of anger. Then, as now, partisan feeling ran high, and many people publicly declared things that in calmer times they would regret. What really distinguishes new anger from the anger circa 1800 is the embrace of anger on a mass scale as a positive sentiment – as a way of feeling good about oneself and coping with everyday life.

I don't mean to say there are no legitimate reasons for political excitement in opposing views and candidates we disagree with. But that excitement has been spiked with a new ingredient that has changed its character. Some observers thought the anger in the 2004, 2016, and 2020 presidential elections was merely especially intense versions of the usual political pulse. But that was a misreading of the situation. What really happened, starting in 2004, was that new anger passed the threshold from being a phenomenon of the political fringe to being mainstream. Major political figures adopted new-anger postures as part of their political repertoire, and advocacy groups that rejected old forms of political suasion in favor of new-anger tactics – groups such as MoveOn.org and America Coming Together – ended up as the dominant voice of the Democratic Party. As a result, even politicians who were not by temperament suited to new-anger theatrics, such as Hillary Clinton, began to adopt the mannerisms of new anger. In 2006, Senator Clinton went to a church in Harlem for the Martin Luther King, Jr., Day celebration and said that the U.S. House of Representatives "has been run like a plantation, and you know what I'm talkin' about."[18]

New anger will continue to add its distinctive kick to the divisive arguments between left and right, turning political defeats into occasions of vicious rebukes and turning victories into fleering smugness. This, indeed, has happened in earlier times in our republic, but never with such relaxed self-approval, as though anger were its own vindication and savory reward. New anger is by no means exclusively or even primarily a political concoction. It is, rather, the expression of a new cultural ideal that emphasizes the importance of individual authenticity achieved through the projection of personal power over others. New anger is a modality – perhaps the most important modality – of an increasingly common personality type. It is the type that the historian Christopher Lasch called "narcissistic" a generation ago, but in the intervening years we have had the chance to get to know these narcissists a little better and, especially, to see how their stance toward the world plays out in their lives and relationships.[19]

But precisely because new anger is everywhere, it is also part of American politics, and in the political context it achieves a kind of mutant grandiosity. New-anger politics is the fusion of the "red state"/"blue state" cultural divide with the narcissism of the 1970s human-potential movement. Differences of political opinion, which were in principle negotiable, are transformed into claims of identity, which cannot be negotiated. We are watching the emergence of a ferocious politics of "I am right because I am me." Cross that line or even hint that a compromise may be in order, and you unleash a political rage founded on the newly angered person's sense of being personally threatened.

New anger is anger that congratulates itself. It is as though the person with the bee in his mouth mistook the repeated stings for the sweetness of the honeycomb. An administrative assistant in Harvard's social studies department, Norah Burch, lost her job in May 2004 when her supervisor read her blog, www.AnnoyYour Friends.com, which was linked to her email signature via her homepage.[20] Her blog contained some disturbing declarations:

I'm two nasty e-mails from professors away from bombing the entire Harvard campus.[21]
I was ready to get a shotgun and declare open season on all senior faculty members and students who dared cross me.

Personnel matters are usually pretty discreet. We know about Burch's dismissal because she published a self-defense in the *Boston Globe*, and her justification captures perfectly the complacencies of the new anger–prone:

I used my online diary as a steam valve for my administrative assistant job. . . . Dealing with obstinate and nasty professors and students, I found that a quick one- or two-minute rant in my blog would calm my nerves enough so that I could return to productivity. . . . To me, blogging became a sort of electronic primal scream, one that saved the eardrums of my neighbors and co-workers.

Her tone of wounded innocence – the death threats were, after all, a service to her employer, since they helped her return to productivity – is the crucial thing. She was admittedly angry, but she wasn't dangerous. Her employer "couldn't prove [her] performance suffered in any way." No harm, no foul, at least in her sense of the situation. Upon getting reprimanded, she "was in shock and felt a little humiliated." She was shocked because she lived in a world where expressing anger – even in the hyperbolic terms of bombs and shotguns – is a legitimate form of self-expression. How can self-expression that doesn't involve actual dynamite or bullets be taken amiss?

Chapter Five

TEMPER, TEMPER

On October 23, 2018, the *New York Times* added to a small genre of fantasy fiction: stories about assassinating Republican presidents. The author this time was Zoë Sharp, an English novelist known for her "Charlie Fox" series of thrillers, such as *Road Kill*, *Riot Act*, and *Killer Instinct*. Invited by the *Times* as one of five writers to imagine Trump's "next chapter," she contributed "How It Ends."[1] In the story, a Russian agent is sent to kill Trump, in order to prevent him from bragging about his having been hand-picked by Putin. At the crucial moment, the would-be assassin's gun jams, but he is helped out by one of Trump's Secret Service agents who presents him his own Glock, butt first: "Here," the agent said politely, "Use mine. . . ."

This wasn't the first time news media were caught thinking aloud about killing Trump. In May 2016, Brad Thor, another novelist known for thrillers – *Hidden Order*, *Use of Force*, *Path of the Assassin* – appeared on Glenn Beck's radio talk show and, after comparing Trump to a Latin American dictator, offered a "hypothetical":

With the feckless, spineless Congress we have, who will stand in the way of Donald Trump overstepping his constitutional authority as president? If Congress won't remove him from

office, what patriot will step up and do that – if, if, he over-
steps his mandate as president? His constitutionally granted
authority, I should say, as president. If he oversteps that,
how do we get him out of office?

With no "legal means available," he added, "I think it will be a
terrible, terrible position the American people will be in, to get
Trump out of office, because you won't be able to do it through
Congress."

An uproar ensued, as many believed that Thor had implied
that assassination would be a legitimate option. SiriusXM Radio
suspended Glenn Beck's show, and Thor took pains to assure
people that his words were "not a defense of assassination."[2]

Sharp and Thor were only among the most visible figures exer-
cising their homicidal imaginations toward Trump. It was
reported that, "Less than a month after Trump's inauguration,
more than 12,000 Tweets had gone out calling for the president's
assassination."[3] The Secret Service had its hands full sorting out
new-anger rodomontade from people actually plotting murder. I
don't doubt that President Obama was also subject to thousands
of social media death threats, but as far as I can tell, mainstream
authors and publishers did not join suit.

Around the time Zoë Sharp published her story, my wife and I
were having dinner with a friend at a modest Indian restaurant in
our Upper West Side neighborhood. Only one other patron was
there, a middle-aged White man talking loudly on his cell phone.
"I'll take him out," he said. "Taking out Trump would mean thirty
years in jail, but I'll take one for the team." I doubt he was an assassin, but the remarkable thing is that this man imagined that such
bluster could only win him approbation from the person he was
talking to on the phone and the other diners.

Sharp and Thor do bring to mind an earlier venture, the 2004
novel *Checkpoint* by Nicholson Baker. It consists of a conversation between two old friends, Jay and Ben, about murdering Pres-

ident George W. Bush with a variety of lethal weapons. It is very hard to imagine that a respectable publisher – *Checkpoint* was issued by Alfred A. Knopf – would have put its name on such a lurid fiction in the days of FDR, Eisenhower, or Kennedy. But Knopf blurbed the book as the "most audacious novel yet" by the "most original writer of his generation." Audacious, apparently, but well within the range of current literary sensibilities. On news of the book's impending publication, Mark Davis, a speechwriter for the first President Bush, took notice of the cultural shift that Baker and Knopf were partly surfing, partly accelerating:

> Checkpoint, *whatever its literary conceits, will be an act of linguistic terrorism.* "He is beyond the beyond," *the* Washington Post *reports the main character saying of Bush.* "What he's done with this war. The murder of the innocent. And now the prisons. It makes me so angry. And it's a new kind of anger, too."[4]

Davis was angry about the book, but clearly he expressed an old anger, one that catches itself and fears excess. He conjured a time when most partisans had "an internalized reality check," and those who didn't were brushed off rather than published by Knopf. He concludes, "Today's Left has lost its way."

Well, yes. The left is lost in new anger, but it is not just the left. New anger is more comprehensive, reaching down to the one- and two-minute anger breaks demanded by administrative assistants like Harvard's Norah Burch.

In broad terms, the left is angry because it had incorrectly assumed that it had won all the important debates and deserved to hold political power. But, in 2001, it found that the House and the presidency were in the hands of Republicans, and the Senate (with the defection of formerly Republican Senator Jim Jeffords of Vermont to the status of "Independent") was evenly divided. Worse still, culturally conservative Republicans held the key positions. The left, comfortable in its long dominance of the media and the universities and convinced that any opposition was founded on some combination of stupidity, ignorance, and corruption, responded to the new situation with incredulity. *How could this have happened?* And it answered its own question by insisting that it hadn't happened. Bush had not been "elected." Rather, he had stolen the election with the help of the U.S. Supreme Court and gained public backing only by deception. Thus, the anger motto of the left became "Bush lies." In the light of unclouded truth, the left would have its legitimate place in command of the government and in the hearts of all worthy Americans.

The emotional center of the left's anger is an unbridled fury at having been dispossessed of a birthright. The left generally cannot conceive that its opponents are intelligent or possess well-reasoned arguments, and losing to an inferior is a bitter thing. The response in the first decade of this century, focusing on President Bush, was to insist ceaselessly that conservatives are inferior, in both intellect ("Bush is a moron") and moral stature ("The murder of the innocent. And now the prisons."). This form of anger combines righteous indignation with utter contempt for the adversary.

It would have been hard to think at that time that such fury could be dialed up any higher, but that's exactly what happened when Hillary Clinton lost the 2016 election to Donald Trump. Where Bush had been seen as "a moron," Trump was seen as a malevolent schemer who had come to power with the aid of the Kremlin and who had the cunning to impose his will on public policies that the left took as settled. The indignation and contempt turned to wrath and to the steely determination to undermine his presidency by any and all available means.

Meanwhile, on the right, a very different set of irritations have produced a different kind of anger. Conservatives have achieved a measure of political power, but they continue to feel their marginalization by the arbiters of culture. Whether they turn to TV news or Hollywood movies, they find their views ignored or derided. In college classrooms, they are often caricatured as racist, sexist, environment-despoiling, militaristic jerks. Intellectually serious conservative arguments are airbrushed out of the *New York Times* picture of America, and the great herd of newspapers, newsmagazines, and TV newsrooms that take their lead from the *Times* follow suit. The conservative churches typically find themselves treated by the leftist establishment as a looming danger to American rights and freedoms. When a cultural event that is rooted in conservative ideals breaks through to a mass audience, the cultural establishment hammers it with full force.

Issues that conservatives take as profoundly serious, such as the defense of the traditional family against court-ordered gay marriage, get muffled and distorted in the mainstream press. In the gay-marriage debate, for example, the mainstream press unrelentingly framed the issue as "civil rights" for gays versus the Religious Right's Biblically based bigotry. Even after the U.S. Senate's two-day debate on the Federal Marriage Amendment put a plainly secular argument on the table (that gay marriage in Scandinavia and the Netherlands sent heterosexual marriage into a nosedive and hugely increased the percentage of children who grow up in one-parent households), the press stuck fast to its presumption that the debate was really nothing but a matter of enlightened advocates of civil rights facing off against a rabble of homophobes.

By the time Trump came to office, the gay-marriage debate had been – for all practical purposes – settled by the Supreme Court, and Trump never indicated the slightest interest in revisiting the issue. Yet somehow the political left added to its indictment of Trump that he was a threat to gay marriage and all other rights enjoyed by people who identify as LGBTQ. Conjuring imaginary threats is a way of keeping a constituency on edge and putting conservatives on the defensive. Conservative views on nearly every topic are treated as rooted in prejudice and menacing.

Conservatives are used to this treatment, and it extends to numerous issues – such as abortion, school prayer, gun ownership, school choice, immigration, and affirmative action. The right responds to this broad exclusion of its views from the zone of cultural respectability partly by evoking a counter-world (Rush Limbaugh in his day, Fox News) where its views dominate and partly by getting angry. The right's anger, however, is heavily tinged with gloom – at least among older conservatives. Even as people on the right press their points, their tone often suggests that the larger battle may already be lost. And the dissonance between these two acts puts bees in their mouths. Their ideal of a world of deeper unity between transcendent ideals (freedom, equality) and ordinary life seems to be hastening away into impossibility. Even with both houses of Congress and the presidency in supposedly conservative hands, the diversity doctrine got elevated to constitutional status by the U.S. Supreme Court in *Grutter v. Bollinger* in June 2003, and gay marriage gathers the momentum of established fact in the wake of the gay nuptials in Massachusetts following the November 2003 *Goodridge* ruling.

The anger of the right, thus, springs from a double resentment: the resentment aimed at the liberal elite's day-in-and-day-out condescension toward hometown America, and the more punishing resentment that is directed inward at the inability of conservatives to win cultural respect and gain any cultural traction even as they win elections. Not all of the right's anger is new anger, but some of it definitely is. The anger of conservative pundits such as Ann Coulter (author of *Treason*) and Mona Charen (author of *Useful Idiots*) is meant to punish the punishers, and it has the quality of unstoppable glee that is the signature of new anger. At one level, the left in the United States is angry and the right is self-effacing; but look again, and the right is rousing itself to anger as well.

Notably, the new-anger conservatives Coulter and Charen were also among the conservatives who turned strongly against Trump. Coulter, a one-time Trump supporter, became a bitter opponent, denouncing him for being all words and no action: "The only people in the world who think saying something is the same as doing something are the media and Trump."[5] Charen is one of the figures featured in Julie Kelly's July 2020 book, *Disloyal Opposition: How the #NeverTrump Right Tried – and Failed – to Take Down the President*, in which her visceral disdain for Trump over five years is catalogued, along with the fumings of other Never-Trumpers such as Bill Kristol, Jennifer Rubin, David French, Bret Stephens, John Podhoretz, David Frum, Jonah Goldberg, and Max Boot. In one of her milder comments, Charen is quoted as denouncing Trump for his self-centeredness: "Trump has made a career out of egotism, while conservatism implies a certain modesty about government. The two cannot mix."[6] The common chord between Coulter and Charen, exemplars of conservative new anger before Trump's candidacy and fierce Trump critics after his rise, is their focus on his words and form of self-presentation, rather than his public policies. There is something about new anger that flattens perspective and judgment in favor of emotional responses to appearance.

Learning to Let Go

One way to draw the contrast between new anger and older forms of anger is to read what people used to say about their emotions and to consider the characters in popular books. But these aren't our only clues.

In *Anger: The Struggle for Emotional Control in America's History* (1986), psychiatrist Carol Zisowitz Stearns and historian Peter Stearns combed through self-help manuals, books of advice to husbands and wives, articles on child care, and magazine fiction to tease out a history of how popular attitudes toward anger developed through American history. The portrait they offer is subtle and complicated, but their essential point is that Americans of generations past saw anger as a powerful and disruptive force that individuals had to learn to control. That lesson was perennial in stories for American children. The Stearnses cited, for example, Louisa May Alcott's *Little Women*, in which Jo's mother counsels her about her "dreadful temper," saying: "You think your temper is the worst in the world, but mine used to be just like it. I've been trying to cure it for forty years, and have only succeeded in controlling it. I am angry nearly every day of my life, but I have learned not to show it; and I still hope to learn not to feel it, though it may take me another forty years to do so."[7]

In fact, the Stearnses divided American history into several epochs characterized by shifting "emotionologies" – their term for the conventions and standards by which people evaluate anger and the institutions that "reflect and encourage these standards." For the period 1750–1860, they found an intensifying effort to banish anger from marital relationships, to prevent children from developing habits of angry expression, and to punish the child who gives in to anger. They noted along the way that the word "tantrum" (initially applied to adults, though the origin is unknown) was coined in the eighteenth century as a way to characterize a kind of overflowing anger.

According to the Stearnses, the period 1860–1940 saw a moderation of the earlier attitude, toward the view that anger was a natural part of the personality and that, rather than strive to eradicate it, we ought to channel anger into constructive activities. This idea applied more to boys than to girls, and it often involved encouraging a spirit of competition in affairs outside the home.[8]

The Stearnses invoked one more epoch, "1940 and following," divided between a "permissive subperiod" ending in the late 1950s and a "somewhat strict subperiod" up to the mid-1980s, when they were writing their book. During the permissive subperiod, they said, Americans abandoned the goal of teaching children to channel their anger and focused instead on showing that anger was an unpleasant experience, best to be avoided. Parents were counseled to show sympathy with angry children, along the lines of "I know how you feel." By the late 1950s, Americans began to feel a need to intervene more actively to control and deflect anger, both among children and between spouses. But, at this point, the analysis seems to blur. The Stearnses were aware that Americans of the 1980s expressed anger a lot more freely than those of earlier generations, but they edged to the conclusion that our society was still too censorious. "One of the most insidious features of the anger-control campaign, certainly," they wrote, "has been its potentially paralyzing insistence that anger is an internal problem rather than a normal response to external stimulus."[9]

The Stearnses' book is more helpful in describing *what* happened than in explaining *why* it happened – although in the opening pages they avowed that "the historian must also shed light on why expressions of anger have changed and how these changes are connected."[10] They gave considerable weight to experts who directly shape emotional attitudes – ministers, psychologists, and other advice-givers – but they also viewed such experts as often racing to catch up with changes that have already occurred in family structure or popular mores. Moreover, the Stearnses said they didn't "aspire to a precision" that would allow them to link specific forms of anger to specific periods of American history, such as "Jacksonian anger and Reconstruction anger." They merely saw some general connection between emotional configurations and, for example, "the excitement of the Civil War," unspecified aspects of Progressivism, and "the steady unfolding of American industrialization."[11]

The Stearnses' reluctance to pursue "precision" or to hypothesize why Americans had reformulated anger leaves a question that, perhaps, anthropologists are better suited than historians to answer. Why have Americans divested themselves of so many of their earlier taboos on how and when to express anger? Because we have – in a slow-moving cultural revolution – redefined the self, its boundaries, and the cultural ideals to which it can aspire. This revolution is necessarily slow-moving, because it takes at least two generations for such a transformation to occur. First, one generation must pioneer a break with the older traditions. But the pioneers, having been nurtured and raised in those traditions, can never entirely divest themselves of the habits of inner governance that those traditions fostered. When the pioneers have their own children and raise them according to their new ideals, however, those ideals themselves define the children's emotional horizons.

The pioneer generation can, and often does, provide spectacular examples of its new ideals: events in which those ideals reach an efflorescence, a Woodstock of perfected expression. But cultural efflorescence doesn't last long enough to plant itself in the personalities of children or to rewrite the rules of social interaction. Those are bigger projects that involve redefining roles in the family, schools, music, work, and other cultural domains. Valuable as I think the Stearnses' contribution is, I don't think they managed the task of tracing the connections across generations and through cultural domains in quite this way.

Perhaps one reason why they missed this larger story is that they emerged, in the end, as apologists for loosening taboos against anger. Since they were partial advocates of the cultural change, they were not well situated to be its critics. They favored a more free-wheeling emotional style as good for individuals and good for society. Individuals had "paid a heavy price in the loss of emotional richness and clarity" because of America's long-standing demand for "facile emotional control." And society, too, suffered as the effort to wean people from anger undermined "the emotional basis for grievance."[12] The Stearnses wrote off the "somewhat strict" approach as hypocritical, covertly hierarchical, and managerial.

I admire much of what the Stearnses accomplished in *Anger: The Struggle for Emotional Control in America's History*, but their concluding comments were wrongheaded. We live in an era flooded with self-indulgent and often trivial claims of grievance, but the Stearnses saw only a parched field in need of irrigation with still more grievance. At a time when millions of Americans were flattening their emotional range into an angry monotone, they called for – what else? – more anger.

The Stearnses, however, were far from alone in endorsing the "richness and clarity" of anger. Since the mid-1970s, a whole academic industry had grown up, composed of specialists who looked on the bright side of anger. A key figure in this shift was James Averill, a University of Massachusetts at Amherst psychology professor. Averill's 1977 questionnaire survey of the 18,000 people in the town of Greenfield, Massachusetts, had revealed that people were angry more often in their day-to-day life than psychologists had supposed – from several times a day to several times a week – and that expressing their anger generally made them feel better. Moreover, expressing their anger "tended to make bad situations much better."[13]

Pulitzer Prize–winning reporter Charles Duhigg, summarizing Averill's work, wrote:

> *Subsequent studies have found other benefits as well. We're more likely to perceive people who express anger as competent, powerful, and the kinds of leaders who will overcome challenges. Anger motivates us to undertake difficult tasks. We're often more creative when we're angry, because our outrage helps us see solutions we've overlooked. "When we look at the brains of people who are expressing anger, they look very similar to people who are experiencing happiness," says Dacher Keltner, the director of the Berkeley Social Interaction Lab. "When we become angry, we feel like we're taking control, like we're getting power over something." Watching angry people – as viewers of reality television know – is highly entertaining, so expressing anger is a sure-fire method for capturing the attention of an otherwise indifferent crowd.[14]*

And "In 1992 alone, social scientists published 25,000 studies of anger." Apparently that was not enough to discover that encouraging anger was a bit like encouraging cigarette smoking, or endorsing the sharpness and clarity that comes from playing catch with vials of nitroglycerine.

Gentlers vs. Purgationists

Anger may have contributed to domestic harmony in 1977 Greenfield, but a little bit seemed to go a long way. As Americans grew angrier, they also grew more divorced, more socially isolated, and more miserable. Maybe the psychologists of the Averill school, who saw all the benefits of communicating anger, would eventually turn their attention to the people who spent their evenings bowling alone. Or, if not those psychologists, then others in the field.

A therapeutic industry burgeoned, with promises to help people get the better of their own anger and to deal more effectively with the anger of their spouses, children, and coworkers.

Of course, the existence of a therapeutic industry implies a substantial number of people who are unhappy with the anger in their lives, and we might take the anger-management movement, at one level, to be a repudiation of the angri-culture. But the situation is actually more complicated. Anger management smooths some of the rough edges of the angri-culture. Most important, it provides help for those whose anger threatens to overwhelm their personal lives. Therapeutic approaches to anger, generally, do not challenge the background radiation of new anger – the bumper stickers, the music, the manners, the clothing, et cetera – its political prominence, or its somewhat disguised role in the workplace. Rather than offering a repudiation of the angri-culture, anger management turns out to be part of that culture: a combination of new anger's designated driver for nights on the town and dry cleaner for the morning after.

The touchstone for this popular therapeutic movement is Carol Tavris's *Anger: The Misunderstood Emotion* (1982), which renewed the call of all those earlier authors to bring anger under control. Tavris's book has remained in print for forty years, and justly so. It is an intellectually rich and wide-ranging exploration of anger. Tavris positioned her advice as a challenge to the view that had gained ground with Duhigg's studies in the 1970s that open expression of angry feelings was generally healthy and often constructive. She had in mind get-it-off-your-chest authorities such as Dr. Theodore Rubin ("blocks of unexpressed anger actually inhibit the free flow of loving feelings") and Paul Popenoe ("Many intelligent men and women are under the mistaken impression that expressing anger is dangerous and destructive to a marital relationship").[15]

Tavris's commonsensical advice about reining in anger inspired a great many similar self-help books in the decades that followed – and, more recently, websites. Among the most popular of the manuals are Harriet Lerner's *Dance of Anger: A Woman's Guide to Changing the Patterns of Intimate Relationships* (1985) and Reneau Z. Peurifoy's *Anger: Taming the Beast* (1999). But it is a crowded field. If Lerner or Peurifoy don't appeal, try Ron Potter-Efron's *Stop the Anger Now* (2001) or Albert Ellis's *How to Control Your Anger before It Controls You* (1998). The genre extends to warnings about the dire health consequences of overindulged anger, such as Redford Williams's *Anger Kills* (1993), and more specialized ventures, such as Suzette Haden Elgin's *You Can't Say That to Me: Stopping the Pain of Verbal Abuse* (1995).[16]

Those who counsel against giving free rein to anger, however, do not have the field to themselves. Dr. Theodore Rubin never relented in his quest to increase our loving feelings by helping us connect with our anger. Rubin's *Angry Book*, first published in 1969, has run through many printings. And various thinkers have offered strangely refined defenses of rage. Clinical psychologist Stephen Diamond, for example, argues for the creative side of choler in *Anger, Madness, and the Daimonic* (1996); and, in *Popular Music, Gender, and Postmodernism: Anger Is an Energy* (1997), Neil Nehring attempted to defend the anger in angry versions of rock 'n' roll from the strictures of postmodernists who find it all too ironic, or insufficiently ironic, or something. Still other writers propose to rechannel anger away from its destructive path into wholesome assertiveness. Neil Clark Warren, for example, in *Make Anger Your Ally* (1990), declared, "I believe anger is a God-given capacity – a neutral force that offers magnificent possibilities."[17]

In the debate between those who hope to gentle us down and those who wish we would unleash our too-hushed hurts, I'd say the Gentlers dominate, though the Unleashers and Purgationists have not fled the field. The relative success of those who would teach us how best to keep a lid on our anger, however, is itself evidence of a widespread sense among Americans that anger is in plentiful supply.

After Tavris, the most important popular writer on anger is psychologist Daniel Goleman, whose 1995 book, *Emotional Intelligence: Why It Can Matter More Than IQ*, remained atop the bestseller list for nearly a year. The title aside, Goleman is a sophisticated writer who lucidly presents an account of recent scientific findings on the physiology of rage, as well as quietly compelling advice on how and why to quell the impulse to get angry. Physiologically, "anger builds on anger." The initial bodily triggers, according to Goleman, prime the body to be extra-sensitive to the next provocation to anger. The individual who gives in to that next provocation, in turn, physically primes his body for an even greater emotional storm. Walk away, Goleman suggests – literally. Walking is one of the best ways to get your mind out of the body's insistence on upping the ante of anger.[18]

Goleman is the Gentler par excellence, so much so that another writer on emotions, Tom Lutz, takes the success of *Emotional Intelligence* as evidence that "we are in the midst of a transition away from the cathartic beliefs of the 1970s."[19] I suspect that is true as far as self-help books go, but not true as a measure of popular attitudes. A book that proposes to explain why "emotional intelligence" matters more than IQ sells because large numbers of people are, in fact, enchanted with the ideal of highly emotive styles of decision-making. Something similar happened with the success of Rick Warren's Christian self-help book *The Purpose-Driven Life* (2002). Its appeal is to those who feel disconnected from a deeper purpose in life, not to self-directed go-getters.

How much weight can we give the proliferation of self-help books and therapeutic services? The best gauge may be the scarcity of self-help books offering counsel about other troubling emotions. Those who feel burdened with an excess of envy, greed, pride, shame, disgust, or apathy, for example, find slimmer pickings in the local Barnes & Noble. Fear and worry, however, do considerably better. W. H. Auden characterized the Cold War era as "the age of anxiety," and his phrase has been lofted into the titles of more than a dozen self-help books. *Consuming Passions: Food in the Age of Anxiety* leads to *Mindblowing Sex in the Real World: Hot Tips for Doing It in the Age of Anxiety*. And if that works out, the reader can turn to *Worried All the Time: Rediscovering the Joy of Parenthood in an Age of Anxiety.*[20]

Part of the anxiety appears to be worry about time itself: the difficulty of scheduling a life that has numerous competing demands between work and family. Can a satisfying emotional life be lived on a corporate schedule? Is "quality time" really what children need? For a lot of people, the answer is a disconcerting "No!" Faced with irresolvable conflicts, they find one more reason to live in a state of near-constant irritation with their spouses and children.

The many books assuaging our many separate worries, however, are really piecemeal approaches to happiness. They deal with troubles that seem within reach of a good, long conversation, but they don't vault to the larger question of how to attain happiness itself – or its darker counterpart, how to overcome the pervasive

sadness and depression that settle over many lives. We do, however, have self-help books that soar to these higher goals, instruct-
ing you how to banish your blues and live a fulfilled life. And these
happy/sad books, it turns out, frequently bring us full circle to
advice about anger. A theory about depression marketed through
much of the therapeutic world is that depression is the result of
anger turned inward. According to this view, someone who suffers
depression can overcome it by figuring out the real target of his
anger (Mom, Dad, spouse, etc.) and then expressing the misdi-
rected emotion to the right cosmic zip code. Thus, within the most
common therapeutic worldview, our two prevailing ailments –
anger and depression – are really two faces of the same thing.
Tavris, incidentally, disagrees with this psychoanalytic cliché, saying that it confuses two separate emotions. "Why not argue anger
is depression turned outward?" In fact, people can be simultaneously angry and depressed, and the two feelings involve different
responses to psychological realities.[21]

The popularity of anger-management therapists, support
groups, self-help books, and websites testify that Americans today
tend to see excess anger as more of a mental-health problem than
a moral issue. If your temper has cost you your job or threatens
your marriage in contemporary America, you will almost certainly be advised by family and friends to seek counseling. In this
case, the shift away from an older approach of moral censure
toward the professional channeler is part of a larger transformation that was noticed and named as long ago as 1966, when Philip
Rieff memorably dubbed it "the triumph of the therapeutic."[22]

Angri-culture leans toward these therapeutic cultural premises
for some purposes and away from them for others. The ambivalence is nicely displayed in the comic movie *Anger Management*
(2003), about a chain of seeming accidents that lead the innocent
and angerless Dave Buznik, played by Adam Sandler, to receive
intensive therapy from a bizarrely uninhibited and confrontational doctor, Buddy Rydell, played by Jack Nicholson. The comic

premise of the movie is that the therapist aims not to cure Dave of his "rage" (he has none) but to help him achieve self-respect, which he can do only by getting appropriately angry at the kid who bullied him in fifth grade, his exploitative boss, his girlfriend's obnoxious ex-boyfriend, and ultimately Dr. Rydell himself.

While the movie makes light fun of anger-management therapy, the plot ultimately vindicates the angri-cultural assumptions that nice guys are simply self-loathing repressors of their authentic angry selves; that no one can really love another person without embracing anger too; and that anger is the true liberating force in our lives. Dave has to be tricked into discovering these "facts," but, once he grasps them, he becomes a full man – tells off his boss, punches out the ex-boyfriend, and wins the girl.

The put-upon and angerless Dave, who inevitably redeems himself by getting angry, also shows us the double-sided quality of "therapy" within the angri-culture. On one hand, we see a version of therapist-driven therapy, which is good-humoredly burlesqued. Nicholson's Dr. Rydell is manic and strange. His therapeutic techniques include teaching his patients to chant a supposed Eskimo phrase ("goosfrabba") to calm them down and interrupting tense moments to have grown men sing Stephen Sondheim's "I Feel Pretty." On the other hand, "therapy" is also the welling up of authentic self-assertion in Dave – with the help of Dr. Rydell's wise provocation.

The comedy in *Anger Management* probably wouldn't work without an audience that already accepts both angri-cultural premises: that formal counseling is a little bit silly, but learning to release one's anger is liberating and good. The Gentlers may be prevailing in the bookstores and actual therapist offices, but, judging by *Anger Management*, the Unleashers generally win at the box office. The 2004 thriller *Paparazzi* can stand for a whole genre of films. It presents a celebrity assigned to anger management for roughing up an intrusive photographer; he finds a more satisfying way to deal with his anger by killing off his tormentors.

American ambivalence about glib, therapeutic approaches received another nice twist in 2005, when freelance journalist Steve Salerno published *SHAM: How the Self-Help Movement Made America Helpless.* "SHAM" is Salerno's acronym for the Self-Help and Actualization Movement. The book is a caustic survey of the fatuities of the self-help industry, which rakes in many millions selling clichés and meaningless nostrums to the gullible. But Salerno's own book, laced with angry indignation at the self-help racket, is yet another exercise in pointing out the obvious; it is a self-help book for those addicted to self-help books.

My survey of books in the self-help category dates mostly from the early 2000s. Some of these books remain in bookstores, but, of course, they have been supplemented in the intervening years by dozens more. Yet the standoff between Gentlers, Unleashers, and Purgationists remains largely what it was. Perhaps the Unleashers have gained ground, since we now have feminists and antiracists who are hard at work advancing their "narratives" about the moral importance of getting and staying angry and expressing that anger at every opportunity.

Legacies

The rise of the angri-culture was helped along by the therapeutic worldview. Even though particular psychologists, such as Carol Tavris, have counseled strongly against the Purgationist approach, modern psychology as a whole seems to have provided the angri-culture with a tissue of rationalizations and excuses for dispensing with the old inhibitions against anger. The figure of Pollyanna comes back to us in Adam Sandler's Dave Buznik – but, this time, instead of Pollyanna teaching her aunt Polly how to overcome anger, the Pollyanna-ish Dave learns how to tap into his long-suppressed, angry inner child.

I don't want to oversimplify angri-culture's origins or flatten it by emphasizing only its personal-liberation side. Anger therapies, whether real or fictional, tend to lift anger out of its historical and social contexts and make it a matter of an individual's efforts to cope with life's checkerboard challenges. But therapeutic assumptions explain only one aspect of our culture's current infatuation with anger. Some other aspects are plainly political, and one of these grew directly out of Cold War divisions in America.

On the Anger Front

During the McCarthy era, many Americans were angry at Communist subversives – angry enough that the government executed Julius and Ethel Rosenberg for spying and blacklisted various academics and, notoriously, a handful of Hollywood screenwriters. And numerous American Communists, ex-Communists, and fellow travelers were angry at both the American government and the citizens who shunned them.

The anger on both sides left wounds that lasted the lifetimes of the participants, and then some. In 1952, movie director Elia Kazan testified to the U.S. House Un-American Activities Committee (HUAC), naming eleven screenwriters and actors as current or former Communists. Kazan never wavered in his conviction that he acted rightly. His longtime friend Arthur Miller, however, sharply disagreed, and he put his anger on stage in 1953 with *The Crucible*, implicitly likening the House inquiry into Communist subversion to the 1692 Salem witch trials. Kazan held his ground. The witches in Salem were a popular delusion; the Communists in Hollywood and elsewhere in American life were real. Kazan put his righteous anger into his 1954 movie *On the Waterfront*, implicitly likening his HUAC testimony to longshoreman Terry Molloy's decision to take a stand against a thuggish and corrupt union. Their friendship was finished, but Kazan and Miller overcame their mutual hostility to the extent that Kazan agreed in 1964 to direct Miller's play *After the Fall*. Nothing, however, could redeem Kazan in the eyes of many on the left, who viewed his willingness to "name names" to the House committee as utterly unforgivable.

The story of these old animosities is well known, and I don't take them as examples of new anger. They were plain old anger to start with, although with a seed of sourness on the left that would eventually ripen into full-blown new anger.

In 1999, Kazan, at eighty-nine, received a Lifetime Achievement Award from the Academy of Motion Picture Arts and Sciences, and the memory of that old anger came flooding back. Not only did it flood back: it was now celebrated, enacted, and put on display, as though it were a national treasure. Some 250 protesters gathered outside the Dorothy Chandler Pavilion on Oscar night to denounce the award. An eighty-year-old screenwriter, Bernard Gordon, who had been blacklisted in the 1950s, led the protest, joined by other octogenarians such as Bob Lees, another blacklisted writer, who said that "Kazan ruined people's lives." The protesters chanted, "No Oscars for rats." Inside the Dorothy Chandler Pavilion, some guests stood up and turned their backs when Kazan received the award. Their staged anger became a news story that won equal billing with the award itself.[23]

Kazan's Oscar also stirred vitriol in some segments of the press. *Boston Globe* columnist Thomas Oliphant, for example, wrote, "Kazan is also a pathetically prototypical rat-fink of the anticommunist hysteria." David Aaronovitch, writing in the *Independent* (London), took the occasion to characterize Kazan's testimony forty-seven years earlier as "a cowardly choice, a choice to be on the side of the bully, and not the bullied."[24]

One of the threads in Aaronovitch's comments is worth following a little further. Aaronovitch recalled that a month after Kazan's HUAC testimony, playwright Lillian Hellman, who was one of the people Kazan named as a former Communist, also testified to the committee. Hellman, however, refused to name names, scornfully telling her interrogators, "I cannot and will not cut my conscience to fit this year's fashions." This sentence is frequently quoted by leftists, both in contrast to Kazan's supposed cowardice and to exemplify a kind of heroism. Aaronovitch does not say but I will add that Hellman, a stalwart Stalinist, was not otherwise known to possess much of a conscience, at least not one that flinched at mass murder or political tyranny. But why do Hellman's fierce words to the HUAC continue to reverberate decades later? Aaronovitch thinks it is because the relativist left, having few firm principles to stand on, has discovered that anger itself can substitute for principle in some situations. How else to explain the admiration accorded to figures such as "that totally uncompromising American feminist, Andrea Dworkin"? These instances, he says, show "how some now value anger and authenticity over respectability."[25]

The word "respectability" isn't exactly right; it is a slightly dismissive substitute for the more daunting word "truthfulness." Because what Hellman exemplifies for the left is a facts-be-damned victory of attitude over substance. Hellman found a way to sound angrily high-minded about covering up Communist subversion.

I don't want to pause at this point for the late and now passé Andrea Dworkin, who built a career on angry pronouncements of risible theories about sex and marriage, except to register Aaronovitch's insight. Dworkin is, perhaps, most famous for her declaration that "Marriage as an institution developed from rape as a practice. Rape, originally defined as abduction, became marriage by capture." Anthropologically speaking, there is no evidence whatsoever that marriage derives from capture, abduction, or rape – but the purpose of making such counterfactual declarations is not to deepen understanding. It is simply to demonstrate the writer's outrageousness as a kind of emotional credential.

The feud between Miller and Kazan is part of the story of anger in America now, because it is one of the events in the historical memory of the left that continues to shape a specific kind of anger. The angri-culture is not a single endlessly repeated jeer but a cacophony of rude noises, blaring insults, and staccato vitupera-tion. The more than half a century that the left spent hating Kazan, praising Hellman, and sentimentalizing Hollywood Communists perfected one distinct note in that cacophony: the angri-culture gained its sense of anger as something one could subscribe to and wear as a badge of membership. The Cold War provided several other events that played in much the same way: former State Department official Alger Hiss's conviction for perjury; the exe-cution of the Rosenbergs for spying; the derailed careers of peo-ple like orientalist Owen Lattimore. But Kazan's longevity carried his case over the decades and made it a particularly powerful opportunity for turning long-standing political enmity into theat-rical new anger.

Chapter Six

SELF-GOVERNMENT

Acting vs. Being Angry

WHEN EXPRESSING ANGER becomes a badge of loyalty to an ideology or a faction, people adopt angry styles even if they do not inwardly feel angry. But only a very talented actor can routinely simulate anger without, in time, feeling the emotion itself. Perhaps not even a very talented actor can do it. In Bernardo Bertolucci's film *Last Tango in Paris* (1972), Marlon Brando gave what many critics regarded as his finest performance, that of Paul (no last name), a man raging "against himself and the women he famously seduced and abandoned." Brando said in his autobiography that when the film was finished, "I decided that I wasn't ever again going to destroy myself emotionally to make a movie."[1]

When politics gets angry, individuals do as well, but their political anger often differs from other forms of anger in their lives. Husbands and wives who are angry with one another may feud, sulk, make up, find practical ways to get along, or separate, all the while nursing their personal grievances. That pattern tends to hold in other family relations as well. Few are moved to announce their anger with family members by declaring it in letters to the editor or postings on Facebook.

Political anger can borrow elements of familial anger, but it tends to project itself outwardly to a larger stage. It isn't left in the kitchen; it appears on the bumper sticker of the family car. Some master an angry public style that they can instantly turn off. They leave their anger on the street corner or at their front door. Others, however, invite it inside. They complicate (and often undermine) their marriages and other relationships by insisting "the personal is political." Cable TV and the internet, both bristling with angry exchanges, have no doubt helped political anger find a place in the living room and the den.

Angri-culture, thus, has a suburban sprawl. It moves beyond the particular issues in their original contexts to clutter the countryside with its pervasive resentments. It is "out there" as well as "in here." Real anger mixes with the imitations of anger – but the imitations, in turn, provoke their own rage, until it is difficult to tell who is really angry and who is just dressing the part.

The mixture of actual feeling and mere acting is nothing new. Social anthropologists (like me) long shied away from emphasizing the emotional side of culture precisely because of this conundrum. When a culture mandates a particular emotional expression – joy at a homecoming, pride at a graduation – do people necessarily feel the emotion? Or do they often just go through the e-motions? In some cultures, people hire professional mourners to weep at funerals. The paid-for tears still express "grief," but in the manner that a prerecorded laugh track on a TV sitcom expresses surprise and delight. The outward form conveys a culturally standardized attitude, but the inner human reality of the hired mourner may be very different.

Not all anthropologists have regarded this disjunction between conventional form and inner feeling as a big issue. In 1934, anthropologist Ruth Benedict wrote one of the discipline's all-time best sellers, *Patterns of Culture*, in which she argued that cultures typically shape the individual's emotions to fit a prevailing ideal. Benedict cited the Zuni tribe of the southwestern United States, for example, as a people who favor tightly self-controlled emotions, and she claimed that all but a handful of "deviant" Zunis mildly fall in line with what is expected of them. Likewise, she described the Melanesian inhabitants of the island of Dobu as schemers who inwardly live in deep fear of the people around them but outwardly express an attitude of polite friendliness. Dobuan culture raises every child to be a conniving hypocrite, and few Dobuans disappoint.

Benedict's approach, which aimed to capture what is central to a culture and to downplay its ambiguities, is very much out of favor in today's anthropology.[2] Not all Zunis are so tightly wrapped or all Dobuans the model of Machiavellian cunning. But Benedict did offer an interesting way to think about group psychology. In effect, she minimized the distinction that psychologists usually draw between emotional dispositions and actual episodes of emotion, usually phrased as the difference between emotional "traits" and emotional "states."[3] And, indeed, new anger involves both traits and states, or dispositions and episodes – as well as a third element that Benedict emphasized and most psychologists do not: the surrounding ambience that teaches, prompts, and continually reinforces the dominant emotional styles.

We should give due weight to both views: the radically skeptical view that anger is often performed according to a cultural script without the performer necessarily feeling it and the Benedict-like view that people generally follow such scripts because they *do* feel the appropriate emotions. On one hand, outward displays of anger are not always what they seem. On the other hand, the angri-culture does impose a kind of conformity. The calmly reflective soul rarely shows up on MSNBC or Fox. We expect titanic clashes. The angri-culture feeds on conflict and rewards those who can best play the role of gladiators – those who, like the professional weepers at funerals, play the role just far enough. The gladiatorial spirit is to play the game roughly but never with total abandon.

The gladiatorial quality of new anger, however, doesn't mean that new anger is always a game or a perpetual conflict. It can, and does, lead to final outcomes: people acting on new anger make key decisions. New anger offers a doctrine of self-empowerment, and all those empowered selves in America are indeed doing something, even if it is mostly contributing to the divorce rate, the number of children raised by single parents, and the fluidity of the job market.

America has an angri-culture, but this doesn't mean that all Americans are perpetually angry or on the verge of anger. Nor does it mean that the angri-culture is the only cultural mode available to us. Rather, it is a kind of emotional air pollution that forms dense smog in some contexts and mere haze in others. The angri-culture doesn't prevent Americans from being friendly to strangers (some of the time) or opening their hearts to victims of tsunamis and hurricanes. But neither does it ever quite go away. Almost any event, from a volcanic eruption in the Caribbean to a polar bear lazing on an ice floe, can be swept up in the grand-standing recriminations of the angri-culture.

Other Angers

Is today's angri-culture really any different from earlier epochs? Are we actually angrier than people were in the 1950s – or 1930s, or 1860s, or 1770s? It is hard to imagine an objective measure of the sheer quantity of anger, or even a subjective measure that could be adjusted for changes in historical circumstances. Were disappointed Confederate veterans angrier than the World War I veterans who camped in Washington, D.C., to demand additional benefits? A popular song in the South in 1870, "Good Old Rebel" by Innes Randolph, offers lines that strut with anger, such as "I killed a chance of Yankees and I wish I'd killed some mo'!" but lyrical defiance and venom are to be found in every decade. A recent book recounts in fine detail the "hardhat riot" of May 8, 1970, when construction workers from the World Trade Center descended on student antiwar protestors in New York's financial district.[4] Explaining the cultural animosities that lay behind this single event takes the author, David Paul Kuhn, hundreds of pages, not least because in the ire of the construction workers he spots one of the origins of Trumpism. That seems fair, although the chasm between the anti-American left and the traditional pro-American public had been growing for decades and could be epitomized by earlier episodes as well.

Can we find benchmarks that distinguish contemporary anger from anger past? Has America always been, at some level, an angri-culture? Or is the era of new anger something different?

The explosion of anger in American politics in the last few years has prompted some scholars to take up the historical question. Some point to the aftermath of the presidential elections of 1800 and 1860 as exceptionally acrimonious. Others have focused on the broader phenomenon of terrorism, including nineteenth-century Russian nihilists, the Irish Fenian dynamiters, the Palestinian Black Septemberists, the European Red Brigades, and many others.[5] America has certainly not been spared the attacks of international terrorists nor the terror campaigns of domestic groups, such as the Molly McGuires and the Weather Underground, but American culture has not proven receptive to political terror – at least not until the summer of 2020. The rise of Antifa and Black Lives Matter that year, combined with the willingness of elected officials and the liberal press to condone their terrorist campaigns, has reset public expectations.[6]

I don't think we can say objectively whether the acrimony during Jefferson's administration, the Civil War, or the Hardhat Riot was more intense than it is today. Perhaps people, like water bottles, can contain only so much, after which the excess just falls away. The sheer quantity of anger, however, is less important than how it is experienced, controlled, and interpreted. My thesis about "new anger" is that it is anger that is experienced as liberating and empowering; that is unmoored from most of the social controls that in earlier epochs treated it as shameful and illegitimate; and that is now interpreted as healthful, constructive, and responsible.

Escalator

A Bee in the Mouth was, I think, the first full-scale attempt to describe the rise of the self-conscious performative new anger. Other observers, however, were soon registering significant changes in American temperament. Writing in the *Atlantic* in 2019, Charles Duhigg summed up a decade in which "evidence of anger's destructive power is everywhere." He cited the confirmation hearings of Supreme Court Justice Brett Kavanaugh, quoting angry comments from Republican Senator Lindsey Graham. And mentioning Attorney General Eric Holder's campaign line: "When they go low, we kick 'em. That's what this new Democratic Party is about."[7] Duhigg mentions violent extremists who shoot and bomb, but he focuses on the "visceral disdain" that both sides have for their political opponents, as well as the marked increase in "partisan nastiness." That increase is not an illusion. Polls showed a dramatic rise over the course of the 2010s in the anger each side had toward the other.[8]

Duhigg accounts for this as a transformation from "ordinary anger" first to "moral indignation – a more combustible form of the emotion," and then, "as the indignant lose faith that their anger is heard," it becomes something else, "a desire for revenge against our enemies that privileges inflicting punishment over reaching accord." Duhigg's three stages are a close parallel between my three-part distinction between old anger, new anger, and wrath. His hopeful prescription is that moral indignation can be turned to "righteous rage" in a good cause, before it ignites into wrath. His example of how that can be done is Cesar Chavez organizing migrant grape pickers in California in 1966 into a small army of self-sacrificial protesters. Duhigg compares the success of this moral-outrage movement to the 1857 mutiny against the East India Company. But even "moral outrage must be closely managed, or it can do more harm than good." Anger has to be channeled, and the leaders of an angry movement have to take care that anger doesn't spill over into violence.

Duhigg then turns his attention to how corporate America ("The New Anger Merchants") have capitalized on anger, and he offers a fascinating account of a debt-collection agency that studied the new research on anger and devised an approach to manipulate the debt-ridden into paying up. "'The trick they were teaching was to use anger strategically,' [researcher Robert] Sutton told me. 'They had it as a formula: when to fake anger, when to cool down, when to give people a bit of forgiveness.'" The collectors pretended to be angry, then offered relief, and most debtors gladly paid. Duhigg disapproves of such manipulation but sees "corporatized outrage" as hugely effective, especially on TV. "Watching anger was entertaining," and getting to participate in it was "irresistible." Duhigg, in other words, found his own path to describing "new anger." He notes that "the targets of our rage" now tend to be strangers – who, rather than appease us, "fire back."

This dynamic, of course, applies to politics as much as to reality TV or Facebook. Duhigg traces efforts to provoking this kind of anger to win political support to George H. W. Bush's 1988 presidential campaign speeches and a Bush TV ad highlighting Willie Horton. Horton, a convicted murderer serving a life sentence in Massachusetts, had been let out of prison on a weekend furlough program. While on furlough, he committed kidnapping, assault, and rape. Bush's Democratic opponent, Massachusetts governor Michael Dukakis, had endorsed the furlough program, and the Bush TV ad used the connection to tag Dukakis as soft on criminals and crime. The connection certainly stirred anger, though it is hard to see that it was a watershed in political-campaign rhetoric.

But Duhigg sees that "anger-mongering in campaigns, whether subtle or overt, has had a corrosive effect on American democracy." On this point, I've come to disagree. Anger-mongering definitely can prompt very bad behavior, but we have discovered that American democracy is much more vulnerable to cool, deliberate deception and ruthless disregard for the impediments posed by honest elections. Against those sorts of chicanery, efforts to rouse public anger are a veritable lesson in basic civics. A complacent public is a public destined to be ruled by usurpers. Anger is the only defense. Blistering essays by Michael Anton, David Horowitz, and other conservative writers have, indeed, aimed at inciting anger that fits entirely in Duhigg's category of "righteous indignation" and my category of wrath.[9]

Duhigg is a perceptive writer on the exact opposite side of this debate. He and I agree that anger can be useful, but the anger that he welcomed in January 2019 was "the moral outrage that motivates citizens to push for a more just society," the anger of "the women of the #MeToo movement, [and] the activists of Black Lives Matter," the latter of which the following year would help unleash a wave of burning, looting, and attacks on police across the country. Duhigg says that "we risk forfeiting the gains that good anger can bring," and he warns against the "the anger merchants' self-serving motives." I warn against being intimidated by the fake righteous anger of movements deployed to undermine core values of our civilization. The great dangers aren't sneaky bill collectors or angertainment TV shows. Rather, the danger lies in the political class intent on dismantling our rights to free speech, free assembly, due process, and self-defense.

I take Duhigg's *Atlantic* essay to be among the most insightful of recent writings on anger. I will deal with another important contribution, Michael Kimmel's 2017 book, *Angry White Men*, in chapter 8. Steven W. Webster's *American Rage: How Anger Shapes Our Politics* (2020) is an academic study of "anger-fueled negative partisan affect" in American political life. It has lots of tables and graphs, and it argues that our national anger does us no good. Steven Levitsky and Daniel Ziblatt, in *How Democracies Die* (2018), found that Trump stirred up a lot of anger that eroded "long-standing political norms," and this pointed the way to his assuming dictatorial powers. Jonathan Haidt's *Righteous Mind* (2012) says little about anger directly but a great deal about the beliefs that underlie anger. It bears on a lot of the topics in this book, especially moral indignation, but Haidt aims for a general social theory, not an account of the changing structure of emotions in our own time. His greatest strength is his analysis of how and why groups create and maintain lockstep agreement on certain beliefs and are roused to fury when someone dissents.[10]

Legendary

Through wars, strikes, riots, and political unrest, anger in the past was either an occasional thing – an eruption of a specific group with a powerful grievance, such as the Pullman Strike of 1894 or the riots at the Chicago Democratic convention in 1968 – or a malady limited to specific people, such as the notorious feud between the Appalachian Hatfield and McCoy families from 1878 to 1890. Sometimes this anger intensified to rage, or even wrath, but it never settled into being a national ideal. We were not a nation known for being full of angry, bitter people or a nation that was always on the verge of blowing its stack.

Even though we created approving legends of vigilantes seeking frontier justice, these sorts of intervention were, on the whole, seen as regrettable and sometimes tragic violations of the standards of civilized life. It is telling that the angriest factions in American society, from Know-Nothings and the Ku Klux Klan to Weathermen and the militia movement, almost always organized themselves as secret societies. In the past, those who decided that they would act on anger hid their faces. The echo of that today is the Antifa movement, but Antifa rioters are far from ashamed of their anger. They are just aware that cameras are now everywhere and that masking is a good way to forestall arrest.

One genre of vigilante tales depicts "Indian haters," who, having lost family members to an Indian massacre, devote themselves to a solitary career of vengeance. Herman Melville, in *The Confidence Man*, captured the genre well when he put the story of the (real-life) Colonel John Moredock in the mouth of an inept hustler. Moredock, an Illinois pioneer in the early nineteenth century, tracked a band of Indians who had killed his mother and siblings. Eventually, having killed all twenty members of the band, Moredock supposedly made a practice of hunting down and killing any Indians he could find.[11]

Moredock-like figures continue to inhabit some dark place in the American soul. Ethan Edwards, in John Ford's classic Western *The Searchers* (1956), reminds some of Moredock, but he is present in any number of revenge movies that have nothing to do with Native Americans. The angry antihero of *Paparazzi* (2004), who dispatches annoying photographers, is a modern Moredock, as are the numerous triggermen of "first-person shooter" video games. The figure has been with us at least since Thomas Kyd wrote *The Spanish Tragedy* (c. 1594), the first Renaissance revenge play.

All this is to say that new anger has one of its roots in an old form of virulent anger in which some Americans imagined an enemy so vile that nothing short of serial or collective murder was warranted. But Moredock was never an American hero. He and his imitators have existed in the American imagination primarily as a type to be repudiated, although the repudiation has recently taken a new direction. A view currently popular within the field of (anti-) American studies is that America has long been a hateful place filled with incitements to genocidal violence. Richard Slotkin's 1973 book, *Regeneration through Violence: The Mythology of the American Frontier, 1600–1860*, provided one of the original sources of this revisionist thesis, and Slotkin built on it in later works, including *Gunfighter Nation: The Myth of the Frontier in Twentieth-Century America* (1992). The latter concludes with images of the My Lai massacre in Vietnam as the practical result of America's supposed obsession with "redemptive" violence. Slotkin himself, however, can stand as the purveyor of a certain version of new anger, one that looks at the history of the United States mainly in order to debunk the nation's older, positive images of itself.

Americans are of two minds about such violence. On one hand, we recoil at mass shooters who unleash their mayhem in public places and who usually plan their own deaths as part of their rampage. On the other hand, a substantial number of Americans consider the mass abortion industry as an incidental cost to be paid for ensuring women's "reproductive freedom," and many others entertain with insouciance the prospect of phasing out White people. A history professor at Drexel University jokingly tweeted in 2016, "All I want for Christmas is white genocide."[12] His jest caused an uproar, and he defended himself by saying that he was mocking "white supremacists" who imagine that their enemies are plotting such a thing. But the joke touches a nerve. Why does our press show such deep interest in the killings perpetrated by White males, while it treats killings perpetrated by Middle Eastern Muslims, Black males, or anyone else as warranting little attention? Why is racism now defined as something inflicted only by Whites against others? Shortly after George Floyd's death, a *Chicago Tribune* columnist declared, "White people, you are the problem," a view that can be found echoed in myriad places.[13] Indeed, the subtext of "Black Lives Matter" is that White lives don't, or at least not as much. A neo-racist Moredockian sentiment has found a respectable place in our cultural commentary.

Thus, contemporary angri-culture has picked up and refurbished some rightfully discarded themes from old anger. The past suffering of oppressed minorities is the source that feeds this angri-culture renaissance. It isn't always an easy card to play, but it is usually in the deck. In October 1995, when Johnnie Cochran convinced the jury in the O. J. Simpson murder trial that his spectacularly unoppressed client was the victim of racist cops, new anger produced a verdict of not guilty. Angri-culture has its uses. The anger of Nicole Simpson's parents has been portrayed as excessively "vindictive."[14]

1619

The anger of oppressed minorities is a story larger than can fit into a single book. Black writers, in particular, span the whole spectrum of America's history of framing the emotion. A short course would lead from Booker T. Washington's titanic effort to exert every ounce of will to control his anger, recounted in *Up from Slavery* (1901); to Ralph Ellison's baffled and abused protagonist in *Invisible Man* (1952), whose anger ultimately makes him visible to himself, if not others; to Malcolm X, in his as-told-to *Autobiography* (1965), discovering the charismatic power of rage, and the paradox that rage is all the more powerful for being conveyed softly.

But the intersection of racial complaint and new anger is nowhere better exemplified than in the *New York Times'* 1619 Project, which attempts to "reframe" all of American history through the lens of White supremacy over oppressed Blacks. As I've devoted a whole book to that subject, *1620: A Critical Response to the 1619 Project*, I'll forebear going at it again except to say that the Project's main editor and lead author, Nikole Hannah-Jones, has proven to be a master pianist at playing the chords of new anger. She assumed responsibility for the riots of 2020 when she assented to having them called the "1619 Riots," and "1619" frequently appeared spray-painted on the statues of American heroes toppled by the rioters. Performative anger won its first Pulitzer Prize when it was awarded to Hannah-Jones for her contributions to the 1619 Project.

To understand the American angri-culture, we will need to

keep in mind the distinction between mere showmanship and expressions of deeply felt human realities. Still, the border between simply acting angry and actually being angry is unmarked, and people stray over it in both directions. This is because of the theatricality of much of modern life. We have learned to live in an unending orgy of self-dramatization and self-creation.

Our historical moment is distinguished by the way we think about anger as much as it is by the magnitude of our ire. We have somehow arrived at a society in which anger has gained a high degree of approval and public respect. Anger is fashionable; within limits, anger is good. Anger has become legitimate and no longer apologetic about itself. This is what it means to have an angri-culture.

Chapter Seven

TAKING CHARGE

ARE THERE WAYS that Americans can escape the cultural lure of anger as entertainment, lifestyle, personal empowerment, and political strategy? Or is new anger a Hotel California that we can enter but never leave? I don't necessarily recommend a remedy for every kind of anger. Sometimes we must fight fire with fire. Everything is a matter of proportion, measure, and self-control. Even wrath needs to be kept under command – not let loose, so to speak, in the corridors of the Capitol.

Founding Anger

We have a plausible standard for the right form of anger in the founding of our republic. It began in a revolution in the anger of men aroused by injustice. That alone is not its distinguishing feature; the French Revolution, also set off by injustice, resulted in fiercer rhetoric and bloodier consequences. The Jacobins were not intrinsically angrier than the Sons of Liberty, but the French Revolution licensed a frenzy of angry expression and cruelty that the American Revolution generally avoided.

The success of the American Revolution in forestalling a descent into unbridled anger is all the more notable in view of the

116

pent-up frustration of the generation of Americans who joined in the revolt against Britain, the angry temperament of some of the leaders, and the quarrelsomeness that flowered in the early Republic. All three factors point to the emotional powder keg that, somehow, did not ignite over eight years of armed conflict.

The first of two conventional explanations for this is that the colonies and their internal factions (with the exception of Tories) united against a common external enemy. Benjamin Franklin's quip at the signing of the Declaration of Independence, "We must indeed all hang together, or, most assuredly, we shall all hang separately," captures that necessary putting aside of local quarrels for the time being. The other explanation is that the Founders were creatures of the Enlightenment who explicitly conceptualized their revolt as founded in law and reason, not on what they called the passions. To a large extent, they played against the anger of their countrymen and took considerable effort to keep their own passions under control.

As far back as John Wise's 1710 admonition that the idea of arbitrary government puts "an Englishman's blood into a fermentation," Americans had shown a readiness to respond to injustice with anger. And the lead-up to the Revolution included plenty of American words and acts redolent with anger. The Boston Tea Party was organized fermentation: anger staged as a public spectacle.

One of the angriest of American leaders was James Otis, the author of the well-worn sentence, "Taxation without representation is tyranny." Otis had been the Crown's advocate general in the Vice Admiralty Court in Massachusetts, but he resigned in 1761 when he was ordered to defend the Writs of Assistance, which in effect allowed colonial officials to search private houses for smuggled goods without evidence of wrongdoing and without search warrants. Otis not only resigned, but also volunteered his services as counsel to some Boston merchants; from this vantage, on February 24, 1761, he gave a five-hour speech in which he expressed –

and evoked in his listeners – fury against the government that had imposed the Writs of Assistance. He said that the writs promoted "revenge, ill-humour, or wantonness" among some, causing others to use the law in self-defense, and so on in reprisal; so "one arbitrary exertion will provoke another, until society be involved in tumult and in blood."[1]

Otis is not well known today, but among those in that audience in 1761 was the young John Adams, who later wrote that "the child of independence was born" in Otis's diatribe against the Writs of Assistance. Otis was provocative on more than one occasion, and through the 1760s he was one of the key leaders in opposition to British impositions. In 1769, however, a customs house official, enraged by one of Otis's newspaper articles, beat him severely over the head with his cane. Badly injured, Otis never fully recovered his intellectual powers but drifted in and out of sanity. During lucid intervals, he still served the cause. He fought, for example, at Bunker Hill. But Otis the revolutionary lightning bolt was dimmed. A dinner with Massachusetts governor John Hancock in 1783 stirred up old memories and so disturbed him that he was put under the watchful care of an old friend in Andover, Massachusetts. Standing in the doorway of the friend's house while telling a story to the friend's family, he was appropriately discharged by a bolt from a passing thunderstorm.

The American Revolution was not lacking for other temperamental hotheads, such as Patrick Henry and Thomas Paine. And it may be that the Revolution would not have succeeded without their capacity to distill the cause down to a fiery essence. But their provocations seem less central to the event than the cerebral coolness of Jefferson, for example, who could calmly subordinate revolutionary anger to abstract principle. Jefferson's Declaration of Independence is a manifesto of revolution, but it deliberately backs away from anger as a reason to rebel. Instead, it advances the claims of "duty":

Prudence, indeed, will dictate that Governments long estab-lished should not be changed for light and transient causes; and accordingly all experience hath shewn, that mankind are more disposed to suffer, while evils are sufferable, than to right themselves by abolishing the forms to which they are accustomed. But when a long train of abuses and usurpa-tions, pursuing invariably the same Object evinces a design to reduce them under absolute Despotism, it is their right, it is their duty, to throw off such Government, and to provide new Guards for their future security.[2]

The call to "duty," of course, does not mean that the American Revolution was anger-free. Otis, the Boston Tea Party, and others had already seen to that. But the word "duty," in a way, repudiates anger (or at least constrains it), even as the Declaration goes on in a litany of twenty-seven clauses naming various abuses by "the present King of Great Britain."

That list accuses the Crown of serious infractions and neglect, and it concludes with reminders that Americans have "Petitioned for Redress" and, when those failed, warned their British brethren of trouble to come. In a sense, the body of the Declaration is objectively angry, in that its details incite a kind of righteous wrath. But the details are also securely under Jefferson's control. This seething list of grievances and might-have-beens is recited under the rubric of performing a public "duty" by showing "a decent respect to the opinions of mankind."

Is the Declaration of Independence an angry document? It is surprisingly hard to say. It contains a cargo of angry complaints in a ship of legal and dispassionate reasoning. Perhaps that's the key to understanding not just Jefferson's view of the Revolution but the guiding ethos of the whole generation of Founders.

This is not to say that the Founders were, as individuals, either angry by nature or cheerful. Individuals varied.

The last of the Declaration's clauses that condemn King George III begins, "He has excited domestic insurrections amongst us," and it goes on to mention frontier wars with Indians. Domestic insurrection was a real possibility. Their Tory opponents often characterized the revolutionaries as wild, intemperate, and willing to license the passions of the mob. The Maryland planter James Chalmers, for example, under the pseudonym Candidus, penned a seventy-page pamphlet titled *Plain Truth* to refute Paine's *Common Sense*. He warned that the revolutionaries were "demagogues" who "to seduce the people into their criminal designs ever hold up democracy to them" but intend really to bring despotism. Chalmers was not eloquent, but he was angry, ending his screed, "INDEPENDENCE AND SLAVERY ARE SYNONYMOUS TERMS."

The revolutionaries, though indeed in love with liberty, also feared what was wild and unrestrained in American life. In the rambunctious history of the quarter-century following the Declaration, the vituperative rivalry between partisans of Adams and Jefferson, as well as Burr and Hamilton's duel to the death, testify to a society in which anger coursed through both public and private life.

One reason for this was that the American Revolution itself aimed at political liberty, not at replacing the basic values of respect, dignity, kindness, and honor that suffused ideals for both political authority and private conduct in eighteenth-century America. The Revolution was intended to create a new regime, not a new culture, much less a new emotional stance toward life. All those emotions that the Founders held at arm's length as "passions" were, in fact, vitally part of their culture and bound to affect the political order. The closest they came to finding a constructive place for the passions was in Federalist No. 10, in which Madison defines a "faction" as a number of citizens "united and actuated by some common impulse of passion."[3] That passion is not necessarily anger, though it might be: Madison mentions, for example, parties inflamed with "mutual animosity." He famously goes on to argue that in the large republic contemplated in the Constitution, the sheer multiplicity of factions will help prevent any one faction – even an angry one – from dominating. Anger will, so to speak, be diffused by its own futility.

Madison's theory is wise statesmanship, but it still leaves a curiously flattened view of human nature – a view that acknowledges the passions but firmly pushes them into the realm of dangers to be managed, not defects to be corrected, not qualities to be cultivated, and not exuberances to be, on occasion, celebrated. Madison aims to address the "factious spirit" that has "tainted our public administrations." But since "the causes of faction" are "sown in the nature of man," we are best advised, as far as politics go, to set aside the causes and focus instead on how to handle the consequences. This framing of the issue politely but firmly closes the door on a deeper inquiry into those human qualities that make us factious.

Lincoln

The inability or unwillingness of Madison, Jefferson, Adams, and their peers to speak more directly about the passionate nature of the Revolution and the buried animosities that reemerged after the nation won its independence left a peculiar gap in our sense of national identity – a gap that the twenty-eight-year-old Abraham Lincoln famously noted in his Lyceum Address in 1838.

In 1836, a mob in Saint Louis had taken hold of an African American freedman suspected of murder and had burned him alive. Lincoln said that this outrage was one of many across the country that demonstrated "the growing disposition to substitute the wild and furious passions, in lieu of the sober judgment of Courts," and he saw disaster ahead for the nation if Americans did not learn to cherish the law. The problem, in Lincoln's view, stemmed from the passing of the generation that had fought for the Revolution.

That revolutionary generation had staked everything on proving *"the capability of a people to govern themselves."* Although they preached reason, they were moved by pride, ambition, and fear of shame if they should fail. "If they succeeded, they were to be immortalized; their names were to be transferred to counties and cities, and rivers and mountains. . . . If they failed, they were to be called knaves and fools, and fanatics for a fleeting hour; then to sink and be forgotten." Lincoln added that the *"passions* of the people" in the American Revolution, "as distinguished from their judgment," were united with the great cause and channeled away from domestic acrimony:

> *By this influence, the jealousy, envy, and avarice, incident to our nature, and so common to a state of peace, prosperity, and conscious strength, were, for the time, in a great measure smothered and rendered inactive; while the deep-rooted principles of hate, and the powerful motive of revenge, instead of being turned against each other, were directed exclusively against the British nation.*[4]

But, as the events of the Revolution receded and the patriots died off ("a forest of giant oaks" swept over by "the all-resistless hurricane" of mortality), the powerful emotions that had held these divisive passions at bay dissipated. "But this state of feeling," said Lincoln, *"must fade, is fading, has faded,* with the circumstances that produced it."

The young lawyer from Springfield, Illinois, had deep admiration for the achievement of the Founders, but he was worlds away from them on the issue of "passion." For the Founders, with their Enlightenment faith in reason, feelings were to be self-governed by the responsible individual and held in check for everyone else by good government. But for Lincoln, the patriots' "passion" was what made them "the pillars of the temple of liberty." He concluded – rather unconvincingly – that the only recourse for his own generation, who could not experience that original passion, would be general intelligence, sound morality, and *"reverence for the constitution and laws."* Perhaps this wasn't an entirely vain hope in 1838, with the Civil War more than two decades away, but it seems unlikely that intelligence, morality, and reverence would ever be enough, by themselves, to galvanize a people into active commitment to the rule of law.

A counsel of temperance in an angry time was surely not out of place. The lynch mobs that prompted Lincoln's speech were, after all, assuming a kind of perverted moral authority, and Lincoln's task was to convince his listeners that that authority was false and illegitimate. The broader problem, of course, has not gone away. Today we have vigilantes of other sorts – radical environmentalists who burn houses and cars, computer hackers who "punish" corporations, animal-rights activists who invade research labs, Black Lives Matter mobs who burn cities, Antifa thugs who attack federal courthouses and murder counterprotesters – turning their anger into lawless attacks on those they accuse of injustice. What exactly do you say to people so convinced of the righteousness of their cause and the lameness of the law that they strike directly at their opponents?

In his Lyceum speech, Lincoln suggested that the Founders had been able to brush aside the complicated issues of the emotional cohesion of the country because the birth pangs of the new republic practically guaranteed an intense common commitment. But the result was a nation in which the bonds of citizenship lacked a certain kind of emotional definition. The cardinal principles articulated in the founding documents and in the nation at large were (and are) liberty and equality. But what was the founding's emotional stance?

Washington

I am not sure this question has an exact answer, but the society that emerged from a long and bloody war was far from a calm, reason-doting constitutional seminar. It had complicated emotional qualities, even if its leaders lacked an overt vocabulary for this aspect of collective life. And the most important of those qualities were, in a way, on display in George Washington, the Founding Father who seems more than any other to have shaped the character of the American people.

Washington was a man burdened throughout his life with a quick temper. In 1748, when he was sixteen, he was hired by Thomas, Lord Fairfax, a relative of his, to survey some property. Fairfax sent Washington's mother a letter, observing: "I wish I could say that he governs his temper. He is subject to attacks of anger on provocation, sometimes without just cause." Fairfax predicted that Washington would get control of his anger but "go to school all his life."[5]

Indeed, all his life Washington did struggle with his tissue-thin sensitivity to slights. The dignified and reserved man who looks out from his portrait on the dollar bill is one who fought his fiercest battles in mastering himself. He was a huge man (for his day) at six foot two, powerfully built, physically tough, and renowned for his horsemanship. Such a man, in a burst of anger, surely intimidates but just as surely is shunned. But Washington didn't become the eighteenth-century equivalent of a Hells Angel on the Appalachian frontier. Instead, he bound his temper with the steel hoops of a code of respect for other people.

This by no means meant that he smothered his temper entirely. Jefferson noted Washington's extreme sensitivity to criticism, and others saw in him a restrained fierceness and a habit of fighting and mastering his passions. In his biography of Washington, Richard Brookhiser remarks, "His temperament had its raw edges, however, and when they were incautiously touched, he could become dangerous to those around him." During the war, Alexander Hamilton, serving as his aide, found him testy and direct, such as when Washington angrily accused the younger man of "disrespect" for being moments late for a meeting, in response to which outburst Hamilton resigned his position. The incident, of course, did not permanently estrange the two men, but Hamilton knew better than most the barely bridled temper in the commanding general.[6]

David Hackett Fischer, in *Washington's Crossing*, describes several episodes of Washington struggling – successfully – to control his rage. On Christmas Eve 1776, as he was about to have his troops cross the Delaware for a surprise attack on the Hessian soldiers in Trenton, New Jersey, Washington received word that a freelancing subordinate, Adam Stephen, had sent his own raiding party across the Delaware on a tit-for-tat mission of revenge. Stephen's raiders had roused the whole Hessian garrison, who chased them away. Washington then summoned Stephen from the column and asked if it was so. Stephen confirmed the truth of it. The general grew very angry. "You, Sir!" he raged. "You, Sir, may have ruined all my plans by having put them on their guard." Others remembered that they had never seen Washington in such a fury. The more he thought about what Stephen had done, the more infuriated he became.

Then something remarkable occurred:

> *But in a moment, Washington mastered his anger. He calmed himself by turning away from Adam Stephen and talking to the bewildered men in Captain Wallis's company [who had carried out Stephen's raid]. He spoke kindly to them and personally invited these proud Virginia soldiers to join his column.*[7]

Yet George Washington comes down to us not as the Enlightenment guru of anger management but as Father of the Country.

The phrase, worn out by repetition, is not easily understood today, but somewhere in it is the sense of a fierce and destructive power held in check by a man determined to do what was right. This determination cost Washington something that today we often value more: his "authenticity." He frequently buried his feelings and retreated behind manners and formality. He adopted a stiff dignity, when all who knew him commented on his physical grace and fluidity. He disappeared behind his mask – almost, because an odd aspect of such masks as public figures wear is that we almost always see behind them. The heartfelt respect that his contemporaries felt for Washington was not just for the figure who defined the plain republican ideal of president of the United States, but also for the man who mastered himself. This would have meant little had self-mastery come easily or had Washington never faced serious temptation. His contemporaries, however, realized that he triumphed by conquering the proud, ambitious, and fierce man that lay within.

Spittoons

Over the last two centuries, Americans have had many occasions to be angry, and they have usually passed the test by not enslaving themselves to anger. They learned, in time, to put it aside and get on with life. They learned to bear with some afflictions; to rise to anger for a just cause and to swallow it sometimes; and, occasionally, to forgive.

I don't wish to make saints out of earlier generations. A great many individuals also lived lives of bitterness, drank themselves to oblivion, or poisoned their lives with unconquerable hatreds. Unable to resolve their differences over slavery and states' rights, one generation precipitated the agony of the Civil War. Unable to open their hearts to African Americans as free and equal fellow citizens, several generations of White Americans angrily impeded the spirit of political and social equality. Anger has been enlisted in many generations both as a motive for transgression and as a fierce determination to end those transgressions.

With that said, Americans have not been, and still are not, by temperament an angry people. Starting in the eighteenth century, foreign observers discerned numerous collective American qualities, not all of them pleasant: Tocqueville was mightily impressed with our individualism; Dickens with our public habit of spitting tobacco juice. A wild rambunctiousness struck many refined visitors. But none of those visitors characterized Americans as a sullen, angry people. Is that what we are now?

George Anderson, the president of Anderson & Anderson, a California-based anger-management firm, told a reporter, "Things really changed after 9–11, and we saw an overwhelming number of referrals. Companies and organizations started to recognize there was a need for this kind of service and that it could be truly beneficial."[8] The terrorist attacks of September 2001 may well have aroused new interest in anger management, as they certainly aroused a lot of new anger. As those "companies and organizations" were busy sending grumpy employees to ten weeks of anger counseling, Toby Keith was selling a lot of copies of his song "Courtesy of the Red, White, and Blue (The Angry American)":

Ohhh Justice will be served
And the battle will rage.
This big dog will fight
When you rattle his cage.
And you'll be sorry that you messed with
The U.S. of A.
'Cause we'll put a boot in your ass;
It's the American way.[9]

That song had its moment. It went platinum in 2012.[10] It is impossible to think that today, some twenty years later, it could be written and performed, let alone strike a chord of public sentiment. Will America fight to preserve itself? That hardly seems the animating idea of the Biden administration. Barack Obama's famous "apology tours" to America's adversaries are now the template for a national government eager to curry favor with Iranian mullahs and Chinese totalitarians. This little dog will whimper and hope for a treat.

Which is not to say that the Biden administration cannot find things to be angry about. Biden began on Inauguration Day by canceling the 1776 Commission amid a flurry of executive orders rescinding Trump administration policies. The National Guard was called out and the Capitol barricaded behind razor-wire fences while rumors of an armed assault by Trumpian forces were circulated. Biden, while saying very little about anything else, found ample time to explain the viciousness of the voters he had triumphed over. When the state of Georgia passed a liberal and expansive election law that nonetheless impeded opportunities for vote fraud, Biden denounced it as "Jim Crow on steroids." Even Democratic legislatures repudiated the slur, but Biden stood by it. This wildness in accusation and manifest disdain for any form of opposition is an embodiment of an intemperate character. The "jealousy, envy, and avarice, incident to our nature" that Madison worried about now has a home in our White House.

Haunting Rage

We possibly have undergone a national metamorphosis, from the admonition "Don't tread on me" to "You wanna piece of me?" Belligerence underlies feelings on both sides of the great cultural divide – which is not to say that the two sides are morally indistinguishable or mirror images of one another.

The left's contempt for the right is comprehensive. Most of those on the right view the left with bafflement and incomprehension, which breaks into episodic anger. Trump gave the populist right a degree of coherence: a story of what had gone wrong in America in which the primary culprit was a greedy and self-interested political class that was advancing its own fortunes at the expense of ordinary people. Conservative intellectuals argued that the left was more than this – that it was moved by a worldview that regarded our whole civilization as a mistake to be rectified. But the conservative intellectuals' warnings about Gramscian takeover of institutions and postmodernist destruction of the moral order do not command any large-scale following. The right continues to feel aggrieved and put upon, but it lacks the left's single-minded determination to seize power and impose its will.

I write that in the present tense, for lack of a tense that expresses the potential for the situation to change very quickly.

In 2017, the cartoonist-turned-political-commentator Scott Adams proposed that Trump's election had split the world into "two realities," which he compared to "two movies on one screen."[11] The conservative "movie" depicted Trump as an aggressive realist. The leftist "movie" depicted him as a moral monster. Glenn Ellmers elaborated Adams's conceit:

> One audience is watching a movie that still accepts – at least to a large degree – traditional morality, even when they don't live up to these ethical principles. This morality includes ideas about men and women, marriage, and children that are either "common-sense," or "outmoded and oppressive." This audience thinks that the natural family is the bedrock of society, and a married husband and wife are the best way to raise a child.

And the audience watching the other movie sees

> basically the reverse. . . . The premises accepted by this other "audience" include group rights and collective guilt, the rule

of experts trained in science, the malleability of nature (including hormone-altering sex "therapy" for children), and the ability of human agency or wisdom to eliminate various evils in the world, such as poverty and injustice.[12]

The gap between these two understandings is profound. It would be a huge error to pretend otherwise, though I encounter smart people who believe, in effect, that the "two movie" interpretation of the cultural divide is an exaggeration. Generally, those who doubt this are men and women of the left who regard the traditionalist view as compounded of ignorance and exaggeration. A liberal acquaintance wrote to me after seeing that I doubted the validity of Biden's election. "Gee whiz," he said. "That is an extraordinary assumption in the face of overwhelming evidence to the contrary." This isn't anger. It is placid self-assurance, rooted in the comfortable sense that the movie he is watching is true. What possibly could perturb that assumption? I am reasonably confident that he paid no attention at all to the details of how vote totals were arrived at during the 2020 election. That's something that only crazy conspiracy theorists would do. Vote fraud, we've been incessantly reminded, is "exceptionally rare" and never enough to actually swing an election.

But to say that the gap between the worldview of those on the left and that of those on the right is profound is not to say that it is forever unalterable. What exactly would change it, I don't know. But emotional regimes, no less than political ones, do change.

In 1963, a twenty-three-year-old Paul Simon wrote "The Sound of Silence" – a protest song of sorts, but more of a lament, perhaps for how difficult it is for people to connect across social boundaries. When Simon and his musical partner Art Garfunkel recorded it in 1964, they gave it the faintest touch of anger in one verse. The song was sadly sweet, even winsome. In December 2015, Disturbed, a heavy-metal band from Chicago, released a new version of "The Sound of Silence." It is word-for-word the same, but it is completely transformed by singer David Draiman's darkly powerful rendition into angry confrontation with despair. "Simon and Garfunkel's version was a warning," wrote one listener; "Disturbed's version is rage."[13] But it is a beautiful, haunting rage.

Chapter Eight

YESTER-ANGER

THE 1994 MIDTERM ELECTIONS were a sharp rebuke to President Bill Clinton. The press dubbed these midterms the Republican Revolution and the Gingrich Revolution, after House Speaker Newt Gingrich. "Revolution" exaggerates the level of change in national politics, but certainly the changes were momentous. The Republican Party gained a majority of seats in the House for the first time in forty years. Republicans also secured a majority in the Senate by gaining eight seats. Republican control of both houses had occurred before, but not often. Between 1933 and 1995, Republicans held both houses for a total of four years. In 1994, they also gained twenty additional governorships from Democrats.

Electoral swings of this magnitude are uncommon in American politics. What happened in 1994 was a political realignment driven largely by the "Contract with America," a legislative agenda proposed by House Minority Whip Newt Gingrich and House Republican Conference Chairman Richard Armey. The *Contract* recycled part of President Reagan's 1985 State of the Union Address. The two-page document is in plain English and sets out eight principles and ten proposed legislative acts.[1] It embeds a few grievances but sounds far more confident than angry. The grievances are limited to a single paragraph:

This year's election offers the chance, after four decades of one-party control, to bring to the House a new majority that will transform the way Congress works. That historic change would be the end of government that is too big, too intrusive, and too easy with the public's money. It can be the beginning of a Congress that respects the values and shares the faith of the American family.

These sentences attack no one by name and don't even mention the party that favors "big government" and a willingness to spend "the public's money" too easily. The principles that follow are likewise anodyne in their enunciation. Here are the first three:

- *FIRST, require all laws that apply to the rest of the country also apply equally to the Congress;*

- *SECOND, select a major, independent auditing firm to conduct a comprehensive audit of Congress for waste, fraud or abuse;*

- *THIRD, cut the number of House committees, and cut committee staff by one third;*

None of this sounds especially angry, but years later this episode in American politics was remembered as one of the mountain peaks of public anger.

In September 2006, William Schneider, writing in the *Atlantic*, devoted an article, "Morphing into Angry Voters," on the torments of that earlier epoch, in which he recalled 1994 as "the year of the Angry White Men." He summoned other memories as well.[2] He mentioned the 1992 Senate confirmation hearings for Supreme Court nominee Clarence Thomas, featuring a belligerent Senator Joe Biden hectoring Thomas, with liberals angry at how Thomas's sexual harassment accuser, Anita Hill, was treated in the so-called

Year of the Woman. He recalled the banking scandal in the House in 1992 that persuaded seventy-six representatives to resign or not to run again, having enriched themselves at public expense. He recalled President George H. W. Bush in 1990 breaking his "Read my lips, no new taxes" pledge. And he touched on President Bill Clinton failing to deliver on his promised "health security for every American" and an aroused public opposed to "Hillary Care." The Hillary Care debacle, more than anything, probably secured the Republican takeover of both chambers of Congress in the November 1994 election.

I suspect that one could choose almost any decade in American history and locate convincing evidence that a substantial number of Americans were angry over political developments at that time. It is the nature of politics that it fosters angry partisanship. And because of that underlying anger, it is difficult to distinguish one political era as angrier than another. Look closely enough and you will find bluster, acrimony, and fury in the dynamics of every election. But "difficult to distinguish" doesn't mean impossible. In fact, the character of anger does change over time, and, because major elections are episodic, they provide excellent mileposts for those changes.

One thing that stands out thematically about the anger in the early 1990s was the element of sexual combativeness. The "Year of the Woman" was followed by what the liberal press dubbed the Year of the Angry White Men. Hillary Clinton's secretive machinations to advance a single-payer health care plan played off against her willingness to cover for her husband's long trail of sexual infidelities. The strident "I believe Anita" theme played discordantly against the Clintons' denials of Bill's twelve-year affair with Gennifer Flowers. Sexual hypocrisy – eagerly crediting flimsy accusations in the case of Anita Hill while staunchly repudiating easily verified claims in the case of Bill Clinton – left liberals in an awkward situation. And, as this played out, the Democratic establishment in Congress crumbled under evidence of massive self-dealing.

The Republican *Contract with America* focused on eight "clean government" principles of a seemingly straightforward nature, such as term limits for all committee chairs and a ban on proxy voting. But the *Contract* also proposed legislation that hinted at the sexual dynamics in the cultural surround. One of the ten proposed bills was the "Personal Responsibility Act," which was partly about welfare reform and largely about discouraging illegitimacy. Another bill was titled the "Family Reinforcement Act"; it was ostensibly about strengthening the rights of parents but plainly also about discouraging behavior that undermines families. The "American Dream Restoration Act," likewise, called for a repeal of the federal marriage tax penalty and created a $500 per-child tax credit. These bills embodied the public worry that the American family was eroding, and a cause as well as a consequence of the erosion was the shift in cultural expectations about the relations between men and women.

So was there anything to the idea that the electoral sweep by Republicans arose from the fury of "angry White men"? The idea was definitely in play at the time. For example, an article in the *Baltimore Sun* in April 1993, "White Men Burdened by the Stress of a Changing Nation," cited a 1993 movie, *Falling Down*, in which a middle-aged White man in Los Angeles (William Foster, played by Michael Douglas) battles his way across the city to get to his daughter's birthday party.[3] Douglas's character is certainly angry, but is he supposed to represent the situation of White males in general? The *Baltimore Sun* article cited a clinical psychologist who confidently explained that White men "will be a distinct minority in the work force" by 2010. If that was what the movie's antihero was worried about, he need not have been. By 2010, according to the U.S. Department of Labor, 82.1 percent of employed Americans were White – and, of those, 54 percent were male.[4]

The Coming Minority Majority?

Let's pause on this for a moment. The offhand comment by that clinical psychologist in 1993 is a lot more important than it might seem. It has a history, and it pointed to a political future in which we are very much involved.

The idea that White males were doomed to obsolescence was launched by a poorly conceived 1987 Hudson Institute report titled *Workforce 2000*. As I recounted in *Diversity: The Invention of a Concept*, the Hudson Institute's fake news played a major part in launching the corporate diversity industry.[5] Suddenly in 1988, in boardrooms across the country, the worry was voiced that by the year 2000 there simply weren't going to be enough White people – especially men – to meet the needs of American employers, and non-White workers were not receiving the preparation they needed to fill the positions either. Industry spoke with one voice: *We need a crash program in "diversity hiring" to secure the economic prosperity of our companies and our country.* This diversity drive was not about dismantling racial bias or eliminating barriers. It was about creating a new regime of racial preferences. This was a crucial moment in the rise of what we now experience as the racial politics of Black Lives Matter, the 1619 Project, critical race theory, and components of the antiracism hysteria.

The jump from corporate diversity trainers, who first appeared on the scene in 1988, to large American companies pledging themselves to antiracism in 2020 may seem large, but it is really just the carrying out of the logic of the original embrace in the late 1980s of the concept that American commerce needed to mold itself to the priorities of racial identitarianism. Corporate America absorbed the idea that the goal was not to eliminate racial discrimination but to discriminate in a new way – though we would wait for another thirty years for Ibram X. Kendi to put it in bald terms: "The only remedy to racist discrimination is antiracist discrimination. The only remedy to past discrimination is present discrimination. The only remedy to present discrimination is future discrimination."[6]

Never let it be said that a think tank's fumes dissipate without consequence. In this instance, the Hudson Institute's 1987 prediction, the falsity of which was evident to anyone who looked beyond the original headline, has continued to reverberate for more than three decades. Politically, it is now a truism: both Democrats and many Republicans now seem to believe that White males are on an inevitable path to sociopolitical marginalization. It has become one of those "observations" so often repeated that most people assume it is true, and it is often used more as a weapon than as a tool of analysis. The message is that political parties should not give much weight to the views of White men or their supposed interests. The future belongs to women and the coming "minority majority."

The trouble with that truism is that it is probably untrue. Unmarried White women do vote in a pattern that contrasts with White men, but married White women vote much like White men. Black, Hispanic, and Asian Americans increasingly do not vote as a unified "minority bloc." Roughly a third of Hispanics vote like White men. And the definition of "White" is considerably more fluid than presented in the official demographics. What counts in the broader culture as "White men" could turn out to include people of rather diverse ancestry.

The inaccuracy of the original prediction was spectacularly underlined by the 2016 election. In theory, the election of Donald Trump could not have happened, and, when facts defy a political theory, the theorists are naturally outraged. Instead of seeing the election as a repudiation of the idea that voters would line up by racial coalition and reliably elect the candidate of the emergent "minority majority," the American left saw Trump's election as a last-gasp resurgence of White male bigotry. Ibram X. Kendi, again, provides the pristine version of the left's baffled outrage:

How could a Donald Trump follow Barack Obama into the presidency? How could the candidate of angry bigots, the Klan's candidate, the stop-and-frisk candidate, the candidate of border walls, the candidate that said a Latino judge can't be objective and that "African Americans and Hispanics" live in "hell" – how could this birther theorist follow the first Black president? How could Trump rise when Obama's rise seemed to make it impossible?[7]

Kendi's answer to his litany of questions, of course, is that America is profoundly and ineradicably racist. No wonder it elected this evil, racist man. He then devotes some five hundred pages in *Stamped from the Beginning* to showing America's racist character.

That indictment by Kendi and others deserves, and has received, plenty of refutation. My point in bringing it up is not to go another round with the critical-race-theory crowd but to note the perfect symmetry with the 1994 midterm elections. The "Year of the Angry White Men" comes round, it seems, whenever voters depart from the approved liberal script. The framing, however, seems a bit doubtful. Sociologist and gender studies professor Michael Kimmel's 2013 book (republished in 2017) *Angry White Men: Masculinity at the End of an Era* proceeds down the same path as the diversity narrative: White men are obsolescent. No wonder they are mad. They now see themselves as victims. In their voices, Kimmel hears "anxiety, vulnerability, and more than just a slight tremor of fear."[8]

Kimmel is a self-declared feminist and a spokesman for the National Organization for Men against Sexism. *Angry White Men* comes with endorsements from figures such as Gloria Steinem, Katha Pollitt, and Madeleine Kunin, so it would be wise not to approach it as an open-minded inquiry into the nature of White male discontent in the age of Obama – or, in its more recent edition, as an assessment of what drove Trump's 2016 election win. With that said, Kimmel's book fills some of the gap in the cultural history of anger between *A Bee in the Mouth* (2006) and *Wrath*. It is the place to turn to learn about angry White men abusing their wives and children, shooting people, joining White supremacist organizations, and arguing for men's rights. These are all, no doubt, topics worthy of examination, but whether they represent the cultural dynamics of twenty-first-century America seems doubtful. Kimmel depicts radio talk-show host Rush Limbaugh, for one, as manipulating unhappy male listeners in order to transform their discontent into rage. The "rise of outrage media," Kimmel says, is a part of an effort to "manufacture rage," through "the cultural construction of aggrieved entitlement."

There is something to this. What I call "new anger" is a performance, and the mass media, including talk radio, are among the stages on which anger is performed for appreciative public audiences. New anger also summons support and sympathy for the performer, and it becomes a means to gain a temporary mask of power. Kimmel notices these things too and touches on some of the same points of origin as I did in *Bee*. Where Kimmel goes wrong is in supposing that this "manufactured rage" is somehow the unique territory of demoralized White men. He sees those White men as suffering from a sense of injury that "mixes hatred and envy"; they want to recover their "dominance." Limbaugh helped them look "back to a time when it was all there, unchallenged, and forward to its restoration."[9] Kimmel, in short, looks with scorn on ordinary White men, whom he depicts as the rightful losers in America's changing culture. They deserve their supposed fate, because

> *the defensiveness of white men is so narcissistic that any criticism of masculinity and male entitlement is seen as the effort to leverage the apparatus of the state in the service of the destruction of an entire biological sex. But these guys aren't really interested in women. They're interested in promoting the interests of white men.*[10]

The theme that Kimmel's book exemplifies is that White men are not only on the way out as any kind of political and social force, but also pathetic in their defeat. Moreover, as a defeated remnant, they harbor destructive views that can, on occasion, harm others, so they need to be kept under close surveillance.

Kimmel's book is valuable as an explicit declaration of this theme, which is widespread in the liberal media but seldom so robustly declared. For Kimmel, even when White males are appropriately defeated as a political force – which is how he depicts President Obama's election wins – they remain behind, like an unsightly tree stump that needs to be pulled up in order to finish the landscaping. The essential problem with Kimmel's analysis is that the performative anger he writes about is by no means limited to White males. It is everywhere. We have abundant testimony to the anger of White women, Black men, Black women, and virtually any other group that can be carved out of the demographic pie. New anger is culturally pervasive and now inseparable from identity-group politics. To expect every other group to self-identify as proudly angry and think that White males will somehow stay off of the angry-go-round is fatuous.

I could well see the case – in fact, I argued it in *Bee* – that making a cultural norm of new anger was foolish and destructive. But even more foolish is saturating the market with books, TV shows, movies, and plays all celebrating the glories of Black rage, feminist rage, anticapitalist rage, and so on and expecting that the demographic group that serves as the all-purpose target of this rage will not absorb the message and reply in kind.

In that light, what stands out is the extraordinary reserve and patience of White males who, contrary to Kimmel, have been mostly stoic under the combined assaults of the designated victim groups. Their stoicism doesn't mean that White males aren't angry. It's just that they're still more rooted in the ethics of the older forms of anger, in which histrionic display is considered weakness. In the meantime, the publishing industry continues to pour out books celebrating women's anger and Black anger. *Pretty Bitches*, for example, is a 2020 compilation of short essays by women, each of whom expresses her ire against some epithet or adjective. The book's subtitle is "On Being Called Crazy, Angry, Bossy, Frumpy, Feisty, and All the Other Words That Are Used to Undermine Women." In her preface, editor Lizzie Skurnick provides the political connection: "When Hillary lost, buried in an avalanche of *flawed* and *shrill* and *ambitious*, I started to think back on those small words again."[11] This is unabashed, proud-of-itself anger that expects a ready market among book-buyers, and it carries no hesitance over the possibility that it will be called out as a mixture of "hatred and envy" or desperate narcissism. It might indeed have as much of those qualities as had the late Rush Limbaugh's primarily male audience, but Skurnick rides in the lane of current cultural approval.

As does Carol Anderson with her book *White Rage: The Unspoken Truth of Our Racial Divide* (2017). Anderson is plainly more interested in blaming Whites than she is in blaming men, but the trajectory is similar. The most interesting part of *White Rage* is an afterword written following Trump's 2016 victory. In Anderson's account, Trump came to office riding a wave of voter suppression aimed at disenfranchising African Americans. The 2017 date of composition is reflected in Anderson's giving full credit to the ideas that Trump was "Putin's puppet"; that the Steele dossier (subsequently revealed as a fabrication commissioned by Hillary) was true and accurate, and that Trump intended to undermine American democracy. One aspect of Trump's road to success, according to Anderson, was the U.S. Supreme Court's decision in *Shelby County v. Holder*, which "gutted the Voting Rights Act." Trump, in turn, "thanked African Americans for not showing up at the polls to vote." And

*[t]he motivation in 2016 was equally nefarious and destruc-
tive. Trump tapped into an increasingly powerful conservative base that had been nurtured for decades on the Southern
Strategy's politics of anti-black resentment.*

In the same vein as Kimmel's analysis, Anderson characterizes
Trump supporters as people who saw him "as 'America's last
chance' to recreate a nation that reminded them of the good ol'
days." These voters opposed "the country's growing diversity."
Where Hillary "spoke forcefully and often about economic anxiety, education, and creating living-wage jobs for a nonindustrial
economy," Trump "dangled a vision before his constituency where
the vast resources of the nation would flow to whites, who in a few
years would be a numerical minority." For Anderson, Trump represented a coming "apartheid regime" and rode "a wave of racial
resentment into the White House."[12]

Anderson was, of course, dead wrong on every single one of
these claims, not least that of Trump's aiming for an apartheid
regime. Under Trump, Black unemployment went to record lows,
Black employment went to record highs, and Trump's support
from the Black community reached heights untouched by any
Republican candidate since Eisenhower.

The facts, however, seldom slow down the proponents of
new-anger mythology.

Escape Velocity

I am skipping over, for the most part, the anger in between the
1994 midterm election and the anger ignited by Trump's election
in 2016. A detailed account of the George W. Bush years is set
forth in *A Bee in the Mouth*, in a chapter titled "Wackadoo Politics: America's Uncivil Liberties." Back then, Democrats and their
supporters were full of righteous indignation; today it is Republi-

cans and Trump supporters. The vitriol of that era, however, has dissipated from public memory.

New anger provides one of the keys to understanding what happened in the four presidential terms following the Bush presidency. New anger, back then, was gleeful in its discovery of the pleasures of uninhibited and highly expressive public hatred. Learning to let go of any and all strictures on what could be said of a Republican president gave Bush's opponents a revelatory moment. There was no going back. It was not just access to a newly scabrous rhetoric of opposition, but also initiation into a new way of feeling politics. It also depended on a perpetual spiral of escalation. New anger created the precedent for an anger that dispensed with virtually all norms. Interestingly, Democrats and Never-Trumper Republicans often attacked Trump as a man who ignored or defied the traditional U.S. political norms. The fairness of that accusation is highly questionable. Trump did not rule by executive order, and he stayed within constitutional limits throughout his term. But accusing Trump of such transgressions was a way of licensing the Democratic Party to do (supposedly) likewise.

At some point in this cycle, new anger reached escape velocity from the gravitational pull of basic civility. I'd say that happened when elected officials and other leaders of the Democratic Party began excusing and even endorsing the post–George Floyd riots. The attempt to make the country ungovernable as a way of undermining the reelection campaign of a president was something new, and it set the stage for moving beyond new anger to wrath.

The left's anger was self-evident at one level, but it was also slightly out of focus for political observers, just as the right's anger had been during the various scandals of the Clinton administration. In both cases, political theory revealed some bafflement at a popular enthusiasm that seemed ill-calculated to achieve any practical end. Had President Clinton been driven from office, Republicans would have faced an incumbent President Al Gore in the 2000 election. Clinton hatred failed to produce the backlash that many

Democrats hoped for, but it did leave conservatives feeling demoralized. In the 1996 presidential election, Republican candidate Bob Dole famously complained, "Where's the outrage?" In fact, Dole handily captured the voters who were outraged by Clinton's dishonesty, but outrage proved too narrow an appeal to win the election, and people who voted their outrage were especially prone to a sense of despondency in defeat. They felt as if the nation had lost its moral center and was making fateful decisions on the basis of expediency rather than judgments of right and wrong.

"Hatred is a very contagious thing," one woman wrote in a 2004 letter to the *Boston Globe* blaming Republicans for her own hatred of President Bush.[13] The *memory* of the conservative anger against Clinton provided a moral justification, though a shaky one, for the grudge match against Bush, fed by the sense that Bush's narrow victory over Gore in Florida in November and December 2000 was illegitimate. The complaints against Clinton and Gore, of course, differed in many ways, but our focus is on emotional styles. In that light, Clinton was attacked by conservatives as *morally* unworthy of his office, whereas Bush was attacked by liberals as intellectually and culturally unfit.

Among the earliest near-recognitions of new anger by a conservative that I have found is an article by Brian C. Anderson in the spring 2001 issue of *City Journal*, published by the Manhattan Institute. In it, Anderson argued that the 1990s had brought an increasing volume of name-calling, mostly by the left. He mentioned the rising use of epithets such as "racist," "homophobe," "sexist," "mean-spirited," and "insensitive," and he immediately apprehended what set these insults apart from normal political raucousness:

> It has become a habit of left-liberal political argument to use such invective to dismiss conservative beliefs as if they don't deserve an argument and to redefine mainstream conservative arguments as extremism and bigotry. Close-

minded and uncivil, this tendency betrays what's liberal in liberalism.[14]

Such invective, Anderson said, destroys the civility on which democratic government depends, and it dismisses the "belief in the superiority of reasoned argument over force." He noted that such attempts to stigmatize the critics of a position rather than answer the substance of their criticism became standard fare on the left in the 1990s.

Anderson provides an answer of sorts to the vexing question of whether this kind of anger in American politics is actually new. Stephen Miller, a few years later, recalled the remarks of nineteenth-century English visitors (Frances Milton Trollope and Charles Dickens) on the "electioneering madness" of Americans and our "injurious Party Spirit" and quoted candidate Rutherford B. Hayes predicting in the 1876 presidential race that a victory by the Democrat, Samuel Tilden, would be an "irretrievable calamity."[15] Yet, said Miller,

in the 19th century there was not what might be called an ideology of anger, as there seems to be now. In the past 40 years, countercultural theorists, psychologists, rappers and talk-show hosts have acted as if expressing one's anger is good for the psyche and good for the nation.

Miller deserves credit for publishing the first full recognition that the Democrats' rage in the 2004 presidential race has to be understood as one manifestation of the broader cultural development of new anger.

Bill Clinton hatred, Bush hatred – do they matter now? Historically, yes, but I don't think they led directly to our current situation. The undercurrent of sexual and racial politics that dates back further is a better touchstone. For millions of conservatives, Clinton stood as an embodiment of a loathsome personality, a man who careened recklessly across the landscape indulging his appetites and, with no twinge of compunction, lying about it. Anger against Clinton was rarely and only superficially directed at his policies – although these, too, could be swept into an indictment of his lack of principles. Bill Clinton, however, was also a revelation for American conservatives. He held up a mirror that showed conservatives that they, too, had been deeply changed by the transformation of American culture, in which everything had somehow become personal. He also showed that almost anything was possible within the office of the presidency. It is hard to imagine that Donald Trump could ever have been elected without Bill Clinton having been elected first. Conservatives saw Clinton as a man seducing the country into a cheaper version of itself. They saw the leaders of elite institutions shrugging off or temporizing with Clinton's personal corruption and feared this meant that older traditions of moral probity had lost their grip on America.

For millions of Democrats, Bush stood as an embodiment of the callow and ignorant side of American life, a man moved by the pursuit of money and cronyism and contemptuous of social justice, international law, and other enlightened ideals. In the place of serious secular thought, he offered evangelical Christian piety; in the place of a sophisticated grasp of culture, he offered catchphrases and slogans. Democrats saw Bush as tricking the country into becoming a meaner version of itself – and using the war on terror to make that change permanent. They feared that he displaced the people who, by virtue of education and commitment to liberal ideals, ought to guide America's institutions.

These are polarized views. It is hard to imagine that any single American subscribes to both of them or that there are large numbers of Americans who do not lean more to one or the other. Each offers a moral picture of the United States as corrupted at the very top. And each invites us to participate as an agent of moral cleansing by joining in a wrathful purging of political opposition. The legacies of Clinton hatred and Bush hatred are still in our political bloodstream, but the more active poison is identity politics. The idea that "angry White men" are fomenting a revolution aimed at installing a regime based on misogyny and racial supremacy is a fever dream of the American left, and it is being used to justify an unconstitutional usurpation of our basic liberties.

Chapter Nine

THE REVOLUTION
IN HOW WE FEEL

AMERICAN TEMPERAMENT changed in the decades following World War II. The key change was that we had moved from a centuries-old culture of regarding anger as something to be carefully controlled – and, in most cases, repressed – to a new culture in which anger was to be celebrated, rewarded, and enjoyed. It is always hard for those living inside a culture to see it as anything other than the "way things are." People usually project contemporary attitudes and values onto the past, and that includes past emotional norms.

Today, for example, we don't just *think* that slavery is unjust; we also *feel* its injustice, and as a consequence we imagine that Americans who lived during the historical epoch of slavery also – or, at the very least, should have – felt this revulsion. And, indeed, we have evidence that some Americans from the late eighteenth century onward did *feel* that slavery was morally repugnant. At first, this was a small minority of Americans, most of whom arrived at these feelings via their religious convictions. The abolitionist movement grew partly from the teachings of Christian ministers, but it really began to gain broad support as a result of the spoken and written testimony of former slaves, and then from the intense dramatizations in books such as Harriet Beecher Stowe's *Uncle Tom's Cabin* (1852).

People seldom all by themselves shed their long-standing emotional attitudes. We need to be taught to question those attitudes and taught again what new attitudes should be adopted in their stead. Changing a culture requires undermining its usual self-satisfaction and replacing that complacency with a stirring new ideal. Emotional revolutions, like political ones, require both a vanguard and a means of propagating the new message.

In *A Bee in the Mouth*, I documented this revolution in a chapter about popular music, a chapter about how experts and authorities justified anger, and a chapter about how people absorbed these lessons. Those chapters looked back at the *advent* of new anger. This book is about what happened after anger arrived, but this chapter offers a compressed account of those three chapters from the previous book.

Anger Music

In 1932, when the Great Depression was settling in for the long haul, a bankrupt electrical supplies salesman named E. Y. Harburg (1896–1981) wrote the lyrics for *Americana*, a musical show that praised the ordinary man beaten down by the capitalists. In one scene, a man standing in a breadline sings:

> *Once I built a railroad,*
> *Made it run,*
> *Made it race against time.*
> *Once I built a railroad,*
> *Now it's done.*
> *Brother, can you spare a dime?*

Though banned by some radio stations, "Brother, Can You Spare a Dime?" became a hit, recorded by Bing Crosby, among others.[1] Both the song and the phrase became inseparable from the national response to the Depression. "Brother, Can You Spare a Dime?" expresses plenty of political anger.

When there was earth to plow
Or guns to bear,
I was always there
Right on the job.
They used to tell me
I was building a dream,
With peace and glory ahead.
Why should I be standing in line
Just waiting for bread?

Quoting the lyrics from this or other angry songs is no substitute for hearing them sung and hearing the instrumentation behind them. Fortunately, YouTube and other social media sites make that easy. "Brother, Can You Spare a Dime?" was composed by Jay Gorney and is said to be based on a Russian Jewish lullaby. It balances between sadness and assertion; perhaps it is *confidently* sad. A reviewer of the original Broadway production called it "plaintive and thundering."[2] Performers varied in the degree to which they voiced the anger in the song, but it was no doubt the anger anthem of the 1930s. After that, it remained in the national repertoire, but it was often layered with irony, smoothed into jazz, or smothered in sentimentality.[3]

Yip Harburg, the song's lyricist, was an avowed socialist, destined to be blacklisted in 1950 from Hollywood, where he had been working on films since 1936. His song about the guy on the breadline did not pull any punches. Yet the tone is somehow slightly wistful, and the singer's reproach to American society is a call on fellow feeling: "Say, don't you remember / I'm your pal." Harburg was, not coincidentally, the author of that other great Depression-era standard of yearning for a better world, "Over the Rainbow."[4]

Harburg voiced the anger of a generation of unemployed men in a manner that a great many singers could capture. "Brother, Can You Spare a Dime?" aimed to wrench sympathy from the supposedly flint-hearted, who needed to be reminded of the sacrifices of the man who was down on his luck. That man once plowed the earth, built a railroad, worked in construction, and served in the army during the Great War. Now, in need, he presses his claims. The appeal worked, at least to the extent that the song gave some everyday emotional definition to the New Deal. The deep message of the song is that we should acknowledge the bonds of shared humanity.

There is an emotional gulf between 1932 and today that is perhaps impossible to capture in any way other than music. But I leave it to the reader to select the exemplar of today's emotional tone.

Music deserves a special place in any attempt to trace how new anger became established as an accepted mode of behavior in American life. That's because, of all the arts, music is the one that speaks most directly to our emotions. Songs get into our heads and stay there. A few notes of a once-familiar song, and it is familiar all over again years – or decades – later. People who never take the trouble to memorize anything remember tunes and lyrics, especially when they capture a particular emotional nuance. Songs constitute a school that teaches young people how to flirt, how to romance, how to feel sorry, and how to hurt. The accumulation of songs in memory and experience becomes a kind of internal repertoire through which we can, in a very subtle shorthand, evoke nuances of attitude. And we can convey those nuances to others who share the repertoire. If we want to experience physical grace, we can go to a pro basketball game or a ballet. If we wish to see beauty or cunning visual artifice, we can view the paintings in a museum. All the arts have, of course, their own command of a range of emotions, including anger. But music is the art that takes us to emotion most directly, and popular music is America's conversation with itself about the right ways to feel.

151

Teaching Anger

New anger came about largely because experts urged on us the idea that anger is good and that expressing it is even better. The family is the school of emotions, as well as the place where we wrestle with our most complex relationships. Ask people almost anywhere about anger, and you generally will hear stories about parents, siblings, spouses, sons, and daughters. The family is too important to allow it to descend into a free-for-all of resentments, accusations, and spite.

For most of our history, the family has sought ways to teach children to control their anger, and we brought considerable pressure on husbands and wives to control their tempers, too.[5] The current profusion of self-help books and anger-management classes testifies that these goals remain valid to many Americans. One major departure, however, is the advent of articles and books urging women to use anger to empower themselves both inside and outside the family.

For example, in *The Anger Advantage: The Surprising Benefits of Anger and How It Can Change a Woman's Life* (2003), Deborah Cox, Karin Bruckner, and Sally Stabb set out to debunk what they saw as myths that stand "in the way of our connection with [our] goals and dreams." They were taught as "little girls," they said, that "we were selfish for feeling angry," and they were scared when their parents were angry. On the whole, they were trained by their families and schools "to put others' emotional needs ahead of our own."[6] Pooling their talents, the three authors created what they call the Women's Anger Project, of which their book is a consequence. Their thesis is plain: "When women attempt to get around their anger without fully acknowledging it, they lose a lot of valuable information and experiences that help them evolve into their full selves."[7]

The Anger Advantage is chock-full of arguments in support of this idea. For example, the authors identify "seven anger myths,"

including "anger is destructive and naughty," "anger ruins relationships," and "anger is avoidable." And they list "Ten Anger Traps
to Avoid," including "Trap #2: Thinking you must justify your
position if you're angry; assuming that you must make logical
sense to yourself or someone else"; and "Trap #10: Trying to force
yourself to forgive and forget."[8]

Cox, Bruckner, and Stabb provide an account of anger, in other
words, that is essentially the complete inversion of traditional
accounts. Anger, in their view, is a power to be tapped to make a
woman a better mother, wife, lover, and friend, and more successful on the job as well. Anger, used astutely, enhances both intimate relationships and worldly pursuits. Readers are advised to
"Revel in it. Wrap yourself up in it. Claim it. Flaunt it. Dream with
it. Go forward with it."[9]

Patti Breitman, one of the feminists who endorsed *The Anger
Advantage*, pronounced, "There are countless, legitimate reasons
for women to be angry today." That was in 2003. Have things
changed? Not too much. We have Soraya Chemaly's book *Rage
Becomes Her: The Power of Women's Anger* (2018); Brittney Cooper's *Eloquent Rage: A Black Feminist Discovers Her Superpower*
(2018), and Lilly Dancyger's edited 2019 volume, *Burn It Down:
Women Writing about Anger*, giving us up-to-date renditions of
the same idea.[10] "No one is served by being afraid of the weight of
anger," counsels Evette Dionne in Dancyger's book. Dionne is
paraphrasing a 1981 speech by angry Black feminist Audre Lorde,
who helped Dionne "locate" her own anger, recognize its "legitimacy," and harness it "in a way that allowed me to show up fully as
myself without fear of confrontation."[11] This is a durable theme:
the Black feminist bell hooks (who eschews capital letters) titled
her 1995 book *killing rage: ending racism*; in it, she explained,
"Renewed, organized black liberation struggle cannot happen if
we remain unable to tap collective black rage."[12]

No doubt women (and men) have always had "countless reasons" to be angry. Life is hard and frequently unfair, but it used to

be a lot harder and vastly less fair. Back in the day, people struggled against anger partly because they understood that anger usually made bad matters worse. Now we have cultural theorists to tell us that (at least for women) anger is "legitimate" and the smart player learns how to use it.

In a 1988 study, two scholars systematically reviewed the advice on "love and anger" in American women's magazines from 1900 to 1979. They found a "zigzag pattern" of change between advice that extolled traditional values (such as patience and self-sacrifice) and what they chose to call "modern" attitudes, which included self-expression, individuality, acting on impulse, expressing anger, and confronting marital problems directly. They determined that articles advising women to express anger in their marriages were scarce from 1900 to 1949 but started to take off in the 1950s and by the 1970s outnumbered articles advising "avoidance."[13] No surprise there.

The idea that women ought to express anger more openly was not solely a conceit of radical feminists. It was quickly establishing itself in mainstream culture. As early as 1972, pop psychologist Dr. Joyce Brothers, in an article on how to keep their marriages vibrant, advised readers of *Good Housekeeping*, "Anger repressed can poison a relationship as surely as the cruelest words."[14] Novelists with a feminist agenda were also popularizing the notion that women who restrained their anger only paid for it down the road. In Marilyn French's 1977 novel, *The Women's Room*, for example, the heroine reflects on her situation in a manner that almost suggests she has been reading a back issue of *Good Housekeeping*: "'Love,' she muttered to herself. It makes you, she felt, hide your own anger from yourself, out of fear, so that by the time it does come out, it is poisonous."[15]

In the 1970s, these were daring new thoughts. American women were, in effect, being challenged, cajoled, and sometimes shamed by the feminist cultural elite into relinquishing older ideals about the importance of repressing anger. By the 1990s, the older ideals had more or less succumbed to the newer standard. Cultural change is always a complex stitching and re-stitching of competing ideals. But it is unmistakable that today the temper of relations between the sexes in America has been deeply altered by an ethic taught to girls at a very early age that encourages confrontational expression of anger within their personal relationships.

Relinquishing anger was never very easy, but the new idealization of anger increases the effort necessary to control it. Many of us seem to feel entitled to strike back verbally and sometimes physically at a world that nips us. Social media all but invites us to hit back at those who post opinions with which we disagree, and TV news suggests we are helpless in a violent and unjust world. Where I live, in New York City, there are reports each week of people being stabbed on the street or pushed onto subway tracks. The attacks are almost never provoked.

We are just adrift in an increasingly lawless society overseen by officials who are determined to void laws that might lead to the arrest and incarceration of violent felons. Why? The anger of the unhinged – some mentally ill, others pursuing their own versions of BLM-style racial justice – is turning my city into a state of seething apprehension. Anger is now a matter of survival against the angrily violent.

The difference is that, in contrast to the old culture's primary emphasis on self-control, our culture now rewards and celebrates anger. The premise that "anger is good" – that it is liberating, wholesome, creative, and empowering – transforms the myriad possible aggravations into welcome opportunities.

Angry Young Men

Feminists in the 1960s and 1970s theorized a variety of reasons why women should get angry. Along with this came a frequent subtext: that men's anger was cruder than women's anger and inherently dangerous for women and the world at large.

In 1983, George Lucas released the third of his Star Wars movies, *Return of the Jedi*, the climax of which must be among the most familiar scenes in the history of Hollywood movies. The Emperor attempts to lure Luke Skywalker to the "dark side," first by offering him his lightsaber:

> *You want this, don't you? The hate is swelling in you, now. Very good, take your Jedi weapon. Use it. Strike me down with it. Give in to your anger. With each passing moment you make yourself more my servant.*

Luke, of course, after partially giving in to the temptation, renounces it rather than kill his father, Darth Vader. But even as Luke escapes, the idea of anger as a deep source of power is registered with cartoon clarity. The overt moral lesson in Star Wars seems thoroughly traditional: anger is actually a lack of self-control that leaves the angry person as an object to be manipulated by others; and the power that comes with anger is, after all, the power of the "dark side."

The writer Caroline Knapp once contrasted women's and men's anger by saying that men have "the male blow-off valve," in which they resolve angry conflicts by pretending they were trivial. She called it the "no-big-deal style of male conflict."[16] The no-big-deal style is a way of diffusing emotions in a culture that has misplaced its sense of how to keep anger in check. Now that every disagreement, no matter how trivial, has the potential to flame up into intemperate display and an opportunity to spelunk in the deeper recesses of one another's subconscious motives, no-big-deal minimization offers a way out. It is not just the "male blow-off valve." It is the necessary complement to new anger, which leaves little room for a middle ground between affected indifference and compounding complication.

Chapter Ten

ANGER AFTER TRUMP

A *BEE IN THE MOUTH* concluded with an exhortation to Americans to get control of new anger lest it overwhelm our good judgment. Too late for that now. This time, I conclude that we should put our national anger to some practical use. I'd like to see the country avoid violent confrontation and channel its wrath into ways that wrest the powers of government back into the hands of those who love our ordered liberty and hold our founding principles in high regard.

But I see around us the possibility of a more catastrophic form of confrontation, and I believe that eventuality is welcomed and encouraged by some of the leading figures on the American left who calculate that they can gain even greater power if they trigger outright rebellion by populists. Some on the conservative right, fearful of such an explosion, seek to marginalize the populists and to restore a more genteel form of political opposition to the radicals who are now in charge. I am arguing for a different avenue: an unabashed nationalism that embraces our constitutional order. Can wrath be channeled into such a thing?

In this chapter, I return to the subject of how performative anger has now burned nearly to the end of its fuse. Donald Trump is a major figure in that story but far from the whole of it.

Trumpian Rage

On September 15, 2020, Simon & Schuster published a new book by Bob Woodward of Watergate fame, titled *Rage*.[1] The cover features a close-up photograph of the right half of Donald Trump's unsmiling face. The nearly four hundred pages of text mostly recount Woodward's seventeen or possibly eighteen interviews with Trump for seven months starting in December 2019. Woodward also interviewed many other people who served at some point in the Trump administration. The book never lays out the actual sequence of interviews, as Woodward splices together bits and pieces from different times and different people. As a source for future historians, it will be a nightmare. But as a register of the emotional climate around President Trump, *Rage* is indispensable.

The book's title is, at first glance, an indictment of Donald Trump as a man of unbridled anger, and Woodward feeds that impression throughout the book, even as his quotations and descriptions veer in other directions. The "rage" in question is not necessarily Trump's rage but the rage he induces in his critics and the rage he incites in his supporters. *Rage* depicts this triangle, starting with the epigraphs on the opening page:

> *"I bring rage out. I do bring rage out, I always have. I don't know if that's an asset or a liability, but whatever it is, I do."*
> Presidential candidate Donald J. Trump
> in an interview with Bob Woodward and Robert Costa
> on March 31, 2016, at the Old Post Office Pavilion,
> Trump International Hotel, Washington, D.C.

In the second quote, Woodward asks Trump whether he stands by those words. "Is it true?" Trump replies:

"Yes. Sometimes I do more things than other people are able to get done. And that, sometimes, can make my opponents unhappy. They view me differently than they view other presidents. A lot of other presidents that you've covered didn't get a lot done, Bob."[2]

President Donald J. Trump

in an interview with Bob Woodward for this book,

June 12, 2020

Neither statement expresses rage or enacts it. In both cases, Trump sounds reflective, even a little ironic. In the second, he is boastful but also somehow detached. The message seems to be *My opponents are full of rage because they are jealous, but that's their problem, not mine.*

On its release, *Rage* became best known for Woodward's account of how much Trump knew early on about the Chinese coronavirus and why he did not tell the American public more about it.[3] Woodward portrays this as active deception rather than uncertainty and prudence, and the left-wing press amplified that message. The book, however, offers a great deal more on the three-part theme of rage: that of Trump, his opponents, and his supporters. Early in *Rage*, Woodward recounts interviews with Senator Dan Coats (R-IN) and his wife Marsha.

Immediately after the 2016 election, Vice President Pence tried to recruit Senator Coats to the new administration, ultimately to the position of director of national intelligence. Both Coats and his wife had reservations about Trump, and Woodward quotes Marsha Coats: "Trump is so controversial. He's the kind of person that would inspire crazy people."[4] Coats himself is described as disoriented by Trump's changing moods. Woodward paraphrases that Trump would "be in a fine mood" one day but other times "lash out abusively."[5]

We learn elsewhere that Trump became angry at his attorney

general, Jeff Sessions. "President Trump had furiously and repeatedly raged against [Sessions]" for not protecting him. Bernstein retells third-hand that Trump was "steaming, raging mad."[6] On another occasion, Trump chewed out Andrew McCabe, acting director of the FBI, for overstepping his bounds. Woodward reports: "Trump flew off the handle. That's not right! I don't approve of that! That's wrong! It seemed that the president repeated himself at least five times, perhaps seven."[7] Woodward recounts perhaps a dozen occasions – but none that he witnessed – in which Trump is described as angry. Trump "tweeted angrily" about Hilary Clinton; "Trump's anger . . . was uncontrollable."[8] "Trump is a large man – around 6-foot-3 and about 240 pounds, almost the size of a football linebacker. On the move and in a rage, he is frightening."[9] "At the next intelligence briefing, Trump blew up in a rage and began to chew them all out."[10]

Not until Chapter 26, based on a December 5, 2019, interview, does Woodward get near the question of America's anger. Woodward, addressing Trump, says:

> *"There is anger out there" in the country, I said. "And the question is, you're sitting here in the Oval Office. Why? Why all that anger?"*

Trump says, "It's for a number of reasons," but his answer veers away from those reasons. Woodward returns to the subject, reminding Trump that the House is about to impeach him (over his July 25 phone call with the Ukrainian president) and "we're sitting in the Oval Office here. And you are content, happy, proud."
Trump: "Yeah."
Woodward: "Any angst?"
Trump: "No."
The conversation wanders off in another direction, in which Trump says "the job of a president is to keep our country safe, to

keep it prosperous." Woodward is annoyed: "As I listened, I was struck by the vague, directionless nature of Trump's comments. He had been president for just under three years, but couldn't seem to articulate a strategy or plan for the country."[11]

So anger finally emerges, but it is Woodward's, not Trump's. Woodward is, in effect, angry because Trump is unperturbed by the left's angry attacks on him and confident of his own and the country's future.

Woodward plays this card again when he recounts an interview he had with Trump on June 22, 2020, after nearly a month of post–George Floyd riots. Woodward tells Trump that people want to hear that Trump is "talking to Black people" and understands what "they've gone through." And Woodward wonders whether someone like Trump will

[s]tep out and say, you know, I've got some breaks, I've had advantages? There are people out there who have not, and I understand their anger and their fierce, fierce resentment of people like you and people like me.

Trump replies, "I feel I do understand it," and he cites his efforts at criminal justice reform. Woodward wants to elicit a new anger–style emotional performance from Trump, which many politicians could produce on cue. Instead he gets Trump's unruffled confidence that fundamentally everything is fine.[12]

Woodward quotes from Trump's Fourth of July speech at Mount Rushmore, that there is "a merciless campaign to wipe out our history. Angry mobs are trying to tear down statues of our Founders," and "this left-wing cultural revolution is designed to overthrow the American Revolution."[13]

This, as far as I can tell, is the sum total of Trumpian anger in *Rage*. It seems a meager harvest, but it doesn't prevent Woodward from concluding that some of Trump's staff concluded "Trump was an unstable threat to their country" and that "half or more of the country seemed to be in a perpetual rage about him, and he seemed to enjoy it." And Trump "enshrined personal impulse as a governing principle of his presidency."[14]

Lost Thread

Woodward's portrait of Trump is etched with acid. It is clear that he neither likes nor respects Trump and that he has taken every opportunity to cast him as unworthy of the presidency. But, as sometimes happens, the attack boomerangs. Trump comes across not as an especially angry man but as one who licenses himself to get angry at those who betray his trust. That he would be angry at the people who staged the slow-motion campaign to undermine him with false accusations about his colluding with Russians to swing the 2016 election is the least we could expect from someone in his position. If he had ruled by "personal impulse," he would have certainly ended the farcical Mueller investigation and cleaned house at the FBI and CIA, which were busy providing a showcase of conspiracy and collusion of their own.

The truth of Woodward's account is not Trump's rage but the rage of others around him: aides who condescended to him and spoke behind his back; avowed enemies who treated his presidency as illegitimate from the outset and mounted a "resistance" movement; and Trump loyalists enraged by the efforts of the "deep state" to undermine his policies. We get glimpses of these kinds of rage in Woodward's book, but they are offstage. They are not the story Woodward wanted to tell.

Glancing Back

Does "rage" differ from "anger" in any important way? I think most people would say something to the effect that rage is excessive anger. Anger can be felt without outward expression. Rage implies something not just felt but outwardly expressed, often with an element of violent aggression. Rage threatens more than anger, in both its intensity and its direction. What I have called "new anger" is often anger pretending to be rage, but the line between pretend rage and actual rage is vague. A tantrum that starts out as show can easily get out of control.

When I started out some twenty years ago to examine American anger from an anthropological perspective, the field of similarly minded observers was very small. Mostly it consisted of historians and psychologists who recognized a shift in American emotionality and saw that this change stood in need of an explanation.[15] Getting up to speed on the subject was like wading across a small stream. As years went on, more and more observers, and not just psychologists, recognized both the growth in angry expression in American culture – and not just American culture – and the absence of a ready explanation for it. Now, instead of wading across a small stream, I am confronted with a raging river of scholarship and opinion.[16]

Much of that raging river deals with identity politics and tribalism. The usual argument is some variant of *We are mad at each other because that's the natural dynamic of groups.* We belong to a group, a "tribe," that defines itself by in-group loyalty and out-group hostility. Such observations have a lot going for them. We are definitely awash in angry identity-group assertions. But tribalism doesn't explain everything. It doesn't explain the pervasiveness and multidimensionality of anger, its contemporary texture, or the broader cultural dynamic of which it is only a part.

163

In recent years, whether the economy did well or poorly, we were angry. Whichever political party commanded the heights, we were angry. Whether we were at war or at relative peace, we were angry. Whether we focused our attention on race, or sex, or immigration, or climate, or COVID, we were angry. Whether we were listening to music, watching sports, going to the movies, worshipping in church, or going on vacation, chances are we were encountering a good bit of anger. Why?

My thesis, argued at length in *A Bee in the Mouth*, is that over the course of roughly four generations, from around 1950 to the present, we transformed ourselves from a culture that elevated the value of self-control into a culture that celebrates self-expression. So why did the culture change? Cultural shifts like this are more like rockslides than like construction projects. The rockslide begins with a few loose pebbles on an unstable slope, dislodges larger stones, and turns into a sudden collapse. A construction project, by contrast, is mapped, planned, and assembled piece by piece by skilled workers. No one planned to turn America into an angri-culture, into warring tribes, or into political parties at the brink of civil war. As we have learned to say, as though no one were responsible, "Well, that happened."[17] But can we say more?

In hindsight, we often imagine a controlling intelligence behind major cultural shifts where there really was only an accident waiting to happen. Most of the consequences of cultural changes are completely unanticipated by the people who set them in motion. Even the people who think they can plan a revolution never get what they want. Think of the Bolsheviks in Russia who imagined a communist utopia but ended up with a corrupt aristocracy presiding over an immiserated empire. Or think of the apostles of the Berkeley Free Speech movement in 1964 who wished for a reform of higher education that would bring unhindered intellectual debate to campus but who ended up laying the foundations for today's cancel culture, dis-invitations, internet censorship, doxing, and intellectual puerility. Long-term plans and even conspiracies are sometimes launched, but they are less like guided missiles than like helium balloons driven by the wind to unknown destinations.

But we can take note of the instabilities that underlie such changes. For example, the shift in America from a primarily rural agricultural economy to a primarily urban industrial economy caused Americans to become more individualistic. The city was a place where men and women could, if they chose, extract themselves from the social controls of family and local community. Living outside those controls appealed to an increasing number of young men and women, and the major cities in the first half of the twentieth century offered economic opportunities unavailable anywhere else.

For America, among the results of World War II were an enormous surge in cultural confidence, a large number of young men pried loose from their families and now experienced in the larger world, a huge increase in educational opportunities thanks to the G.I. Bill, and an influx of important European intellectuals. In that milieu, Americans got their first taste of European existentialism and their first serious introduction to Freudian psychoanalysis. The lure of existentialist philosophy was that it urged the importance of seeking "authenticity" in one's life. Psychoanalysis taught the enlightened that neurosis is the result of repressing anger. These ideas were in circulation in the late 1940s, and by 1950 they crystallized as a new emotional tone: authenticity through anger.

This was, at first, a cultural novelty found mostly in New York and on the West Coast, mostly among sophisticates. It was not predestined to become culturally dominant – but, over the course of a few decades, that is exactly what happened. I won't repeat here the story of subsequent developments. The key is that this loosening of old restrictions, combined with a positive injunction to pursue anger as personally empowering and healthful, turned out to be both attractive and useful. On one hand, it offered an exciting new way to live, and it gained adherents who made it a lifestyle. On the other hand, it offered protest groups cultural permission to transgress more loudly, more self-righteously, and more angrily. New anger fed the "expressive individualism" of the 1960s, which is one of the roots of modern identity. But it also fed the springs of identity-group grievance.

Superficially, these look like diametrically opposed developments. Putting a supreme value on self-expression and submerging one's identity into a group defined by the wrongs it has suffered would seem to involve very different emotional trajectories. But that's hardly the case.

An early contribution to conceptualizing new anger shows us how. Ralph Ellison published his great novel *Invisible Man* in 1952. It traces some twenty years in the life of the unnamed narrator, a Black man from the South. He suffers some racial indignities as he graduates from high school but wins a scholarship to an elite Black academy (a fictionalized Tuskegee Institute), from which he is expelled after angering the headmaster. From there, he goes to New York City, where he tries and fails to advance himself in the White-dominated world of paid employment. Accidentally, he is discovered by radical White activists (plainly communists) as he ignites a small-scale protest against a Harlem landlord who is evicting an elderly woman. Soon he is taken up as a well-paid community organizer whose job it is to build a radical Black movement in solidarity with other communist factions – which was the United Front communist strategy of the time. The narrator grows in his personal anger toward Whites, including the communists who manipulate him and betray the Harlem Blacks, but he proves to have a remarkable talent for stirring up racial anger in Harlem. One of his speeches sets off a major riot, in which he participates. After that, however, he turns his back on the outside world to live in a basement and to embrace his identity as an "invisible man."

This invisible man is not just angry; he is existentially angry to the depth of his whole being. But, along the way, we have seen him provoke anger against himself (his headmaster; his short-term employers; and leaders of rival groups in Harlem, especially the Garveyesque Black nationalist "Ras the Destroyer") and solicit anger as a tool of protest and group solidarity. He doesn't start out angry; he starts out as innocent and naïve. The novel traces his achievement in becoming a living rebuke to the society that has no place for him, an achievement gained by becoming a master of the full spectrum of anger: from insult to insolence, to rabble-rousing, to riot, to total disdain.

Invisible Man demonstrates that angry expressive individualism and angry identity-group grievance are not opposites. They are just two modes of the same effort to summon power to oneself. That self can navigate from angry individual to group solidarity with perfect fluidity. Indeed, the angry group is the perfect platform for the angry leader who can dazzle followers with rhetoric and violence (feigned or real) that embodies his own charismatic anger and invites others to warm themselves in its glow. This is perhaps the best way to understand figures such as Nikole Hannah-Jones and – hold yourself – Donald Trump. This may be the first time anyone has compared him to Ellison's Invisible Man.

But Trump, for all his media visibility, is a lot like the Invisible Man. He is a man who, despite his remarkable abilities, has been subject to scorn and dismissal and who profoundly resents that treatment. Like the Invisible Man, he has turned his resentment into public complaint by allowing others to project their own resentments into his narrative. When Trump tweeted a picture of himself pointing into a camera, captioned "In reality they're not after me. They're after you. I'm just in the way," millions of his supporters knew exactly what he meant. Trump's tormentors in the media, in politics, and in the "deep state" bureaucracy were their tormentors too. But to the extent that Trump made himself the embodiment of that humiliation, the real person vanished into the persona. That is what comes across in Woodward's book. The famous journalist who enjoyed extraordinary personal access to Trump ends up with four hundred pages in which the man behind the public persona never appears.

Play Angry

Anger, it is often said, is a "primitive" emotion. Be that as it may, it is a powerful and showy emotion. It is a lot easier to gain positive attention by displaying anger to an audience than to enact happiness, sadness, disgust, fear, or surprise – the usual list of basic emotions.[18] Those emotions get performed, too, in our age of expressive individualism, but they don't lend themselves very well to publicly enacted lifestyles. Anger does.

Once the old restraints and taboos fell, anger stepped in as a medium for defining personal and group identity. Anger by its nature is oppositional, so it lends itself to groups that are attempting to declare their difference. "I am woman, hear me roar," sang Helen Reddy in 1971.[19] "Say it loud: I'm Black and I'm proud!" sang James Brown in 1968.[20] These were anger anthems aimed at group identity. But virtually any angry song is about opposition and boundaries. And many songs that aren't really about anger play with anger as a device for asserting personal identity – for example, Alicia Keys's 2012 single "Girl on Fire," in which anger seems indistinguishable from sex appeal.[21]

For a while, a common piece of golf apparel was a hat that advised "Don't play mad . . . PLAY ANGRY."

Playing angry has become a dominant theme in sports, dating back to the racket-throwing, verbally abusive tennis star John McEnroe.[22] McEnroe thrilled audiences in the early 1980s, but he has been superseded by any number of show-offs who have abandoned the quaint idea of sportsmanship. That John McEnroe could emerge not only as a champion in his sport but also as the object of a kind of dark and enduring public admiration speaks more clearly than any opinion survey about anger's acceptance in the culture at large. On his way to winning seven Grand Slam tournaments and seventy-seven singles titles, McEnroe screamed obscenities at umpires, opponents, fans, and even himself. One writer assessed McEnroe's behavior:

> *Behind the blowups was a self-loathing narcissism ("I'm so disgusting, you shouldn't watch. Everybody leave!" he screamed between points during the '81 Wimbledon tournament) and a class resentment in reaction to tennis' pretension. He would rail against the sport's "phonies and elitists," earning him antihero status.*[23]

McEnroe's contempt for the people who shared an interest in his sport (and who provided him with fame and fortune) has since been echoed in the careers of other sports icons. In *A Bee in the Mouth*, I dealt at some length with the exceptionally angry Olympic ski champion Bode Miller, known for his sneering contempt for racing officials, reporters, sponsors, fans, and even his own ghostwriter.[24] I presented him as second-generation new anger: raised in a family commune by hippie parents who, as a longtime acquaintance of his put it, gave him "unbridled freedom."[25] His parents valued emotional expressivity and "honesty" over self-control, and that's what they got.

The idea of playing angry has become a semi-humorous trope. Dozens of games are now marketed as pretend anger, including "Angry Moms" (a card game); "Angry Dice" (a dice game); and a host of video games, including the immensely popular "Angry Birds," as well as "Angry Teacher," "Angry Shark," "Angry Neighbors," "Angry Gran," and "Angry Worms." One video-game company, Angry Mob, specializes in anger games, such as "Brawlout," "Predators," and "Guerrilla Bob."

In writing *Bee*, I went to considerable lengths to present examples of new anger, and that book is valuable as a warehouse of a moment when America was exuberantly exploring new media for showpiece anger. But new anger today is no longer especially new. It is the norm and has settled into recognized forms. It has been domesticated sufficiently to be treated as an idle amusement while also growing stranger, meaner, and more destructive. The anger of today is also Black Lives Matter, Portland riots, Never-Trumpers, social media censorship, and the left's unceasing effort to cancel all avenues of open expression by conservatives. The seemingly trivial anger-for-amusement aspect of our comprehensive cultural revaluation of anger is not to be dismissed as a factor in habituating Americans to the thrill of unleashing their angry impulses in real life.[26] This is not to say that violent video games or violent sports *cause* real-world violence. But they plainly create a strong sense of familiarity and even comfort with anger as self-empowerment. And that bears on the way in which anger has saturated our politics.

As I said in the opening chapters of this book, the angry left has provoked a reciprocal anger on the right – an anger now rising to wrath. But the right's current anger is new territory, not an extension of expressive individualism or performative anger.

Populist Anger

Some scholars have ventured explanations of today's anger, mostly treating it as the opposition between an established elite (supported by a client underclass) and a disenfranchised Middle America aligned with a populist movement. The term "populism" is used by both sides: with scorn by the elite and with pride by "deplorables" who have rallied to the Trumpian cause. Whether the "Trumpian cause" will remain the right expression for this movement is hard to say, but as I write, Trump is clearly its central figure. The divisions between left and right – between liberal and conservative, Democrat and Republican – were always rough approximations of the fault lines in American life, but they seem especially poor today. Elite vs. populist comes closer, but that distinction also requires some refinement.

Some observers of the American political scene complain that these binary distinctions invariably distort a picture in which many factions are readily identifiable and even the larger categories break down into a spectrum of enthusiasms. But our system of government is at bottom binary, and any particular faction or group of enthusiasts gains ground only by allying itself with one side or the other. The question, then, is whether we can describe the overall character of a side composed of disparate parts. Of course we can. We do so intuitively all the time, with a high degree of accuracy.

The left is secular (and has been since the French Revolution), globalist, post-nationalist, elitist, statist, environmentalist, and strongly attached to victim-group politics. The left opposes almost anything that could bear the label "traditionalist" – as in religion, custom, constitutional law, borders, family structure, sex roles, moral standards, and curricula. The right is open or committed to religion, is nationalist, is oriented to the middle class, is strongly in favor of individual rights, and is devoted to the family and the integrity of local communities. The right holds traditional moral standards in high regard. It opposes open borders, efforts to diminish the authority of the American Founding, racial preferences and other identity-group privileges, federal intrusion into private property, and high-handed and self-serving officialdom.

All four of these lists – what the left and right generally support and what they oppose – could be expanded, of course, and all four could be picked apart by citing exceptions. But the omissions and exceptions would do nothing to upset the underlying cogency of the two positions. The left is running pell-mell toward what it imagines is a glorious future of perfect fairness under an enlightened system of political and social control. The right is desperately trying to preserve what it believes is the fairest, most free, and flourishing republic ever known. The left is a coalition that pursues "social justice" by the accumulation of state power; the right pursues "greatness" by trying to restore the foundations of American liberty.

The two sides don't agree on much. It is possible to depict this as a tribal situation, but I don't think that clarifies anything. The left and the right (for simplicity's sake) are opposed on the basis of conflicting worldviews and principles. In many cases, they are even opposed on the basis of epistemology (i.e., what legitimately counts as knowledge). The left leans toward relativism, a high value on what people feel, and what they have experienced.[27] The right leans toward established facts, principles that have stood the test of time, and revealed (by religion) truth. The left favors a form of science in which truth is determined by consensus. The right favors a form of science in which hypotheses remain open for challenge no matter how many people regard a matter as settled. These epistemological differences turn out to have far-reaching consequences for topics such as "gender reassignment" and "climate change."

Moreover, the division between a feeling-oriented, experience-enamored left and a fact-oriented, tradition-regarding right plays out dramatically in the realm of anger. For the left, anger is a versatile tool ready at hand in any dispute. For the right, anger is a dangerous weapon that one resorts to reluctantly but, once picked up, is hard to lay down. The most successful users of new anger on the right are those who channel it into humor, which was the late Rush Limbaugh's burnished skill.[28] It might be said to be Trump's great skill as well. His famous tweets that drove his opponents to fury were mostly well-aimed arrows of jest.

Anger on both the left and the right often takes the form of righteous indignation, but with a noticeable difference in character. The righteous indignation of the left usually focuses on charges of unfairness. The righteous indignation of the right usually focuses on charges of betrayal. For example, the left is indignant that the United States has not allowed undocumented immigrants from

Central America to cross the border into the United States from Mexico. It's "unfair." The right is indignant that President Biden decided to ignore U.S. law and open the border to all comers. It's a "betrayal." The reactions are both about injustice, but they are emotionally quite different. Unfairness is something you expect from a system you don't trust. You are angry in a manner that empowers you to fight for what you think is right. Betrayal is the injustice you never expected, and it tears up the possibility of accommodation. Your anger aims at ending an abused relationship, not so much at righting a wrong – though you may hope for that too.

Populist anger in America right now is all about betrayal. It centers on the belief that the 2020 election was stolen. I personally know many conservatives who do not share that belief or who stand off from it and say: "Maybe. I don't know." Those are not the people whose anger is on the edge of wrath. I personally know many other conservatives who are profoundly convinced that unwarranted and extralegal manipulation of voting laws, as well as outright fraud in counting ballots, swung the election to Biden and Harris. While I am in no position to adjudicate what actually happened in the election, I take very seriously the views of those who say it was stolen.

Angrier

The German word *Rechthaberei* refers to the attitude "I'm right and everyone else is wrong." It is a dangerous place to sit. In *Bee*, I scavenged a quote from a blogger named "Wally" at *Wally Whateley's House of Horrors*, who wrote from a defiantly anti-Bush leftist position. His expostulation could easily have come from a pro-Trump supporter today:

Once again, when you force a huge chunk of the population to be voiceless and powerless, when you ignore their concerns

173

and lie almost constantly, you can expect those people to get angrier and angrier and angrier. The issue shouldn't be "Why do those uncouth liberals say swears?" but "Why is the fucking media so goddamn fucking awful?"

The angry left in 2006, of course, had open access to the internet and used it freely. No one was trying to silence Wally and the many thousands like him. Websites such as the *Daily Kos* specialized in giving them a platform that was essentially wall-to-wall virulence. The "voiceless and powerless" population today is a lot more voiceless and powerless, as it is censored by virtually all the major social media, much of corporate America, and the government. President Bush didn't put barbed wire and the National Guard around the Capitol. Democrats did exactly that in the weeks and months following the Capitol Hill riot. And people have gotten "angrier and angrier and angrier."

In *Bee*, I devoted space to the rise of angry talk radio and to the increasing prominence of the internet as a medium for expressive anger and the creation of anger coalitions. I have skipped that in this book, on the grounds that it is too familiar and too well-documented to stand in need of further comment. Whole books, including Martin Gurri's *Revolt of the Public and the Crisis of Authority in the New Millennium*, are devoted to it. Gurri's work, which first appeared as an ebook in 2014, is celebrated as the first to predict the rise of the Trumpian populist movement and Trump himself. Gurri, a former CIA analyst, set out what at the time was a peculiar argument in which he linked disparate developments, including technological advances, the soaring popularity of social media, and the undertow of populist disaffection with establishment politicians. Essentially he argued that after the "Rathergate" scandal of 2004, in which anonymous bloggers destroyed the credibility of a major news network anchor, the lid was off establishment control of what could be thought and said. He claimed that "the old entrenched social order is passing away."[29]

What he saw ahead was "the grinding struggle of negation" as "the central feature of our time." Mostly what he saw as ripe for negation was the authority of "institutions," and he specifically named

> *government – office holders, regulators, the bureaucracy, the military, [and] the police, [as well as] corporations, financial institutions, universities, mass media, politicians, the scientific research industry, think tanks and "nongovernmental organizations," endowed foundations and other nonprofit organizations, [and] the visual and performing arts business.*

Each of these, he said, "clings to a shrinking monopoly over its field of play."[30]

The Revolt of the Public is more about the interplay of information, protest, and mass mobilization than it is about anger, but Gurri presupposed anger and disaffection at every point, and he drew a worldwide picture, touching Iran, China, Turkey, Tunisia, and Egypt before getting anywhere near the United States. When he did get to America, it was to mention the disintegration of "the daily newspaper" and "the political party."[31] Following his argument from this point on would carry me too far from the topic at hand, but this is enough to give credit to an eccentric visionary who caught on to the fuller implications of the declining credibility of those who used to sit atop the hierarchy of establishment authority in our political system. Gurri recognized that these authority figures still exist and still imagine they are in control, but he maintained that this is an illusion.[32]

Gurri's work is on "the new information technologies" that had unleashed "powerful political forces." But I think it could be read alternatively as describing how anger and disaffection leveraged those new technologies to achieve cultural dominance. The delegitimation of the old institutions happened partly thanks to new digital media, but the technology was deployed for angry purposes because new anger had already established itself as the legitimating force *par excellence.* In other words, the psychological basis for tearing down the old institutions was in place before the technology came along to make the task easier and more scalable.

By this point, millions of words have been written by and about supporters of Donald Trump who were disappointed in the outcome of the 2020 election. I'd like to capture the distinctive quality of their anger without adding too many words to the subject. A self-taught folk artist with a bent toward fantasy, Richard Bledsoe also blogs occasionally at a site he calls "Remodern America." On November 17, 2020, he posted "The Difference between Totalitarian Tantrums and Righteous Rage," an essay that captured the populist moment as well as anything I've seen. It began, "We are in the midst of the greatest manipulation attempt in history," which is to say that Bledsoe started out with an angry declaration. His essay was not an attempt to compare the manipulation of the 2020 vote with other manipulations. It was a way of expressing his outrage. He continued:

> *President Donald Trump won the election, probably with 75 million plus votes, once all the fraudulent switching and destruction of ballots is taken into account. The corrupt establishment cabal of the media, globalist corporations, and the deep state are expending all efforts to suppress reality and replace it with their preprogrammed fake narrative.*[33]

Bledsoe presented no evidence for this, nor needed he do so. He was writing to an audience that already accepted these assertions as true, largely because they paid assiduous attention to the testimony and reports from people who had watched the original events unfold. But the key to this opening is that Bledsoe was reciting the core narrative of national betrayal, which is the very center of anger on the American right.

His next step was to connect this betrayal to earlier betrayals, "the wacky woo hoo virus hysteria" that "exposed massive corruption and Chinese influence in our traitorous elitists" and the race riots that he saw as part of the "planned and prepared Postmodern assault on the United States."

Putting the three pieces together – stolen election, Chinese virus, and race riots – signals that Bledsoe was deep into what the press likes to call a "conspiracy theory." One doesn't have to see a "planned and prepared" web of connections to recognize that three events are laced together. The coronavirus shutdown was a coordinated act of state power, and it was state power that prevented an effective response by law enforcement to the wave of riots across the country. As we have seen, Kamala Harris, among others, welcomed the race riots. And both the shutdown and the riots were used as compelling reasons for states to extend absentee balloting and other measures that conduced to electoral mischief. It isn't hard to construct a "conspiracy theory" around these pieces, especially after February 2021, when *Time* magazine published Molly Ball's "Secret History of the Shadow Campaign That Saved the 2020 Election," which plainly acknowledged – or, rather, boasted about – some of the "shadowy" steps that were taken.

Thus far, Bledsoe had stayed within the narrative that became common property to all who doubted the legitimacy of the election. His next several steps, however, ventured into speculation about the inner nature of the "postmodern" leftists who had engineered this coup:

Postmodernists pretend to feel whatever their situational ethics informs them is the politically correct way to feel. Their stance is perpetual posturing.

In this delusional state, they misname their ravenous appetite for domination as "pragmatism." Their version of pragmatism basically means they get their way, always.

It's hard for normal people to cooperate with this hunger,

177

since Postmodernists are fundamentally bottomless maws in desperate need of validation.

Well before the mainstream media began to censor any suggestion that the election was stolen, and before such suggestions were being met routinely with expressions of outrage, Bledsoe observed, "They whip their unregulated emotions into what they hope is an intimidating frenzy." He likewise saw leftists "gloating across all media platforms" that Trump supporters were "beaten, depressed, and incoherent," and he rejoined that not only did he not feel that way, but also he saw "a heightened sense of awareness and determination," which he distinguished from "impotent rage." He invoked something another blogger called "Cold Anger" – which is more purposeful than hatred, acts prudently, and is "strategic." Bledsoe believed the left sought to "create hopelessness" among its opponents but that somehow Trump supporters would "bring the criminals down."

As predictions go, Bledsoe's failed. But as a characterization of the emotional climate on the right, Bledsoe's was meteorologically accurate. Weather reports come and go. The Biden-Harris White House and its supporters in Congress have not only ridden out the initial storm but used it to their advantage by aggregating even more police power to the state and fostering even greater levels of censorship in the media. Is there any reason why they should fear people like Richard Bledsoe and the (perhaps) seventy million Americans who share some measure of his "righteous rage"?

"Cold Anger" is, I take it, another way to say *wrath*.

Mrs. Mitchell

A society awash in anger is also drenched in real-world consequences of fatherless children, frivolous litigation, needless automobile accidents, and rage that escalates to violence.[34] In 1849,

New England clergyman John Mitchell (1794–1870) published a memoir, *My Mother; or, Recollections of Maternal Influence*, in which he attempted to sift from his childhood the most enduring moral lessons. Among these was his mother's self-control:

> *She never lost her temper with us. I have heard her say that she was naturally quick, and somewhat violent, in her resentments, but that the feeling of anger was so painful to her that she set herself to correct it; and such was the self-control she early acquired, by God's assistance, that, from the time of her professing religion, I presume no one ever saw the least appearance of anger in her, under whatever provocation. Such self-command is a great matter in the governing of children.* [35]

Mitchell, of course, may have idealized his mother's success, but the ideals themselves are perfectly clear – and worlds away from the expressive individualism that predominates today.

The picture that Mitchell paints of his mother, however, is more than a parade of pious generalities. The family endured smallpox, impoverishment, and discord. But smaller incidents perhaps reveal a great deal more about the ordinary emotional dynamics of the household. Once, as a child, Mitchell lost his temper at a maid who had crowded his tiny room with an extra piece of furniture. "Who keeps putting that plaguy chair between the bed and my trunk?" he demanded to know. His mother ironically commanded the maid not to "inconvenience" her son; at which point he

> *felt ashamed, went and restored the chair to its place, reflecting once for all, that there were others besides [myself] whose convenience was to be regarded, and that domestic order, and the comfort of all, are to be promoted by each member, though at some sacrifice of individual convenience.* [36]

On another occasion, Mitchell, his older brother, and a visiting cousin sat in the yard watching the bees one summer afternoon and were taken with the idea of overturning one of the hives. They thought the bees would fly away and they would then be able to help themselves to the honey. Mitchell pushed the hive over and the bees swarmed out: "It was we that flew away, and not the bees." His mother rushed out and set the hive aright without getting stung. She expressed no anger at the three boys, whom she trusted to draw their own conclusions. Mitchell added:

> *Do you know that bees have a special antipathy to some people, and will sting them almost unprovoked, while others can do any thing with them with impunity? She was one of their favorites, as they were hers.*[37]

Mitchell's book, which was printed in a few thousand copies and then seemingly forgotten, sums up the older tradition of suppressing anger. In his preface, Mitchell presented his mother (who is never named; he published the memoir anonymously) as devout but "nothing very novel or extraordinary" and suggested that "the wisdom and experience of such as are in the ordinary walks of life" are most likely to help others. He thus offered the memoir to a young woman ("Mrs. ———— ") to aid her "in the discharge of your own responsible duties as a mother."[38]

The attitude toward anger that Mitchell portrayed as ordinary at the beginning of the nineteenth century remains alive in America to this day, but it is rare. Mrs. Mitchell may have found the feeling of anger "painful"; today, most people find that feeling empowering.

The consequence of our revaluation of anger is plain: we have to live in a culture in which many of the people around us act out their sense of entitled rage; their belief that they cannot be authentically themselves unless they feel their anger and give it voice;

and their idea that their vision of the world can be brought to pass by sheer assertion of angry will.

We seem to be at a point where the angrified utopian left, burning with frustration at its inability to remove Trump by scandal or impeachment, burst its chains. It now intends to impose its agenda on the country heedless of any restraint of law or any concern about the views of others. The concept of a nation that respects the rights of those out of power has been vanquished. At least as I write this, there seems no plausible legal check on the new regime.

Some, however, believe the left is so overplaying its hand that it will falter. Dan Gelernter, writing about attempts to "whitewash our cultural history" by censoring the past, for example, suggests that

> [t]he self-important, self-indulgent, bloated and buffoonish legacy media and entertainment industries are imploding. They have reached the red giant phase. Out of ideas, out of fuel, they can do nothing but consume themselves, swelling with impotent rage until, one day in a flash, they collapse and become white dwarfs: lifeless reminders that a star once was there.[39]

This is an encouraging prophecy in the vein of Martin Gurri, and I would apply it as well to much of contemporary higher education. Presumably as the cultural institutions that are both the instruments of the left's power and its Pretorian Guard lose their grip, the figurehead politicians will slip in turn. But will that be an opening for the dispossessed right? Were it so, through the midterm 2022 elections or the 2024 presidential election, we might prevent a far worse catastrophe. We need Mrs. Mitchell to set the beehive aright. But I fear we are more likely to see a cage match between the BLM left and militant right-wing groups. There are plenty of Americans who are not only familiar with but enthusiastic about deploying violence. And there are plenty of other Americans on both sides who are increasingly willing to stand back and let it happen.

Feeling Justified

When the satisfactions of expressing anger outweigh the disadvantages of venting dissatisfactions, we are in the territory of new anger – our distinctive cultural form of an old emotion. New anger prefers to boil rather than simmer; to count to one rather than to ten; and to preen itself on its cleverness. New anger does not regret that it has brushed aside old caution; rather, it views that shrug as a magnificent display of strength. New anger sees political division as an opportunity, not a failure. It simultaneously feeds the left's sense of righteous indignation and the right's sense of being unable, despite all its political gains, to stop the vulgarization of American culture and the erosion of American values. Its counsel makes both left and right act foolishly. But follies committed out of new anger never worry the newly angry, who exculpate themselves by returning to the fight less in sorrow than in even more intense anger.

The grievances of the newly angry are often vague and elastic. Appease one, and it will expand to include more. New anger feels liberating; it is exhibitionist and theatrical, even as it lodges deep claims to authenticity. Is theatricality consistent with authenticity? No matter.

Somewhere in new anger is a thirst for revenge, and it takes an unseemly delight in the prospect. Michael Datcher, writing in the *San Francisco Focus* in 1992 in response to the Rodney King riots, presented a letter he had written to a friend on April 29, thirteen minutes after the reading of the not-guilty verdict for the police officers accused of unlawfully beating King. Datcher wrote:

I know there will be riots in the streets of L.A. tonight. I know
that people will die tonight. I want them to be white people,
Kevin. I want white people to die.... and experience injustice.
To experience the land of equality like we experience it.[40]

New anger consists not just in Datcher's feeling these things or
even in his saying them in the heat of the moment to his friend.
Rather, new anger is most fully visible in his choosing to keep that
letter and to publish it months later, and then to republish it years
afterward in a collection of African American statements on
"self-discovery."

Some selves, once discovered, should appall us. That they no
longer do is a reason to worry.

That new anger is about to or already has tipped into Cold
Anger or *wrath* is an even greater cause for worry. That wrath is, I
said at the beginning of this book, justified – at least at some level.
Our republic is under an unprecedented assault, which is not to
say like Bledsoe that the election represented the "greatest manipulation attempt in history." But self-governing republics under the
rule of law are not a fact of nature. Our Founders knew that
republics have a poor track record and are typically undone by
one faction or another gaining too much power and overwhelming all the rest. To prevent that, they wrote a constitution that set
up elaborate checks and balances amid and within the three
branches of government. The Founders, however, failed to anticipate a giant federal bureaucracy able to act autonomously and even
in defiance of the elected government. Nor did they anticipate a
Supreme Court that would simply choose to turn a blind eye to
massive electoral fraud. And they never anticipated a political party
that would shrug off all legal and procedural limits and proceed to
act on unchecked ideological impulse. Those are conditions that
are ripe for insurrection, if not revolution. Trying to head off
those eventualities by censoring channels of communication,
sneering at the opposition, and assembling a show of military

force strikes me as a poor way to go about restoring the necessary degree of mutual reserve that would prevent such a calamity.

Black and White

On the opening page of his 2020 book, *The Age of Entitlement: America since the Sixties*, Christopher Caldwell refers to how that decade has "given order to every aspect of the national life of the United States – its partisan politics, its public etiquette, its official morality."[41] The phrase *public etiquette* is striking. It includes the emotional volatility that we first allowed and then came to expect in the way many people behave in public.

In his last chapter, titled "Losers," Caldwell summarizes the great chain of transformations he traced to the sixties. The sixties brought the civil rights revolution, the sexual revolution, and massive immigration. The "losers" in Caldwell's reading were mainly White and mainly conservative. He examines the Tea Party movement, begun in 2009 in the first days of the Obama administration; he notes that Whites as a category had seen a fifty-year "steep decline in their social status and a degradation of their way of life," and for the first time "a critical mass of whites [began to] conceive of themselves as a race."[42] Caldwell connects this White racial consciousness to changes in the ethnic composition of America, in which many of the new immigrants were disinclined to assimilate to the old American culture. On top of this, younger White Americans began dying at a high rate from drug addiction, an epidemic that had spread to the suburbs and countryside.[43] The breakdown of the nuclear family also reached Whites at the lower end of the income and class scales.[44]

Caldwell's chapter on "losers" recapitulates how this demoralization of Whites was reinforced by a new form of aggressive cultural assertion by Blacks, culminating in the "Ferguson Uprising" of 2014 and the rise of Black Lives Matter as an organizational force.[45] Caldwell also pauses to describe the 2015 incident at Yale in which a mob of Black students surrounded, baited, and humiliated professor Nicholas Christakis because his wife had written a memo saying that students should exercise their own judgment about what Halloween costumes to wear. The Yale event serves Caldwell as a capstone, showing both the unleashed performative anger of the Black students and the pathetic inability of this senior White faculty member to mount an effective defense: "His demeanor was meek, even sycophantic."[46]

The incident was among the reasons I made Yale the centerpiece of a project I was working on at the time to examine the rise of a new kind of racial disparity in American higher education. In *Neo-Segregation at Yale*, Dion Pierre and I traced the origins of Christakis's mobbing back to – where else? – that moment in the 1960s when Yale president Kingman Brewster decided to capitulate to the radical members of Black Students at Yale (BSAY) who insisted that the only way Blacks could thrive at the Ivy League institution was if the university agreed to and funded measures that would enable them to self-segregate from the White community. The logic of this was absorbed by other minority groups, and – year by year, decade by decade – Yale abandoned the ideal of a single cohesive community in favor of becoming an archipelago of quasi-autonomous ethnic and sexual tribes.[47]

The ideologies at play in these retreats into ethnic enclaves owe a great deal to the emotional volatility of our public etiquette. The video of the verbal assault on Christakis (available on YouTube) features several especially vulgar and vituperative students. One of them declares to Christakis, "I am sick looking at you. I am disgusted watching [students] argue with you. . . . I am disgusted knowing that you work at Yale University where I will get my degree, where I will look back and think, I have to argue with you."[48] In May 2017, Yale conferred its Nakanishi Prize on two graduating seniors, Abdul-Razak Mohammed Zachariah and Alexandra Zina Barlowe, who had been active participants in the mob; Zachariah had taken a leading part.[49]

The dynamics of anger in America right now include this asymmetrical racial division. Blacks and some other minority groups feel licensed to shame White people. In New York City, where I live, random attacks by Blacks on Whites and Asians are now an everyday occurrence. Elders are casually thrown to the ground, young women are shoved down subway steps, and people of all ages are punched for the attacker's sheer pleasure in the act. But while this epidemic of racial assaults by Blacks continues, the "narrative" asserts a very different path, one on which Black and Asians are perpetually endangered by Whites. Treating Whites – especially White liberals who are eager to be counted as free of the taint of racism – as vile transgressors who deserve public humiliation is now part of "public etiquette" and "official morality." Day after day, unsuspecting individuals are called out, fired, and written off for minor or even imaginary transgressions against racial dignity. The firing (actually forced resignation) in February 2021 of *New York Times* forty-five-year-veteran science reporter Donald McNeil for having repeated "the N-word" in a student's question on a 2019 field trip in Peru can stand as the exemplar of this kind of racial shaming.[50]

Angry Economics and Angry Politics

Humans are, by nature, easily aroused to anger. We have abundant scientific support for that observation, which also comports with common sense.[51] Inability to experience anger is a significant impairment. And we now have a rich body of biomedical studies on what anger consists of physiologically. Yet anger remains somehow a mystery. Many people speak of it as a force that overwhelms them, as though it comes from outside. And many people struggle to control that force, fearful that under its influence they will do foolish things or hurt people they love. Yet anger is also culturally malleable. The style of anger that prevailed one hundred years ago in your own family is probably very different from what prevails today. That isn't exactly a matter of your choice. Your anger has been shaped by your parents, your teachers, your peers, music, the arts, the media, and the larger (nearly invisible) surround of cultural expectations. Public etiquette and official morality, as Caldwell puts it, play their part. Our ideas about what is just and unjust, our feelings of having been victimized or scorned, and our sense of being in charge of our own lives also shape how we feel and how we express anger.

My account in this book is that many Americans, believing the 2020 election to have been turned by manipulation and fraud, are on the verge of distinct escalation of anger into wrath. But I am an observer, not a prophet, and I think it wise to acknowledge other views about the emotional situation.

Eric Lonergan and Mark Blyth published a book in 2020 with the arresting title *Angrynomics*. Lonergan is a fund manager in London, and Blyth is a professor of economics at Brown University. "Angrynomics" is their word for a type of economic analysis that takes fully into account our "experience of the world" as a place full of upsetting inequalities, disconnection between elites and ordinary people, and the distressing uncertainties of our age. They also intend the word to cover not just the analysis of these forms of distress but the distress itself.

Angrynomics is here and now. It is determining elections. It is recasting party politics across the world – not just Trump and Brexit, but in countries as diverse as Germany, Brazil and Ukraine, and in the revival of nationalism in Hungary and Poland, Russia's foreign policy, Turkey's growing anti-Europeanism, and in the collapse of traditional centre parties everywhere.[52]

Lonergan and Blyth, to put it mildly, are no fans of nationalism, and their view of populism is even worse. "Populism is incoherent, but the energy of tribes and moral mobs are clearly identifiable." Their book is essentially about "who gets what, where, when, and why."[53] And they pay a lot of attention to how "wealth inequality" and other such economic matters shape anger. They know we ordinary people "crave security" and that technological change and globalist policies make us feel insecure and therefore angry. To remedy this, they want to teach us "how to profit from uncertainty while hating it."[54] And they have recommendations for an assortment of redistributive economic policies intended to remedy that.

Their book is useful for anyone who seeks a more global – or, at least, international – perspective on what has happened. Economic insecurity was plainly a factor in Trump's electoral success in 2016, and it is very much in play as Democrats, centrist Republicans, and populists debate our economic priorities today. An open border with Mexico is probably the most important dividing line between the progressives and the populists on this. But note also that Lonergan and Blyth have the usual Euro-disdain for nations and nationalism, as well as the usual condescension toward those who are not eager to embrace whatever technological and administrative "advances" the elites are eager to impose next.

They do, however, recognize the potency of populist anger. "Anger," they say, is "the most powerful human emotion," and through "moral outrage" it is shaping real-world events.[55]

R. R. Reno, writing in February 2021, began his essay "Anger-Politics on the Right" by quoting the oft-repeated claim, "Populism is a threat to democracy." In my view, populism, far from being a threat to our democracy, is the best hope we have for restoring our self-governing republic. Reno says the "threat to democracy" line and similar declarations puzzled him when he first heard them, but he now has an explanation. People are "panicked" about "the continuity and integrity of our basic institutions."[56] And "Populism is a politics of anger and frustration." Trump "stoked populist anger and openly represented it." These seem to be accurate and well-put observations.

But Reno, in this short article, offers something more: an explanation of the particular animus of the "liberal-progressive establishment" and its "junior partner," the conservative establishment against the Trumpian populists. As Reno sees it, the liberal-progressive establishment, since the time of Franklin Delano Roosevelt, has ruled by serving as a bulwark against the angry and violent far left. That establishment managed also to domesticate Black rage in the 1960s by accommodating enough of its demands to dilute its most radical agenda. The conservative establishment played its subsidiary role "to preserve and protect hierarchies of wealth and power" by holding back the crazies on the right. Both establishments work together to maintain the status quo, and both depend on the threat of unleashed anger from the extremes, where the far left seeks revolution and the far right is depicted as "racist, bigoted, authoritarian, or fascist."

But now the populists see that the accommodations the establishment parties have made for the radical left "may have tipped into capitulation." It seems that Democrats are no longer actively opposing any demands by radicals. Reno finds that populists are "rightly" angry about this and no longer accept the conservative establishment as a legitimate voice. Rather, we are at the point of "counterrevolutionary anger," aka "Cold Anger," aka wrath. "That rage is well founded":

> *Our country is plagued by deaths of despair, substance abuse, family breakdown, de-industrialization, futile foreign conflicts, a loss of transcendence, and a legitimate fear that our ruling elites are not loyal to their country.*

Populist anger, however, "can be impotent." Trump gave it a focus and became its "voice." But whatever dangers populist anger poses – and Reno says it does pose a threat – they are not because of Trump. The anger comes from a great many people who feel *betrayed*. Reno distinguishes the anger of the left, which is based on claims of exclusion and oppression, from this angry-right feeling of betrayal, which cannot be bought off with social welfare programs or COVID checks. He argues that this anger, which "runs deeper" than anything the establishment has met before, stands mainly in need of leadership that will temper it with faith and with prudence. He hopes "a conservative FDR will emerge" to fill this role.[57]

Reno has provided a political-checkerboard analysis of the situation that seems plausible and congruent with my own observations, except that I view the current political crisis as arising from cultural sources that are deeper than political scare tactics. I've argued in this book that we made ourselves susceptible to the lure of anger before it was recruited as the dominant idiom of our politics. And that means politics is unlikely to extract us, even if a magical conservative FDR does emerge.

January 6, 2021

In Chapter 2, I reviewed the part played by Jacob Chansley, the "QAnon Shaman," in the January 6, 2021, riot at the Capitol. Democrats, the press, and a fair number of Republicans deemed the riot an "insurrection" and used the threat of further insurrection as grounds for tough new security measures. The Insurrection Narrative also became a justification for vigorous pursuit and prosecution of that day's trespassers, often on fantastically inflated charges and with brutally excessive tactics.[58] And it was used to propel restrictions of free expression, especially the voicing of any doubts about the legitimacy of the 2020 election. Even to hint of such a thing, it was said, was to invite further efforts by "armed insurrectionists" to overthrow the government.

Nothing of the sort happened on January 6, 2021, even though what did happen was lawless and inexcusable. The ensuing impeachment of Trump, after he left office, on the grounds that he had incited the "insurrection," was more new-anger showmanship on the part of House Speaker Nancy Pelosi. The question of whether America now faces a wrathful response to the 2020 election and to the sense of betrayal on the part of many millions of populists does, however, turn on how Americans come to regard the January 6 riot. Did it reveal the utter irresponsibility and madness of the Trumpian right? Or was it a combination of a "few hundred street brawlers" mixing in with a milling crowd that had no particular objective?[59]

In 2020, the American people endured a long season of riots, some of them sustained over weeks and months, that tore apart cities and towns across the country. To most Americans, that not only looked like but actually *was* an insurrection, and in most cases governing leaders made minimal effort to meet it with adequate law enforcement. We heard Democratic leaders at municipal, state, and federal levels excuse and even justify it. Then, in the run-up to the election on November 3, 2020, we were informed that the rioters were armed and ready to resume their "protests" if the election didn't go their way.

The contrast between the angry left and the Trumpian right seems pretty clear-cut to most populists. The leftists destroyed massive amounts of property, destroyed businesses, and killed more than a dozen people with impunity. The Trumpian rioters inflicted relatively minor property damage, destroyed no businesses, and killed no one. They did, however, strike terror into the hearts of legislators, who never imagined that violence would come so close to their workplace. And the rioters insulted the nation by violating the sanctity of an important symbol of our country's lawfulness.

The symbolic violation is real and important. That was a trespass that will not easily be forgiven or forgotten. The issue is really this: who were these trespassers? The QAnon Shaman should summon our pity for the mentally disturbed and our doubts about the competence of the Capitol Hill police and/or the authorities who oversee them. Subsequent reports from the FBI that Pelosi and others had been warned more than a week in advance of the impending intrusion and had decided not to take more vigorous steps to protect the Capitol raise other questions, as does Pelosi's reported rejection of steps to involve the National Guard on January 6 after the riot began. Claims and denials have flown back and forth, and at this point we are left with murkiness.[60]

To populists, the January 6 riot has an odor of official mischief, as if Pelosi and others hoped for and to some degree abetted the disorder. Which is to say that the January 6 riot does not mean the same to many Americans as it does to Democrats in Congress and the national media.

Charles Kesler, head of the Claremont Institute and no populist, offers a sober assessment, "After January 6th," in the *Claremont Review of Books*.[61] Having established that "No citizen, no constitutionalist, no conservative could regard that day's outrages with anything but dismay and indignation," Kesler proceeds to dismiss the grounds for Trump's second impeachment. Trump was "reckless" in calling for that rally while Congress was meeting, but he didn't invite or encourage anyone to "trash the Capitol." Trump did believe the election was corrupt, and he encouraged others to believe that too, though indisputable evidence had not emerged. The hectoring by Pelosi and others that Trump's claims were "baseless," says Kesler, has to be taken in the context that

> *Pelosi and [Senate Majority Leader Chuck] Schumer and [President] Joe Biden continue to speak of "Russian collusion"' as though it were real. Nothing is true or false until they say so, apparently. Thus they treat electoral fraud in 2020 not as an empirical question open to proof or disproof but as a superstition or delusion "discredited" in advance.*

Other words also lose their moorings:

"Insurrection" [is] now defined as governing in ways of which the Democratic Party heartily disapproves.

Kesler finds the question of the "extent and significance of election fraud in 2020" to end in murkiness. *Murkiness*, a populist might be expected to rejoin, is exactly what those who perpetrated fraud would aim for. The sheer implausibility of the vote count in key precincts and key states invites doubts in many and incredulity in still more – but, without forensic evidence, murkiness is all we have. And every step has been taken to ensure that such forensic evidence will never be found.

Kesler believes that Trump himself is finished, or nearly so. "An erosion [in support for Trump] has begun," Kesler claims polls show. He foresees, as does Reno, "an impending feud between pro- and anti-Trump forces [within the GOP]," which could play into the hands of progressives by splitting the conservative vote. But he concludes that "Trumpism has a future, even without Trump's continuing political presence."[62]

Wrath

After reading a draft of the opening chapters of this book, a long-time friend of mine, on whom I rely for wise counsel, advised: "As a writer, you don't do wrath well. It's not who you are. You don't even really do anger." I accept his criticism, but here I am – as I think a good portion of the country also is – trying to deal with what we take to be a gross abuse of our electoral system.

We conservatives don't "do wrath well" and aren't even very good at anger. Achilles isn't our ideal; neither is Medea. We worship a merciful God. We view unleashed anger with suspicion, doubt, and misgiving. That doesn't mean we don't feel it. But we don't idolize it, and we don't treat it as recreation. There are higher values and better ways to rule your life than to give in to anger. If we splurge on anger, we soon regret it. That euphoric high that some get from performative new anger is not for us, or not for long. The temptations are all around us to indulge in sportive anger, and sometimes we give in. New anger is contagious. We are familiar with it now. How could we not be? We may admire it from a distance. But at some level, we know better than to center our lives on this folly. The righteous indignation of a truly righteous man inspires us. The righteous indignation of a truly righteous woman summons deep respect. But righteous indignation isn't a diet on which most of us choose to live.

But what happens when we see our country captured by people who mean to tear it down? What do we do with this gnawing feeling of betrayal? How do we act? What do we say? We might stand frozen in indecision for a while. We are not used to starting fights. But we don't see ourselves as having started this one. We are wary of those on our own side who are ready to "finish it," because we know that will probably lead to violence and harm to the innocent.

But we believe that woke progressivism must be stopped, and we have not a penny's worth of confidence in the hapless old conservative establishment that has bowed to, excused, and accommodated the leftists who are imposing their will on the country with the thinnest pretext of democratic process.

It is up to us to do something. Just getting angry has limited value. Let's face up to our duties. We may not do wrath well, but at some point it is all we have: just stone-cold refusal to do what an illegitimate government demands. We have seen it in other countries around the world. It could, it might, and I suspect it will happen here.

Acknowledgments

ALL BOOKS EMBODY the conversations that their authors have had with friends and acquaintances. Some books – including this one – benefit as well from keen-eyed and informed critics who have read chapters in their early drafts and have pointed out important omissions and errors of fact and emphasis. I have benefited from both such conversations and criticisms, and this ordinarily would be the place to name my benefactors and thank them publicly.

But, on reflection, I have decided to break with custom by not naming any of the people whose ideas and insights have helped me to shape the arguments in *Wrath*. At the moment, acknowledging their help would inevitably mean exposing them to attack. Some of them are indeed willing to deal directly with the assaults on their characters and livelihood, but I see no reason to make things easier for cyberbullies and cancel-culture enforcers. Exposing those who have helped me to the personal attacks that have become the stock-in-trade of disordered progressive activists would be a poor way to show my gratitude. Doxing, vituperation, social media mobbing, and worse are now the near-automatic response of many who uphold views that I dispute in this book.

Thus I offer only a general acknowledgment. You, my good friends and brave correspondents – you know who you are – are the basis of my hopes for the restoration of this great republic against the forces that are bent on its destruction. I'm deeply grateful for your trust and support, and this book is much the better thanks to your decisions to help.

Notes

PREFACE

1. Jason G. Goldman, "I'll Bee There for You: Do Insects Feel Emotions?" *Scientific American*, September 30, 2016, https://www.scientificamerican.com/article/i-ll-bee-there-for-you-do-insects-feel-emotions; Jason Castro, "Do Bees Have Feelings?" *Scientific American*, August 2, 2011, https://www.scientificamerican.com/article/do-bees-have-feelings.

CHAPTER 1

1. Jesse O'Neill, "Photo Reveals Couple Slaughtered over Snow Shoveling Dispute," *New York Post*, February 5, 2021, https://nypost.com/2021/02/05/picture-shows-pennsylvania-couple-killed-in-snow-shoveling-dispute.
2. Chris Flannery, "Battle Hymn of the Republic," March 9, 2021, in *The American Story*, produced by Derek Wood, podcast, 6:00, https://theamericanstorypodcast.org/episode/battle-hymn-of-the-republic.
3. The full text of the original song transcribed in Black dialect can be found in John Stauffer and Benjamin Soskis, *The Battle Hymn of the Republic: A Biography of the Song That Marches On* (New York: Oxford University Press, 2013), 297.
4. John Stauffer, "The Song That Marches On: History of the Battle Hymn of the Republic," HistoryNet, https://www.historynet.com/the-song-that-marches-on-history-of-the-battle-hymn-of-the-republic.htm.
5. Stauffer & Soskis, *Battle Hymn of the Republic*, 60.
6. Stauffer and Soskis, 118, 327.
7. Dominic Tierney, "'The Battle Hymn of the Republic': America's Song of Itself," *Atlantic*, November 4, 2010, https://www.theatlantic.com/entertainment/archive/2010/11/the-battle-hymn-of-the-republic-americas-song-of-itself/66070.
8. Stauffer, "The Song That Marches On."
9. Tierney, "The Battle Hymn of the Republic."
10. Stauffer & Soskis, *Battle Hymn of the Republic*, 212.
11. Martin Luther King, Jr., "Address at the Conclusion of the Selma to Montgomery March," https://kinginstitute.stanford.edu/king-papers/documents/address-conclusion-selma-montgomery-march.
12. Babylonian Talmud, Sanhedrin, fo. 102b.
13. Sadi, *Gulistan* (c. 1258), Book 8, Maxim 20.
14. Because this book is addressed to a general audience, I have steered away from engaging the handful of other scholars who have most directly taken up the

topic of what to do, philosophically, religiously, and politically, with our excess anger. Among these most prominently is Martha Nussbaum, a progressive law professor who has published numerous books on topics that involve how our feelings bear on questions of justice. Her relevant works include *Hiding from Humanity: Disgust, Shame, and the Law* (2004) and *From Disgust to Humanity: Sexual Orientation and Constitutional Law* (2010). But the most directly relevant is Martha C. Nussbaum, *Anger and Forgiveness: Resentment, Generosity, Justice* (New York: Oxford University Press, 2016).

In this book, Nussbaum elaborates distinctions between different kinds of intensities of anger, all from the perspective that anger is always an impediment to justice and should be made to give way to reconciliation. She opposes punishment of wrongdoers by the state or by individuals who have suffered at their hands. She even opposes being angry at oneself, anger being always "a trap" (91). Anger may be "well-grounded" (35, 49, 52, 93, 97, 140) in Nussbaum's terms, but even then it gets in the way of "forward-looking" (6, 50, 95) approaches she favors. Empathy, forgiveness, and reconciliation comprise the whole of Nussbaum's sense of legitimate emotional responses to provocation. She sees no place for retribution either in law or in personal relationships. She criticizes our "cultural reluctance to pursue no-anger" (248). She does distinguish between various shades of anger and between anger and other "reactive emotions" (50), and she particularly condemns anger about status and rank. She confesses to have her own susceptibilities to anger, her "pet peeve" being "large men, usually very out of shape, who grab one's suitcase without asking permission first and try to hoist it into the overhead rack" (139, 149). Nussbaum also briefly touches on the idea that anger can be used "as an attention-getter" (141) or as a "performance" (150). These are, in my view, central characteristics of today's "new anger," but she makes little of them.

I disagree with Nussbaum about many matters, large and small, but I recommend *Anger and Forgiveness* as an excellent source for the reader who wishes to learn more about the philosophical and theological background to the issues I discuss in *Wrath*. It is a deeply learned book and a good way to become acquainted with how progressive ideology distorts clear thinking about justice.

15. Strong opinions are found on both sides of the question, not always congruent with the usual political divisions. Some writers usually classed as conservatives reject the view that voter fraud played a significant role in the 2020 election. See Andrew C. Eggers, Haritz Garro, and Justin Grimmer, *No Evidence for Voter Fraud: A Guide to Statistical Claims about the 2020 Election*, February 3, 2021, https://www.dropbox.com/s/0120sormtbw9w10/fraud_extended_public. pdf; Patrick Byrne, *The Deep Rig: How Election Fraud Cost Donald J. Trump the White House, by a Man Who Did not Vote for Him* (n.p.: Deep Capture, 2021); Jay Valentine, "The Sovereign Crime of Industrial Scale Vote Fraud," *American Thinker*, March 16, 2021, https://www.americanthinker.com/articles/2021/03/

the_sovereign_crime_of_industrial_scale_vote_fraud.html.

16. Molly Ball, "The Secret History of the Shadow Campaign That Saved the 2020 Election," *Time*, February 4, 2021, https://time.com/5936036/secret-2020-election-campaign.

17. Audra D. S. Burch, Weiyi Cai, Gabriel Gianordoli, Morrigan McCarthy, and Jugal K. Patel, "How Black Lives Matter Reached Every Corner of America," *New York Times*, June 13, 2020, https://www.nytimes.com/interactive/2020/06/13/us/george-floyd-protests-cities-photos.html.

18. Derrick Bryson Taylor, "George Floyd Protests: A Timeline," *New York Times*, January 6, 2021, https://www.nytimes.com/article/george-floyd-protests-timeline.html.

19. Jennifer A. Kingson, "$1 Billion-Plus Riot Damage Is Most Expensive in Insurance History," *Axios*, September 16, 2020, https://www.axios.com/riots-cost-property-damage-276c9bcc-a455-4067-b06a-66f9db4cea9c.html.

20. The number may be significantly higher, as the key source of the statistic, the international group ACLED (Armed Conflict Location and Event Data), decided to discount killings "carried out in the vicinity of protests" that it judged were not part of a political demonstration. Lois Beckett, "At Least 25 Americans Were Killed during Protests and Political Unrest in 2020," *The Guardian*, October 31, 2020, https://www.theguardian.com/world/2020/oct/31/americans-killed-protests-political-unrest-acled; David Bernstein, *Reason*, January 11, 2021, https://reason.com/volokh/2021/01/11/gaslighting-last-summers-riots-and-the-law-enforcement-response. These include David Dorn, a retired seventy-seven-year-old police captain whom looters shot and killed when they broke into a pawn shop; Secoriea Turner, an eight-year-old girl who was killed during a shooting incident involving armed rioters in Atlanta; and Aaron Danielson, conservative counterdemonstrator, whom a leftist rioter stalked and murdered. The overall death toll was about double the dozen, including individuals shot and killed by police and armed civilians in self-defense, people killed by right-wingers reveling in the chaos, and people killed by automobile drivers who were trying to escape the rioting.

21. Andrew M. Baker, M.D., *Hennepin County Medical Examiner's Office Autopsy Report for George Floyd*, ME NO. 20-3700, May 26, 2020, https://www.hennepin.us/-/media/hennepinus/residents/public-safety/documents/floyd-autopsy-6-3-20.pdf; Lou Raguse, "New Court Docs Say George Floyd Had 'Fatal Level' of Fentanyl in His System," KARE 11, August 26, 2020, https://www.kare11.com/article/news/local/george-floyd/new-court-docs-say-george-floyd-had-fatal-level-of-fentanyl-in-his-system/89-ed69d09d-a9ec-481c-90fe-7acd4ead3d04.

22. Frances Robles and Audra D. S. Burch, "How Did George Floyd Die? Here's What We Know," *New York Times*, June 2, 2020, https://www.nytimes.com/article/george-floyd-autopsy-michael-baden.html.

23. Steven A. Camarota, "Births to Unmarried Mothers by Nativity and Education," Center for Immigration Studies, May 5, 2017, https://cis.org/Camarota/Births-Unmarried-Mothers-Nativity-and-Education.

24. Federal Bureau of Investigation, *2019 Crime in the United States*, U.S. Department of Justice, https://ucr.fbi.gov/crime-in-the-u.s/2019/crime-in-the-u.s.-2019/topic-pages/expanded-homicide.

25. Glenn Loury, "Unspeakable Truths about Racial Inequality in America," *Quillette*, February 10, 2021, https://quillette.com/2021/02/10/unspeakable-truths-about-racial-inequality-in-america.

26. Heather Mac Donald, "Taking Stock of a Most Violent Year," opinion, *Wall Street Journal*, January 24, 2021, https://www.wsj.com/articles/taking-stock-of-a-most-violent-year-11611525947.

27. Mac Donald.

28. Devin Foley, "Chicago: 75% of Murdered Are Black, 71% of Murderers Are Black," *Intellectual Takeout* (blog), July 27, 2016, https://www.intellectualtakeout.org/blog/chicago-75-murdered-are-black-71-murderers-are-black.

    Analyzing 2011 data for Chicago, Foley found "87% of all [homicide] offenders had a prior arrest history. Offenders were 88% male." 53.22 percent of the killers were aged 17 to 35, and 26.32 percent were aged 26 to 35; 71.2 percent were Black. "Based on the data on the victims, that means young, Black males are primarily killing other young, Black males."

29. Jake Lahut, "Obama releases statement on George Floyd: 'For millions of Americans, being treated differently on account of race is tragically, painfully, maddeningly 'normal,'" *Business Insider*, May 29, 2020, https://www.businessinsider.com/obama-releases-statement-on-george-floyd-amid-minnesota-protests-2020-5.

30. Jonathan Martin and Katie Glueck, "'The Pain Is Too Intense': Biden Challenges White Americans," analysis, *New York Times*, May 29, 2020, https://www.nytimes.com/2020/05/29/us/politics/joe-biden-george-floyd.html.

31. Heather Mac Donald, "The Myth of Systemic Police Racism," opinion, *Wall Street Journal*, June 2, 2020, https://www.wsj.com/articles/the-myth-of-systemic-police-racism-11591119883.

32. Barry Latzer, *The Rise and Fall of Violent Crime in America* (New York: Encounter, 2016).

33. Alice Chughtai, "Know Their Names: Black People Killed by the Police in the U.S.," Al Jazeera, https://interactive.aljazeera.com/aje/2020/know-their-names/index.html, retrieved February 2, 2021.

34. Janelle Monáe, Deep Cotton, St. Beauty, Jidenna, Roman GianArthur, and George 2.0, "Hell You Talmbout," video, 6:38, uploaded by reggaematicltd, c. 2015, https://www.dailymotion.com/video/x31032h.

35. Monáe et al., "Hell You Talmbout." Northwest Tap Connection, "a social justice

oriented dance studio" in Seattle, went on the road with its version of "Hell You Talmbout." "The taps of their toes are like the walks and talks of those chained and silenced – but at the very same time, an embodiment of revelry and resilience. It's a cry to say their names, see their names and feel their names ... and it's a declaration that the list of lives lost to police brutality ends today." "Hell You Talmbout," co-directed by Denzel Boyd, Tyler Rabinowitz, and Joseph Webb, produced and edited by Tyler Rabinowitz, music by Janelle Monae and Wondaland Records, YouTube video, 8:18, uploaded by YoungArts, November 25, 2016, https://www.youtube.com/watch?v=17KyuCd8nlo.

36. John Powers, "David Byrne and Spike Lee Conjure Up a Joyous Vision of 'American Utopia,'" movie review of *David Byrne's American Utopia*, NPR, October 13, 2020, https://www.npr.org/2020/10/13/923258756/david-byrne-and-spike-lee-conjure-up-a-joyous-vision-of-american-utopia.

37. "Hell You Talmbout – David Byrne's American Utopia," YouTube video, 4:44, uploaded by David Byrne's American Utopia on Broadway, June 1, 2020, https://www.youtube.com/watch?v=wVQdXB9xgpw.

38. "Sen. Kamala Harris: The Nationwide Protests Are a Movement. They're Not Going to Stop," YouTube video, 6:22, uploaded by The Late Show with Stephen Colbert, June 22, 2020, https://www.youtube.com/watch?v=NTg1ynIPGls, at 5:34.

39. "Donald Trump Rushed to 'Terror Attack' Bunker as Violent George Floyd Riots Rage near White House," YouTube video, 3:04, uploaded by The Sun, June 1, 2020, https://www.youtube.com/watch?v=ut1-1MOcxsE.

40. Mollie Reilly and Nick Visser, "Donald Trump Vows to Crack Down on Anti-Racist Protests in Surreal Rose Garden Speech," *HuffPost*, June 1, 2020, https://www.huffpost.com/entry/donald-trump-protest-crackdown-minneapolis-george-floyd-protests_n_5ed57ce3c5b642ed75ab6582.

41. "You Won't Be Safe in Joe Biden's America," YouTube video, 0:30, uploaded by Donald J Trump, July 15, 2020, https://www.youtube.com/watch?v=JK6K-sWTAtM.

42. Ross Douthat, "The Case against Riots," *New York Times*, May 30, 2020, https://www.nytimes.com/2020/05/30/opinion/sunday/riots-george-floyd.html.

43. Zak Cheney-Rice, "The Rioters Aren't Here to Convince You," *New York Magazine*, June 1, 2020, https://nymag.com/intelligencer/2020/06/rioters-at-the-george-floyd-protests-dont-want-sympathy.html.

44. Tony Thomas, "'Time' Returns to the Scene of the Crime," *Quadrant* Online, February 7, 2021, https://quadrant.org.au/opinion/america/2021/02/like-a-criminal-time-returns-to-the-scene-of-the-crime.

45. Charles Dickens, *Barnaby Rudge: A Tale of the Riots of 'Eighty*, Chapters 57 and 60, https://www.gutenberg.org/files/917/917-h/917-h.htm

46. "The Harlem Riot," excerpt from the American Masters film *Ralph Ellison: An*

American Journey, https://ny.pbslearningmedia.org/resource/aml15.ela.lit.riot/
the-harlem-riot.

47. Nat Brandt, *Harlem at War: The Black Experience in WWII* (Syracuse, NY: Syracuse University Press, 1996), 184–94; Dominic J. Capeci, *The Harlem Riot of 1943* (Philadelphia: Temple University Press, 1977), 100–107; Charles R. Lawrence, Jr., "Race Riots in the United States 1942–1946," in *Negro Year Book: A Review of Events Affecting Negro Life, 1941–1946*, ed. Jesse P. Guzman (Tuskegee, AL: Tuskegee Institute, 1947), 242–43.

48. "The Harlem Riot."

CHAPTER 2

1. James Gordon, "QAnon Snowflake Shaman! Jacob Chansley, 33, Makes First Court Appearance by Video Link on Federal Charges for MAGA Riot – as His Mom Moans He Hasn't Eaten since His Arrest Three Days Ago Because the Jail Won't Serve All-Organic Food," *Daily Mail*, January 12, 2021, https://www.dailymail.co.uk/news/article-9136479/QAnon-Shamen-Jacob-Chansley-makes-tele-court-appearance-today-Phoenix.html.

2. Gordon.

3. McKenna Moore, "What You Need to Know about Far-Right Conspiracy QAnon," *Fortune*, August 1, 2018.

4. Robert Walker, "Video Shows Capitol Police Giving Approval for January 6th Protesters to Protest Inside U.S. Capitol," Shore News Network, May 17, 2021, https://www.shorenewsnetwork.com/2021/05/17/video-shows-capitol-police-giving-approval-for-january-6th-protesters-to-protest-inside-u-s-capitol.

5. Zachary Stieber, "Sen. Graham: Calling 'QAnon Shaman' as Impeachment Witness Would Turn Trial into 'Circus,'" *Epoch Times*, January 30, 2021, https://www.theepochtimes.com/sen-graham-calling-qanon-shaman-as-impeachment-witness-would-turn-trial-into-circus_3678301.html.

6. Peter W. Wood, "I Paid for This Microphone," *National Review Online*, August 10, 2007, https://www.nationalreview.com/2007/08/i-paid-microphone-peter-wood.

7. Peter W. Wood, "Donald Trump and the Weak Man's Vanity," *National Review Online*, August 20, 2015, https://www.nationalreview.com/2015/08/donald-trump-and-new-anger-peter-wood.

8. Peter W. Wood, "The Gilded Rage: Why Is America So Angry?" *Spectator USA*, October 7, 2019, https://spectator.us/topic/gilded-rage-america-angry.

9. Karen Tibbals, *Persuade, Don't Preach: Restoring Civility across the Political Divide* (n.p.: Ethical Frames, 2020).

10. Recent statistics show that people who classify themselves as "very liberal" profess a much greater willingness to endorse the use of violence to pursue political goals than do conservatives. A third of the "very liberal" cohort in 2020 recog-

nized violence as a legitimate tool. Five percent of conservatives agreed. The numbers come from the "2020 Times Series Study" by the American National Elections Studies, funded by the National Science Foundation (https://election studies.org/data-center/2020-time-series-study), summarized here: "Will Left's Violent Tendencies Lead to U.S. Breakup or Dictatorship?" *Issues & Insights*, March 16, 2021, https://issuesinsights.com/2021/03/16/will-lefts-violent-tendencies-lead-to-u-s-breakup-or-dictatorship.

11. "President Trump News Conference," C-SPAN video, 23:48, August 15, 2017, https://www.c-span.org/video/?432633-1/president-trump-there-blame-sides-violence-charlottesville; Glenn Kessler, "The 'Very Fine People' at Charlottesville: Who Were They?" *Washington Post*, May 8, 2020, https://www.washingtonpost.com/politics/2020/05/08/very-fine-people-charlottesville-who-were-they-2.

12. Dominick Mastrangelo, "Washington Post Adds Lengthy Correction to Report on Trump Call with Georgia Elections Investigator," *The Hill*, March 15, 2021, https://thehill.com/homenews/media/543271-wapost-adds-lengthy-correction-to-story-on-trump-georgia-call.

13. Andrey Mir, *Postjournalism and the Death of Newspapers: The Media after Trump: Manufacturing Anger and Polarization* (Author, 2020).

14. Martin Gurri, "Slouching toward Post-Journalism," *City Journal*, Winter 2021, https://www.city-journal.org/journalism-advocacy-over-reporting.

15. Robert Stacy McCain, "Why Is Identity Politics Destroying America? Tribalism Has Turned Toxic in the Age of Social Media," *American Spectator*, February 5, 2021, https://spectator.org/identity-politics-media.

16. No Glory for Hate Act, H.R. 484, 117th Cong. (2021), https://www.congress.gov/bill/117th-congress/house-bill/484; Victoria Taft, "Unity Watch: Democrats Introduce a Bill to Punish Trump When He Dies," PJ Media, February 18, 2021, https://pjmedia.com/news-and-politics/victoria-taft/2021/02/18/unity-watch-democrats-introduce-a-bill-to-punish-trump-when-he-dies-n1426572.

17. Thomas Paine, "The American Crisis," *Pennsylvania Journal*, December 19, 1776, https://www.gutenberg.org/files/3741/3741-h/3741-h.htm#link2H_4_0002.

CHAPTER 3

1. The *Guinness Book of World Records* says that a man has held 109 honeybees in his closed mouth for ten seconds. In August 1997, David Skorupa of Glasgow, Scotland, died of anaphylactic shock after being stung by a bee in the mouth. A passenger on a bus in Laurie Fox's novel *My Sister from the Black Lagoon* (1999) explains that "Certain people scream because of what's inside them. Like, you know, having bees in the mouth." The horror film *Candyman 2* features a sequence in which a character has live bees in his mouth. The "beewrangler" who managed that special effect had to vacuum them out afterward.

2. "S7E10: *The Simpsons* 138th Episode Spectacular," video, 0:10, https://comb.io/t5HFLs.

3. John Walsh, "The Fall of *The Simpsons*: How It Happened," YouTube video, 31:07, uploaded by Super Eyepatch Wolf, August 12, 2017, https://www.youtube.com/watch?v=KqFNbCcyFkk.

4. Nicolaus Mills, *The Triumph of Meanness: America's War against Its Better Self* (Boston: Houghton Mifflin, 1997), 1–5, 15.

5. "True Crime Series 1 1992 Eclipse Complete Base Card Set of 110 at Amazon's Entertainment Collectibles Store," Amazon, accessed April 14, 2021, https://www.amazon.com/TRUE-CRIME-1992-ECLIPSE-COMPLETE/dp/B01LA2LHIA.

6. Chris Rodkey, "Ice Cream Icon Has Fiery Message," *Boston Globe*, July 22, 2004, http://archive.boston.com/news/politics/president/bush/articles/2004/07/22/ice_cream_icon_has_fiery_message.

7. Doreen St. Félix, "'The Rachel Divide' Review: A Disturbing Portrait of Dolezal's Racial Fraudulence," *New Yorker*, April 26, 2018, https://www.newyorker.com/culture/culture-desk/the-rachel-divide-review-a-disturbing-portrait-of-dolezals-racial-fraudulence.

8. Poppy Noor, "White US Professor Jessica Krug Admits She Has Pretended to Be Black for Years," *The Guardian*, September 3, 2020, https://www.theguardian.com/world/2020/sep/03/jessica-krug-white-professor-pretended-black.

9. Andre Ricketts, "Why White Women Keep Getting Caught Pretending to Be Black," *Daily Beast*, November 27, 2020, https://www.thedailybeast.com/why-white-women-keep-getting-caught-pretending-to-be-black.

10. Hira Humayun and David Williams, "University of Wisconsin-Madison Grad Student Admits Pretending to Be a Person of Color," CNN, September 17, 2020, https://www.cnn.com/2020/09/17/us/wisconsin-grad-student-race-trnd/index.html.

11. Colleen Flaherty, "More White Lies," *Inside Higher Ed*, September 10, 2020, https://www.insidehighered.com/news/2020/09/10/more-allegations-racial-fraud-academe.

12. "Don't Push Me," featuring Lloyd Banks and Eminem, on 50 Cent, *Get Rich or Die Tryin'*, Shady/Aftermath/Interscope, 2003.

13. "ARGH! 11 Rage Anthems to Listen to When You're Angry," BigTop40, accessed April 14, 2021, https://www.bigtop40.com/features/songs-to-listen-to-when-angry.

14. "So What," on Pink, *Funhouse*, LaFace/Zomba, 2008.

15. "The Angry Playlist – Angry Classic Rock," Audacy, accessed April 14, 2021, https://www.audacy.com/angryplaylist/listen#schedule.

16. "Mean," on Taylor Swift, *Speak Now*, Big Machine, 2010; "Picture to Burn," on Taylor Swift, *Taylor Swift*, Big Machine, 2006; "Better Than Revenge," on Taylor Swift, *Speak Now*, Big Machine, 2010; Halsey, "Nightmare," Capitol, 2019.

17. Aaron Nicodemus, "Agents' Visit Chills UMass Dartmouth Senior," *South Coast*

NOTES

Today, January 14, 2011, https://www.southcoasttoday.com/article/20051217/news/312179988.

CHAPTER 4

1. Eleanor H. Porter, *Pollyanna* (Boston: Page, 1913), 43.
2. Quoted in James R. Mellow, *Nathaniel Hawthorne in His Times* (Boston: Houghton Mifflin, 1980), 551–52. According to Mellow, "Hawthorne confessed that he was not one of Brown's admirers; he described the abolitionist, in fact, as a 'blood-stained fanatic.' Nor could he believe that Brown's death had 'made the Gallows as venerable as the Cross' – which was, reportedly, Emerson's view. 'Nobody was ever more justly hanged,' Hawthorne countered." Mellow also quotes Hawthorne on the topic of Brown's execution: "Any common-sensible man, looking at the matter unsentimentally, must have felt a certain intellectual satisfaction in seeing [Brown] hanged, if it were only in requital of his preposterous miscalculation of possibilities."
3. Owen Wister, *The Virginian: A Horseman of the Plains*, with illustrations by A. I. Keller (New York: Macmillan, 1902), 29.
4. Joel Chandler Harris, *The Complete Tales of Uncle Remus*, compiled by Richard Chase (1955; Boston: Houghton Mifflin, 1983), 8–9.
5. Dashiell Hammett, *The Maltese Falcon* (1929; San Francisco: North Point Press, 1987), 271.
6. Clif Garboden, "Screw You, America," *Boston Phoenix*, November 12, 2004, https://bostonphoenix.com/boston/news_features/other_stories/multi_3/documents/04256169.asp
7. Geoffrey Norman, "Dead Ball," *Wall Street Journal*, May 7, 2004, https://www.wsj.com/articles/SB108389097578204875
8. Jeff Benedict, *Out of Bounds: Inside the NBA's Culture of Rape, Violence, and Crime* (New York: HarperCollins, 2004), xv.
9. "NBA When the Anger FINALLY Comes Out Moments," YouTube video, 11:25, uploaded by NothingButAmazing, October 31, 2019, https://www.youtube.com/watch?v=28KfQE-Fw6E.
10. Michael Katz, "The Joel Embiid vs. Karl-Anthony Towns Fight Is Pretty Funny, Actually," SBNation.com, October 30, 2019, https://www.sbnation.com/nba/2019/10/30/20941095/joel-embiid-karl-anthony-towns-fight-video-reaction.
11. Kyle Neubeck (@KyleNeubeck), Twitter, October 30, 2019, 7:43 p.m., https://twitter.com/KyleNeubeck/status/1189719476163489797
12. Kyle Neubeck (@KyleNeubeck), Twitter, October 30, 2019, 7:45 p.m., https://twitter.com/KyleNeubeck/status/1189720135902384130
13. Jonathan Welsh, "Why Cars Got Angry," *Wall Street Journal*, March 10, 2006, W1, https://www.wsj.com/articles/SB114195150869994250.

14. Rose Eveleth, "For Experts, Cars Really Do Have Faces," *Smithsonian Magazine*, October 2, 2012, https://www.smithsonianmag.com/smart-news/for-experts-cars-really-do-have-faces-57005307.

15. Jack Baruth, "You Can't Be Tough All the Time, and You Shouldn't Be," *Road and Track*, May 9, 2014, https://www.roadandtrack.com/car-culture/a7834/avoidable-contact-tough-all-the-time-may-2014.

16. Clemsie McKenzie, "Why Do Modern Cars Look Angry?" *Drivetribe*, 2018. https://drivetribe.com/p/why-do-modern-cars-look-angry-L_Zc8_TvT-WHbjiBBEhmzQ.

17. Renee Nelson, "Why Are Cars Looking So Angry?" 92 Moose, October 29, 2020, https://92moose.fm/why-are-cars-looking-so-angry.

18. The speech was widely reported, but for a comment on Senator Clinton's phrase "you know what I'm talkin' about" see Mark Goldblatt, "You Go Girl! A Missing Consonant and the Race Card," *National Review*, January 27, 2006, https://www.nationalreview.com/2006/01/you-go-girl-mark-goldblatt.

19. Christopher Lasch, *The Culture of Narcissism: American Life in the Age of Diminished Expectations* (New York: Norton, 1978).

20. Norah Burch, "Rant and Rage. Harvard Fired Me after Reading My Online Diary; I Didn't Really Want to Bomb the Campus, But There's a Reason I Wrote That in My Blog," *Boston Globe*, June 27, 2004, Magazine, 7.

21. Burch quotes herself as having written the words "I'm two nasty e-mails...," but the *Harvard Crimson* quoted her blog with a slightly different phrasing:

> *"Work is aggravating me,"* she wrote in an April 28 entry on the publicly accessible journal, the contents of which have since been taken offline. *"I am one shade lighter than homicidal today. I am two snotty e-mails from professors away from bombing the entire Harvard campus."*
> Leon Neyfakh, "Online Weblog Leads to Firing,"
> *Harvard Crimson*, May 26, 2004.

I am not sure what to make of Burch's gentle suppression of the phrase "I am one shade lighter than homicidal today" or why she apparently shifted "snotty" to "nasty" in her retelling of the incident.

CHAPTER 5

1. Zoë Sharp, "How It Ends," in "Five Novelists Imagine Trump's Next Chapter," *New York Times Book Review*, October 23, 2018, https://www.nytimes.com/2018/10/23/books/review/trumps-next-chapter.html.

2. Jesse Walker, "SiriusXM Suspends Glenn Beck for Brad Thor's Comments on Trump; Brad Thor Responds to His Critics," *Reason*, May 31, 2016, https://reason.com/2016/05/31/glenn-beck-suspended-for-brad-thors-comm.

3. Michael Gordon, "When Feds Came to Discuss His Post about Trump, He Cursed Them. Now He'll Talk to a Judge," *Charlotte Observer*, March 30, 2018, https://www.charlotteobserver.com/latest-news/article207176974.html.

4. Mark W. Davis, "Shoot to Sell: Knopf's Tangos with Presidential Assassination," *National Review*, July 15, 2004, http://www.nationalreview.com/comment/davis200407150818.

5. Jonathan Kyncl, "'Going on with Trumpism without Trump,' Ann Coulter Speaks at OU Turning Point USA Student Event," *Oklahoma Daily*, November 6, 2020, https://www.oudaily.com/news/going-on-with-trumpism-without-trump-ann-coulter-speaks-at-ou-turning-point-usa-student/article_c8d5cb34-1ff0-11eb-ad16-2357d3c4ab89.html.

6. Julie Kelly, *Disloyal Opposition: How the #Nevertrump Right Tried – and Failed – to Take Down the President* (New York: Encounter Books, 2020), 11.

7. Carol Zisowitz Stearns and Peter N. Stearns, *Anger: The Struggle for Emotional Control in America's History* (Chicago: University of Chicago Press, 1986), 74.

8. Stearns and Stearns. On the periodization of American anger, 10–11, 36–109, 241; on the etymology of the word "tantrum," 29.

9. Stearns and Stearns, 238.

10. Stearns and Stearns, 9.

11. Stearns and Stearns, 11.

12. Stearns and Stearns, 239.

13. Charles Duhigg, "The Real Roots of American Rage," *Atlantic*, January/February 2019, https://www.theatlantic.com/magazine/archive/2019/01/charles-duhigg-american-anger/576424.

14. Duhigg.

15. Quotation from Duhigg, "The Real Roots." The Rubin quotation is originally from the *Ladies' Home Journal*, November 1975, 32; the Popenoe quotation is also from the *Ladies' Home Journal*, June 1975, 18. The Stearnses claim that such permissiveness failed to shake the older consensus that anger is dangerous and best kept in check.

16. Harriet Lerner, *The Dance of Anger: A Woman's Guide to Changing Patterns of Intimate Relationships* (1985; New York: HarperCollins, 1997); Reneau Z. Peurifoy, *Anger: Taming the Beast* (New York: Kodansha International, 1999); Redford Williams, *Anger Kills* (1993; New York: HarperCollins, 1994); Suzette Elgin, *You Can't Say That to Me: Stopping the Pain of Verbal Abuse* (New York: John Wiley & Sons, 1995).

17. Theodore Rubin, *The Angry Book* (New York: Simon & Schuster, 1998); Stephen Diamond, *Anger, Madness, and the Daimonic: The Psychological Genesis of Violence, Evil, and Creativity* (Albany: State University of New York Press, 1999); Neil Nehring, *Popular Music, Gender, and Postmodernism: Anger Is an Energy* (Thousand Oaks, CA: Sage Publications, 1997); Neil Clark Warren, *Make Anger Your Ally* (Wheaton, IL: Tyndale House Publishers, 1990).

18. Daniel Goleman, *Emotional Intelligence: Why It Can Matter More Than IQ* (1995; New York: Bantam Books, 1997), 56–65.

19. Tom Lutz, *Crying: The Natural and Cultural History of Tears* (New York: W. W. Norton, 1999), 300.

20. Sian Griffiths and Jennifer Wallace, eds., *Consuming Passions: Food in the Age of Anxiety* (Manchester, UK: Manchester University Press, 1998); Sari Locker, *Mindblowing Sex in the Real World: Hot Tips for Doing It in the Age of Anxiety* (New York: HarperPerennial Library, 1995); David Anderegg, *Worried All the Time: Rediscovering the Joy of Parenthood in an Age of Anxiety* (New York: Free Press, 2004).

21. Carol Tavris, *Anger: The Misunderstood Emotion* (New York: Touchstone Books, 1982), 108.

22. Philip Rieff, *The Triumph of the Therapeutic* (New York: Harper & Row, 1966).

23. Bernard Weinraub, "Amid Protests, Elia Kazan Receives His Oscar," *New York Times*, March 22, 1999, E3; Michelle Caruso, "Kazan Draws Applause, Protest for Special Honor," *New York Daily News*, March 22, 1999, 4; Jerry Schwartz, "Kazan Honor Stirs Firestorm in Film World," *Atlanta Journal and Constitution*, March 22, 1999, 1C; Benedict Nightingale, "Legacy of a Hollywood Witchhunt," *The Times* (London), March 4, 1999.

24. Thomas Oliphant, "Honoring a Dishonorable Man," *Boston Globe*, March 2, 1999, A15; David Aaronovitch, "An Oscar That Reminds Us of a Cowardly, Shameful Little Episode," *The Independent* (London), March 23, 1999, 3, https://www.independent.co.uk/arts-entertainment/an-oscar-that-reminds-us-of-a-cowardly-shameful-little-episode-1082420.html.

25. Aaronovitch.

CHAPTER 6

1. David Edelstein, "Marlon Brando: The Largest Actor of Them All," obituary, *Slate*, July 2, 2004, https://slate.com/news-and-politics/2004/07/brando-the-largest-actor-of-them-all.html.

2. See, for example, Maruska Svasek, "Introduction: Emotions in Anthropology," in *Mixed Emotions: Anthropological Studies of Feeling*, ed. Kay Milton and Maruska Svasek (New York: Berg, 2005), 6.

3. A *trait* is a long-standing component of an individual's personality (e.g., "Tulip is a generally angry person"). A *state* refers to the short-term experience of an actual emotion (e.g., "Tulip was furious when Land's End delivered the wrong color sweater"). For accounts of emotions as traits, see Carroll E. Izard and Brian P. Ackerman, "Motivational, Organizational, and Regulatory Functions of Discrete Emotions," in *Handbook of Emotions*, ed. Michael Lewis and Jeannette M. Haviland-Jones, 2nd ed. (New York: Guilford Press, 2000), 253–64; Carroll E. Izard, *The Psychology of Emotions* (New York: Plenum Press, 1991);

Jeannette M. Haviland-Jones and Patricia Kahlbaugh, "Emotion and Identity," in *Handbook of Emotions*, ed. Lewis and Haviland-Jones, 293–305. For an account of emotions as states, see Michael Lewis, "The Emergence of Human Emotions," in *Handbook of Emotions*, ed. Lewis and Haviland-Jones, 265–80. The trait/state distinction, however, doesn't seem to offer a very useful way to decipher new anger, which involves both well-developed psychological dispositions and transitory episodes of extreme excitement, and is thus both trait and state. Moreover, new anger involves a third quality, which is neither trait nor state but a repertoire of symbols, acts, clichés, gestures, words, and expressions that together constitute an external world – the angri-culture – which individuals, regardless of their personalities or their momentary feelings, must negotiate.

Psychologists who specialize in the study of emotion will find that in this book I have bypassed most of the current theoretical controversies in the field about the nature of emotion. My analysis of new anger in America is closer in spirit to the anthropological study of emotion; see, e.g., Catherine Lutz and Geoffrey M. White, "The Anthropology of Emotions," *Annual Review of Anthropology* 15 (1986), 405–36; but here, too, I have attempted to steer clear of academic debates and technical issues.

4. David Paul Kuhn, *The Hardhat Riot: Nixon, New York City, and the Dawn of the White Working-Class Revolution* (New York: Oxford University Press, 2020).

5. Michael Burleigh, *Blood & Rage: A Cultural History of Terrorism* (New York: Harper, 2009).

6. Andy Ngo, *Unmasked: Inside Antifa's Radical Plan to Destroy Democracy* (New York: Center Street, 2021).

7. Aaron Blake, "Eric Holder: 'When they go low, we kick them. That's what this new Democratic Party is about,'" *Washington Post*, October 10, 2018, https://www.washingtonpost.com/politics/2018/10/10/eric-holder-when-they-go-low-we-kick-them-thats-what-this-new-democratic-party-is-about.

8. Charles Duhigg, "The Real Roots of American Rage," *Atlantic*, January/February 2019, https://www.theatlantic.com/magazine/archive/2019/01/charles-duhigg-american-anger/576424.

9. Michael Anton, "Why Do the Election's Defenders Require My Agreement?" *American Greatness*, February 23, 2021, https://amgreatness.com/2021/02/23/why-do-the-elections-defenders-require-my-agreement; David Horowitz, "The Fascist Democrats & the Fake Insurrection," *Frontpage Mag*, February 24, 2021, https://www.frontpagemag.com/fpm/2021/02/fascist-democrats-fake-insurrection-david-horowitz.

10. Steven W. Webster, *American Rage: How Anger Shapes Our Politics* (Cambridge, MA: Cambridge University Press, 2020); Steven Levitsky and Daniel Ziblatt, *How Democracies Die* (New York: Crown, 2018); Jonathan Haidt, *The Righteous Mind: Why Good People Are Divided by Politics and Religion* (New York: Pantheon, 2012).

11. Melville's source for Moredock's life was James Hall, *Sketches of History, Life, and Manners in the West* (1835). Hall complained that Moredock was omitted from a recently published account of the early history of Illinois, and it is Hall's vindication of Moredock that Melville puts in the mouth of a callow flimflam man.

12. Gabriel Samuels, "'All I Want for Christmas Is White Genocide': Professor Receives Death Threats after Mocking Supremacists," *The Independent*, December 27, 2016, https://www.independent.co.uk/news/world/americas/history-professor-twitter-storm-white-genocide-death-threats-george-ciccariello-maher-a7497301.html.

13. Dahleen Glanton, "White America, if You Want to Know Who's Responsible for Racism, Look in the Mirror," *Chicago Tribune*, May 31, 2020, https://www.chicagotribune.com/columns/dahleen-glanton/ct-racism-white-people-george-floyd-20200531-tmdbj52ownc7fegdargh75k4qq-story.html.

14. See, e.g., H. K. Khalifah and Marsha Stewart, *O. J.'s Double Jeopardy: Revenge Lynching* (Hampton, VA: U.B. & U.S. Communications Systems, 1997).

CHAPTER 7

1. James Otis, *On the Writs of Assistance*, https://www.hazlet.org/userfiles/31/Classes/1172/james%20otis-writs%20of%20assistance-primary%20source.pdf?id=3246, 5.

2. *Declaration of Independence: A Transcription*, National Archives, https://www.archives.gov/founding-docs/declaration-transcript.

3. "Federalist Nos. 1-10," Library of Congress, https://guides.loc.gov/federalist-papers/text-1-10.

4. Abraham Lincoln, "The Perpetuation of Our Political Institutions: Address before the Young Men's Lyceum of Springfield, Illinois," January 27, 1838, http://www.abrahamlincolnonline.org/lincoln/speeches/lyceum.htm.

5. Richard Brookhiser, *Founding Father: Rediscovering George Washington* (New York: Simon & Schuster, 1996), 116; Richard Norton Smith, "The Surprising George Washington," *Prologue* 26, no. 1 (Spring 1994), https://www.archives.gov/publications/prologue/1994/spring/george-washington-1.html.

6. Brookhiser, *Founding Father*, 115–17.

7. David Hackett Fischer, *Washington's Crossing* (New York: Oxford University Press, 2004), 232–33.

8. Peter Sanders, "Anger Management," *Daily Breeze* (Torrance, CA), February 29, 2004.

9. "Courtesy of the Red, White, and Blue (the Angry American)," on Toby Keith, *Unleashed*, DreamWorks/Interscope, 2002.

10. "American single certifications–Toby Keith–Courtesy." Recording Industry Association of America, https://www.riaa.com/gold-platinum/?tab_active=default-award&ar=Toby+Keith&ti=Courtesy#search_section.

11. Scott Adams, "Good Example of Our Two-Movie Reality," *Scott Adams Says* (blog), February 12, 2017, https://www.scottadamssays.com/2017/02/12/good-example-of-our-two-movie-reality.

12. Glenn Ellmers, "The Other Americans," *American Mind*, April 1, 2021, https://americanmind.org/salvo/the-other-americans.

13. "Disturbed – The Sound of Silence [Official Music Video]," YouTube video, 4:19, uploaded by Disturbed, December 8, 2015, https://www.youtube.com/watch?v=u9Dg-g7t2l4.

CHAPTER 8

1. "Republican Contract with America," *McClatchy DC*, n.d., http://media.mcclatchydc.com/static/pdf/1994-contract-with-america.pdf.

2. William Schneider, "Morphing into Angry Voters," *Atlantic*, September 2006, https://www.theatlantic.com/magazine/archive/2006/09/morphing-into-angry-voters/305251.

3. Wayne Hardin, "White Men Burdened by the Stress of a Changing Nation," *Baltimore Sun*, April 12, 1993, https://www.baltimoresun.com/news/bs-xpm-1993-04-12-1993102073-story.html.

4. U.S. Bureau of Labor Statistics, *Labor Force Characteristics by Race and Ethnicity, 2010* (Report 1032), U.S. Department of Labor, August 2011, https://www.bls.gov/opub/reports/race-and-ethnicity/archive/race_ethnicity_2010.pdf.

5. Peter Wood, *Diversity: The Invention of a Concept* (New York: Encounter Books, 2003), 204–5.

6. Ibram X. Kendi, *How to Be an Antiracist* (New York: One World, 2019).

7. Ibram X. Kendi, "Preface to the Paperback Edition," *Stamped from the Beginning: The Definitive History of Racist Ideas in America* (New York: Hachette Book Group, 2017), ix.

8. Michael Kimmel, *Angry White Men: American Masculinity at the End of an Era* (New York: Nation Books, 2017), 32.

9. Kimmel, 41.

10. Kimmel, 43.

11. Lizzie Skurnick, ed., *Pretty Bitches: On Being Called Crazy, Angry, Bossy, Frumpy, Feisty, and All the Other Words That Are Used to Undermine Women* (New York: Seal Press, 2020), xiii.

12. Carol Anderson, *White Rage: The Unspoken Truth of Our Racial Divide* (New York: Bloomsbury, 2017), 161–63, 166–67, 169–73.

13. Jeanne Stapleton, letter to the editor, *Boston Globe*, July 23, 2004, A20.

14. Brian C. Anderson, "Illiberal Liberalism," *City Journal*, Spring 2001, 42–53, https://www.city-journal.org/html/illiberal-liberalism-11983.html.

15. Stephen Miller, "Anger Mismanagement," *Wall Street Journal*, March 19, 2004, W13, https://www.wsj.com/articles/SB107966979329060137.

CHAPTER 9

1. Bing Crosby, "Brother, Can You Spare a Dime?" YouTube video, 3:11, uploaded by src66, n.d., https://www.youtube.com/watch?v=eih67rlGNhU; Al Jolson, "Brother Can You Spare a Dime," YouTube video, 3:17, uploaded by isthisnametook, n.d., https://www.youtube.com/watch?v=4F4yToKAMyo; Rudy Vallee, "Brother, Can You Spare a Dime," YouTube video, 3:37, uploaded by Rudy Vallee – Topic, May 7, 2020, https://www.youtube.com/watch?v=Cgl1NFRGgRk.

2. Brooks Atkinson, "The Play: Design and Dance in an *American Revue* That Represents Modern Taste in Artistry," *New York Times*, October 6, 1932.

3. See Judy Collins, "Brother Can You Spare a Dime," YouTube video, 3:16, uploaded by pingolfin, n.d., https://www.youtube.com/watch?v=yCtIEeO-NrY; George Michael, "Brother Can You Spare a Dime (Audio)," YouTube video, 4:25, uploaded by georgemichael (Official Artist Channel), October 19, 2016, https://www.youtube.com/watch?v=keuyx-ROUA0.

4. William Zinsser, *Easy to Remember: The Great American Songwriters and Their Songs* (Jaffrey, NH: David R. Godine, 2000), 145–48; Robert Gottlieb and Robert Kimball, eds., *Reading Lyrics* (New York: Pantheon Books, 2000).

5. The comparative study of emotions in different cultures has precedents in anthropology going back to the nineteenth century, but the field has grown substantially since the 1970s. See Catherine Lutz and Geoffrey M. White, "The Anthropology of Emotions," *Annual Review of Anthropology* 15 (1986): 405–36. The "universality" of emotions, including anger, is widely accepted by contemporary anthropologists, who, however, dispute the degree to which the experience of emotional states is shaped by culture. Anthropologists are also divided on whether emotions are better viewed as internal states or as attributions that people make about each other's behavior. And, within anthropology, there are some sharp differences of opinion over whether to give primary emphasis to the biological side of emotions, such as hormones; the cultural definitions of anger; or the social rules that govern the expression of anger. I have sidestepped these debates to focus in this book on an ethnographic account of new anger in America, but it should be clear that I regard anger and other emotions as multidimensional. This book, however, focuses on the cultural transformation of the United States as we went from one way of regarding anger to another.

   Anthropologists are not alone in emphasizing the cultural patterning of emotions. Harvard psychology professor Jerome Kagan, a pioneer of developmental psychology, argues vigorously against reductive theories of emotion – i.e., theories that reduce all emotions to a few basic types rooted in the nature of the nervous system. Kagan sees human emotions as complex and complexly changing according to cultural and historical circumstances. For example, he discerns an emotion for which we do not yet have a name but which is partially captured in words like "*confused, rudderless, uncertain,* and *spiritually empty*

NOTES

[that] do not fully capture its meaning, [which is] a coherent state and not the sum of several elementary basic emotions." Jerome Kagan, *What Is Emotion? History, Measures, and Meanings* (New Haven, CT: Yale University Press, 2007), 201.

6. Deborah Cox, Karin H. Bruckner, and Sally Stabb, *The Anger Advantage: The Surprising Benefits of Anger and How It Can Change a Woman's Life* (New York: Broadway Books, 2003), 1.

7. Cox, Bruckner, and Stabb, 5.

8. Cox, Bruckner, and Stabb, 76–77.

9. Cox, Bruckner, and Stabb, 281.

10. Soraya Chemaly, *Rage Becomes Her: The Power of Women's Anger* (New York: Atria, 2018); Brittney Cooper, *Eloquent Rage: A Black Feminist Discovers Her Superpower* (New York: Picador, 2018); Lilly Dancyger, ed., *Burn It Down: Women Writing about Anger* (New York: Seal Press, 2019).

11. Evette Dionne, "Unbought and Unbossed," in Dancyger (pp. 81–90), 87.

12. bell hooks, *killing rage: ending racism* (New York: Henry Holt, 1996), 20.

13. Francesca M. Cancian and Steven L. Gordon, "Changing Emotion Norms in Marriage: Love and Anger in U.S. Women's Magazines since 1900," *Gender and Society* 2, no. 3 (September 1988): 308–42.

14. Joyce Brothers, "When Your Husband's Affection Cools," *Good Housekeeping*, May 1972.

15. Marilyn French, *The Women's Room* (New York: Summit Books, 1977), ch. 14.

16. Caroline Knapp, "Grace Notes: An Ode to Best Friends," *The Merry Recluse: A Life in Essays* (New York: Counterpoint, 2004), 41 (First published in *Siren Magazine*, 2000).

CHAPTER 10

1. Bob Woodward, *Rage* (New York: Simon & Schuster, 2020).

2. Woodward, xi.

3. Jamie Gangel, Jeremy Herb, and Elizabeth Stuart, "'Play It Down': Trump Admits to Concealing the True Threat of Coronavirus in New Woodward Book," *CNN Politics*, September 9, 2020, https://www.cnn.com/2020/09/09/politics/bob-woodward-rage-book-trump-coronavirus/index.html.

4. Woodward, *Rage*, 28.

5. Woodward, 29.

6. Woodward, 45.

7. Woodward, 53.

8. Woodward, 61.

9. Woodward, 62.

10. Woodward, 118.

11. Woodward, 186–89.

12. Woodward, 366–67.

13. Woodward, 375.

14. Woodward, 387, 392.

15. See Peter N. Stearns and Jan Lewis, eds., *An Emotional History of the United States* (New York: New York University Press, 1998); Peter N. Stearns, *Jealousy: The Evolution of an Emotion in American History* (New York: New York University Press, 1989); Carol Zisowitz Stearns and Peter N. Stearns, *Anger: The Struggle for Emotional Control in American History* (Chicago: University of Chicago Press, 1986); Norbert Elias, *The Civilizing Process: The History of Manners*, trans. Edmund Jephcott (New York: Urizen, 1978); Arlie R. Hochschild, "Emotion Work, Feeling Rules, and Social Structure," *American Journal of Sociology* 85 (1979): 551–75.

16. Douglas Axe, William M. Briggs, and Jay W. Richards, *The Price of Panic: How the Tyranny of Experts Turned a Pandemic into a Catastrophe* (Washington, D.C.: Regnery, 2020); Christopher Caldwell, *The Age of Entitlement: America Since the Sixties* (New York: Simon & Schuster, 2020); Soraya Chemaly, *Rage Becomes Her: The Power of Women's Anger* (New York: Simon & Schuster, 2018). See Jessica C. E. Gienow-Hecht, ed., *Emotions in American History: An International Assessment* (New York: Berghahn Books, 2010); Paul E. Griffiths, *What Emotions Really Are* (Chicago: University of Chicago Press, 1997); Jonathan Haidt, *The Righteous Mind: Why Good People Are Divided by Politics and Religion* (New York: Vintage, 2012); Ezra Klein, *Why We're Polarized* (New York: Avid Reader Press, 2020); Eric Lonergan and Mark Blyth, *Angrynomics* (Newcastle on Tyne: Agenda Publishing, 2020); Lilliana Mason, *Uncivil Agreement: How Identity Politics Became Our Identity* (Chicago: University of Chicago Press, 2018); Joshua Mitchell, *American Awakening: Identity Politics and Other Afflictions of Our Time* (New York: Encounter Books, 2020); Davin L. Phoenix, *The Anger Gap: How Race Shapes Emotion in Politics* (New York: Cambridge University Press, 2020); Bobby Soave, *Panic Attack: Young Radicals in the Age of Trump* (New York: All Points Books, 2019); Carolyn Strange, Robert Cribb, and Christopher E. Forth, eds., *Honour, Violence and Emotions in History* (New York: Bloomsbury, 2014).

17. The phrase has been traced to a 2000 movie, *State and Main*, in which one of the characters wrecks his car and treats it nonchalantly as just an event that had to happen sooner or later. The implication is that the event was random and inexplicable.

18. That list, however, is strongly disputed by Jerome Kagan, the Harvard psychologist whose book *What Is Emotion? History, Measures, and Meanings* (New Haven, CT: Yale University Press, 2007) rejects the idea of a small number of "basic emotions" from which the emotions we experience derive by combination. "Humans are capable of an extraordinary variety of emotions. The demands, threats, moral values, and social structure of a society select from the large

number of possibilities a smaller number for elaboration. The size of the potential set and the scientist's desire for parsimony motivate theorists to invent a rationale that might legitimate a privileged list of 'basic emotions.'" Kagan, 196–97.

19. Reddy's lyrics include these:

> *You can bend but never break me*
> *'Cause it only serves to make me*
> *More determined to achieve my final goal*
> *And I come back even stronger*
> *Not a novice any longer*
> *'Cause you've deepened the conviction in my soul*

https://genius.com/Helen-reddy-i-am-woman-lyrics

20. Brown's lyrics include these:

> *Some people say we've got a lot of malice*
> *Some say it's a lot of nerve*
> *But I say we won't quit moving until we get what we deserve*
> *We have been 'buked and we have been scorned*
> *We've been treated bad, talked about as sure as you're born*
> *But just as sure as it takes two eyes to make a pair, ha*
> *Brother we can't quit until we get our share*

https://genius.com/James-brown-say-it-loud-im-black-and-im-proud-lyrics

21. Keys's lyrics include these:

> *Oh, she got both feet on the ground*
> *And she's burning it down*
> *Oh, she got her head in the clouds*
> *And she's not backing down*

https://genius.com/Alicia-keys-girl-on-fire-lyrics

22. "Play Angry" has been institutionalized as well. The college basketball team, the Wichita State Warriors, for example, uses it as its motto. Ron Baker, "Play Angry," *The Players' Tribune*, March 17, 2017, https://www.theplayerstribune.com/articles/ron-baker-wichita-state-shockers-basketball-play-angry.

23. Larry Platt, "John McEnroe," *Salon*, July 11, 2000, https://www.salon.com/2000/07/11/mcenroe.

24. Devin Gordon, "You Don't Know Bode," *Newsweek*, January 23, 2006, 40.

25. Tony Chamberlain, "Remarks Have Created Uphill Climb," *Boston Globe*, January 12, 2006, C11.

26. Jody M. Roy, *Love to Hate: America's Obsession with Hatred and Violence* (New York: Columbia University Press, 2002).

27. Dominic Green, "Meghan 'n' Joe's Empire of the Sentiments," *Spectator*, March 12, 2021, https://spectator.us/topic/meghan-markle-joe-biden-empire-sentiments. Green observes in reference to President Biden's March 11, 2021, primetime address to the nation, watched by 32 million people, and Prince Harry and Meghan Markle's two-hour interview with Oprah Winfrey broadcast on March 7, watched by 17 million people:

> [Biden] *knows how it feels, he said with that now-customary surge of anger, as if he's not fully in control of his frontal cortex. And we know how it feels when someone says they know how we feel. Consider everything fixed: COVID, racism, opioids, deficits, the collapse of the schools, the children at the border. The Therapeute-in-Chief is here, dispensing serotonin the way Barack Obama dispensed drone strikes.*
>
> *It doesn't matter whether Biden means what he says, any more that* [sic] *it matters whether Meghan Markle told the truth when she implied that her son was denied a prince's title because he might have dark skin. It's the feelings that matter: feelings of security, empathy and contentment, and especially the feeling that Nietzsche correctly foresaw as the root feeling of modern life, resentment.*
>
> *The result is the rule of sentiment over thought and symbols over reality. Given the complexities of the facts and the appeal of a flight into sentiment, it's no wonder that this week the administration and media did direct us to pity the children.*
>
> *Biden's increasingly vague routines of empathy are the symbolic face and velvet glove of a bureaucracy of the sentiments whose offices run from government to the media.*

28. Limbaugh was a master of comic tone and timing. He told stories and reads from articles with exactly the right pauses and intonations to suggest a much richer picture than the words alone conveyed. He aimed at provoking extreme responses from his critics and often succeeded. Jose Barreiro, among others, rose to attack Limbaugh for his "Bigotshtick," as he titled a 1995 essay on Limbaugh's attitude toward Native Americans. Before becoming a Democratic senator from Minnesota, comedian Al Franken published a best-selling book, *Rush Limbaugh Is a Big Fat Idiot and Other Observations* (1996). Molly Ivins preceded Franken in 1995 with an article, "Lyin' Bully," in the far-left magazine *Mother Jones*. Ivins began with a lament for what Limbaugh had done to the nation's civility: "One of the things that concerns a lot of Americans lately is the increase in plain old nastiness in our political discussion. It comes from a number of sources, but Rush Limbaugh is a major carrier." In the spirit of overcoming that nastiness, Ivins gently reproved him: "I object because he consistently

targets dead people, little girls, and the homeless – none of whom are in a particularly good position to answer back." After Limbaugh's death from lung cancer in February 2021, he received many tributes, but he remained the target of leftist abuse. HuffPost headlined the story, "BIGOT, MISOGYNIST, HOMOPHOBE, CRANK: RUSH LIMBAUGH DEAD." Even *New York Times* writer Frank Bruni, no fan of Limbaugh, thought the venom went too far, as he wrote in "Must We Dance on Rush Limbaugh's Grave?" https://www.nytimes.com/2021/02/20/opinion/sunday/rush-limbaugh-dead-reaction.html

29. Martin Gurri, *The Revolt of the Public and the Crisis of Authority in the New Millennium* (San Francisco: Stripe Press, 2017).

30. Gurri, 30–31.

31. Gurri, 66.

32. Gurri's book is, no doubt deliberately, posed as something outside the usual channels of publication. It was published by a technology company, Stripe, rather than a well-known press. It lacks an ISBN number and other standard bibliographic data. There are no notes on the author and no index. The text is supplemented with numerous photographs, many of which appear superfluous, such as portraits of President Kennedy and Albert Einstein. And the endpapers, table of contents, titles, and chapter notes are printed in magenta, and the graphs in lavender. As a physical object, the book is ostentatiously odd, as if to say "So there!" to the conventions of modern publishing.

33. Richard Bledsoe, "The Difference between Totalitarian Tantrums and Righteous Rage," *Remodern Review* (blog), November 17, 2020, https://remodernreview.wordpress.com/2020/11/17/the-difference-between-totalitarian-tantrums-and-righteous-rage.

34. Abigail R. Esman, *Rage, Narcissism, Patriarchy, and Culture of Terrorism* (Washington, D.C.: Potomac Books, 2020). Esman puts fatherlessness at the center of the kind of radicalism that breeds terrorists.

35. John Mitchell [published anonymously], *My Mother; or, Recollections of Maternal Influence* (Boston: Gould and Lincoln, 1855), https://books.google.com/books?id=2eETAAAAYAAJ, 155–56.

36. Mitchell, 162–63.

37. Mitchell, 179–80.

38. Mitchell, vii–viii.

39. Dan Gelernter, "Cancel Culture's Newest Victims," *American Greatness*, March 9, 2021, https://amgreatness.com/2021/03/09/cancel-cultures-newest-victims.

40. Michael Datcher, "The Fire This Time," reprinted in *Testimony: Young African-Americans on Self-Discovery and Black Identity*, ed. Natasha Tarpley (Boston: Beacon Press, 1995), 24–25.

41. Christopher Caldwell, *The Age of Entitlement: America since the Sixties* (New York: Simon & Schuster, 2020), 3.

42. Caldwell, 234, 238, 239.

43. Caldwell, 241.

44. Caldwell, 244.

45. Caldwell, 262–69.

46. Caldwell, 271.

47. Dion J. Pierre and Peter W. Wood, *Neo-Segregation at Yale* (New York: National Association of Scholars, 2019).

48. "Yale University – Full Version – New Videos of The Halloween Email Protest," YouTube video, 23:44, uploaded by TheAsianRepublican, September 20, 2016, https://www.youtube.com/watch?v=hiMVx2C5_Wg.

49. Pierre and Wood, *Neo-Segregation at Yale*, 37.

50. Marc Tracy, "Two Journalists Exit *New York Times* after Criticism of Past Behavior," *New York Times*, February 5, 2021, https://www.nytimes.com/2021/02/05/business/media/donald-mcneil-andy-mills-leave-nyt.html; Lia Eustachewich and Jackie Salo, "*New York Times* Reporter Donald McNeil Defends Himself in Private Email," *New York Post,* February 17, 2021, https://nypost.com/2021/02/17/new-york-times-donald-mcneil-defends-himself-in-private-email.

51. Stuart Walton, *A Natural History of Human Emotions* (New York: Grove Press, 2004); Otniel E. Dror, Bettina Hitzer, Anja Laukötter, and Pilar León-Sanz, eds., *Osiris, Volume 31: History of Science and the Emotions* (Chicago: University of Chicago Press, 2016); Paul E. Griffiths, *What Emotions Really Are* (Chicago: University of Chicago Press, 1997).

52. Eric Lonergan and Mark Blyth, *Angrynomics* (Newcastle on Tyne: Agenda Publishing, 2020), 11.

53. Lonergan and Blyth, 19.

54. Lonergan and Blyth, 10.

55. Lonergan and Blyth, 7–8.

56. R. R. Reno, "Anger-Politics on the Right," *First Things*, February 2021, 63–66, https://www.firstthings.com/article/2021/02/anger-politics-on-the-right.

57. Reno.

58. For example, Joshua James, an Iraqi war veteran, was lured from his house in Alabama by an FBI agent pretending to be a customer and was met with "an Army armored vehicle with a turret on top, 2 FBI vans, 6 FBI vehicles, 3 local police and sheriff's vehicles." Authorities "ransacked" his home, dispossessing his wife Audrey James and their three-year old child. He was arrested on charges that impute he played some role in the January 6 Capitol Hill riot, but he did not commit any violent crime. As of this writing, he is being held without bail awaiting trial. James's situation is similar to that of many other of the four hundred people arrested in connection with the January 6 riot. Jim Hoft, "FBI Sends in Armored Vehicle with Turret, 2 Vans, 6 FBI Vehicles, 3 Local Police Vehicles to Arrest Young Father Who Attended Jan. 6 Rally," *Gateway Pundit*, March 12, 2021, https://www.thegatewaypundit.com/2021/03/

shock-report-fbi-sends-military-vehicle-turret-2-vans-6-fbi-vehicles-3-local-police-vehicles-arrest-young-father-attended-jan-6-rally-unbelievable-interview.

59. Steve Sailor, "Trump's Luck," *iSteve Blog, Unz Review*, January 13, 2021, https://www.unz.com/isteve/trumps-luck-2.

60. Robert Farley, "Timeline of National Guard Deployment to Capitol," *FactCheck.org*, January 13, 2021, https://www.factcheck.org/2021/01/timeline-of-national-guard-deployment-to-capitol; Jemima McEvoy, "House Republicans Claim Pelosi May Be Responsible for Delaying National Guard Deployment on Jan. 6," *Forbes*, February 15, 2021, https://www.forbes.com/sites/jemimamcevoy/2021/02/15/house-republicans-suggest-pelosi-may-be-responsible-for-delaying-national-guard-deployment-on-jan-6; Tom Kertscher, "Only Nancy Pelosi Is 'Responsible for What Happened at the Capitol' on Jan. 6, 'Security at the Capitol Is Her Job,'" *PolitiFact*, February 25, 2021, https://www.politifact.com/factchecks/2021/feb/25/facebook-posts/no-capitol-security-not-only-pelosis-responsibilit.

61. Charles R. Kesler, "After January 6th," *Claremont Review of Books* 21, no. 1 (Winter 2020/21): 28–34, https://claremontreviewofbooks.com/after-january-6th.

62. Kesler.

Index

Aaronovitch, David, 100–101

abortion industry, 113

Adams, John, 77, 118, 120, 121

Adams, Scott, 129

"Address at the Conclusion of the Selma to Montgomery March," 4

Aemilianus, Scipio, 6

Afghanistan war, 60

After the Fall, 100

Age of Entitlement: America since the Sixties, The, 184–85

Alcott, Louisa May, 88

ALF, 41

America Coming Together, 78

Americana, 149

"American Crisis, The," 38–39

American Idol, 56

American Library Association, 61

American Rage: How Anger Shapes Our Politics, 110

American Revolution, the, 38–39, 45, 66, 77; Abraham Lincoln on, 122–23; founding anger and, 116–21; George Washington and, 124–26

American Utopia, 15

Anderson, Brian C., 144

Anderson, Carol, 141–42

Anderson, George, 127

Andros, Edmund, 66

Angeli, Jake. *see* Chansley, Jacob Anthony

anger. *see also* wrath: Abraham Lincoln and, 121–23; academic studies of, 91–92, 163; American temperament and, 127–28, 182; angri-culture, 59, 62, 98–99, 105–6; authenticity and, 165–66; cars and, 74–75; Cold War era,

99–102; "de-fund the police" campaigns, 57; depicted in movies, 42–43; Donald Trump and, 29–31, 77, 111, 158–62; due to political polarization, 76–79; earlier epochs of, 106–8; in economics, 186–90; expressed in fashion, 50–52, 55–56; expressed in music, 44, 52–55, 127–28, 149–51, 168; expressed in popular culture figures, 58, 63; feelings of entitlement about, 76, 90–91, 180–81; flamboyant American, 25–29; founding, American Revolution and, 116–21; in games, 169; Gentlers on, 94–95; George Washington and, 124–26; "going postal," 49–50; in heroic figures, 65–66, 76; Hillary Clinton and, 48–49, 77, 78; history of popular attitudes toward, 87–90, 148, 154–55, 164; Howard Dean and, 58, 59–60; individualism and, 165–67; intensified by the media, 35–36; justified and congratulating itself, 79–80, 182–84; of the left, 8–9, 13–16, 35–36, 59–62, 78; literary portrayals of, 63–68, 81–83, 112; and malice in public, 43–45; moral outrage, 108–9, 110; new, 77–80, 87, 100, 107–8, 139, 140, 144–45, 166, 169–70; over hypocrisy, 47–48; over politics and elections, 45–49; over small provocations, 47; over the 2020 election, 22–25, 174, 176; performative, 48–49, 104–5, 114–15, 168–70; political polarization and, 76–79; populist, 170–73, 188–89; portrayed in films, 67–68, 71–74, 96–97, 112, 135, 156;

INDEX

INDEX

INDEX

INDEX

A NOTE ON THE TYPE

WRATH *has been set in Adobe's Warnock Pro, a type family begun in 1997 by Robert Slimbach. Named for John Warnock, one of Adobe's co-founders, the roman was originally intended for its namesake's personal use, but was subsequently developed into a comprehensive range of faces. Although the types are based firmly in Slimbach's calligraphic work, the completed family makes abundant use of the refinements attainable in the OpenType format. With its range of optical sizes, Warnock Pro is elegant in display settings, warm and readable at text sizes – a classical design with contemporary adaptability.* ✱ *The display type is Rudolf Koch's Antiqua, first issued by the Klingspor foundry in 1922.*

DESIGN & COMPOSITION BY CARL W. SCARBROUGH